Food in 5 languages

AN INTERNATIONAL MENU GUIDE

ENGLISH · GERMAN · FRENCH · ITALIAN · SPANISH

Elis

CW01095959

GRUB STREET · LONDON

Published by Grub Street
The Basement, 10 Chivalry Road
London SW11 1HT

Copyright this edition © Grub Street 1995
Originally published by Carl Gerber Verlag GmbH, Germany
Jacket illustration and design: Nicci Walker

British Library Cataloguing in Publication Data

Neiger, Elisabeth
  Food in Five Languages: International
  Menu Guide
  I. Title
  641.59

  ISBN 1-898697-22-1

Printed and bound in Great Britain by
Biddles Ltd, Guildford and King's Lynn

Contents

Conversion Chart

Weights

1 kilogram or kilo (kg) = 1000 grams (g)

100-125 g = 4 oz   225 g = 8 oz

450 g = 1 lb   1000 g = 2.2 lb

Fluid measures

1 litre = 1000 millilitres (ml)

= 0.2462 US gallons

= 0.2200 UK gallons

= 1.760 UK pints (approx 1¾ pts)

1 fluid ounce (fl oz) = 28.41 ml

1 US pint = 16 fl oz

1 UK pint = 568.2 ml = 20 fl oz

½ UK pint = 284 ml

¼ UK pint = 142 ml

½ litre = 0.88 pts

Temperatures

°C	0°	5°	10°	15°	20°	25°	35°	40°	45°	50°
°F	32°	41°	50°	59°	68°	77°	95°	104°	113°	122°

To convert °C to °F – multiply the centigrade figure by 9; divide by 5 then add 32.

To convert °F to °C – subtract 32 from farenheit figure, multiply by 5 and divide by 9.

Boiling point of water is 100°C or 212°F.

Freexing point of water is 0°C or 32°f.

Abbreviations used in the book

m = masculine; f = feminine; n = neuter; pl = plural; Am = American

FOREWORD

This handy pocket book has now sold over 100,000 copies worldwide.

It contains everything you want to know when you sit down to read a menu in German, French, Spanish, Italian or English. Uniquely, all the words and phrases are listed side by side.

The book is an essential companion for anyone travelling throughout Europe.

It will also be of inestimable help for those whose job it is to compile and write menus as well as providing a useful teaching resource to the many students and teachers in catering colleges around the world.

Sauces	Saucen	Sauces	Salse	Salsas
Aïoli sauce (garlic mayonnaise)	Aïoli-Sauce (Mayonnaise mit Knoblauch)	Sauce aïoli[1] (mayonnaise au coulis d'ail)	Salsa aïoli (maionese all'aglio)	Salsa ajiaceite o alioli (mayonesa al ajo)
American sauce (tomato sauce with lobster butter)	Amerikanische Sauce (Tomatensauce mit Hummerbutter)	~ américaine (sauce tomate et beurre d' homard)	~ americana (salsa di pomodoro e burro di astice)	~ americana (salsa de tomate con manteca de bogavante)
Anchovy sauce	Sardellensauce	~ aux anchois	~ d'acciughe	~ de anchoas
Apple sauce	Apfelmus	~ aux pommes	~ di mele	~ de manzanas
Béarnaise sauce (Hollandaise sauce with tarragon)	Béarner Sauce (Holländische Sauce mit Estragon)	~ béarnaise (sauce hollandaise á l'estragon)	~ bearnese (salsa olandese al dragoncello)	~ bearnesa (salsa holandesa con estragón)
Béchamel sauce	Béchamelsauce	~ Béchamel	Besciamella	~ bechamel, ~ besamela
Bercy sauce (butter, shallots, white wine)	Bercy-Sauce (Butter, Schalotten, Weißwein)	~ Bercy (beurre, échalotes, vin blanc)	Salsa Bercy (scalogno, burro e vino bianco)	~ Bercy (manteca, vino blanco, escaloñas)
Bigarade sauce (orange sauce)	Bigarade-Sauce (Orangensauce)	~ bigarade (sauce à l'orange)	~ bigarade (salsa all'arancia)	~ bigarade (salsa de naranjas)
Bordelaise sauce (wine sauce with beef marrow)	Bordelaise-Sauce (Weinsauce mit Rindermark)	~ bordelaise (sauce au vin avec moelle de bœuf	~ bordolese (salsa di vino con midollo di bue)	~ bordelesa (salsa de vino con tuétano)
Bread sauce	Brotsauce	~ au pain	~ di pane	~ de pan
Brown sauce	Braune Sauce	~ brune, ~ espagnole	~ bruna	~ española
Burgundy sauce (red wine sauce)	Burgunder Sauce (Rotweinsauce)	~ bourguignonne (sauce au vin rouge)	~ alla borgognona (salsa di vino rosso)	~ borgoñona (salsa de vino tinto)
Butter sauce	Buttersauce	~ au beurre	~ al burro	~ de mantequilla
Caper sauce	Kapernsauce	~ aux câpres	~ di capperi	~ de alcaparras
Cardinal sauce (béchamel & lobster butter)	Kardinals-Sauce (Béchamel u. Hummerbutter)	~ cardinal (Béchamel et beurre de homard)	~ cardinale (besciamella e burro d'astice)	~ cardenal (bechamel y manteca de langosta)
Chateaubriand sauce (meat glaze enriched with butter & parsley)	Chateaubriand-Sauce (Fleischglace, Butter, Petersilie)	~ Chateaubriand (glace de viande beurrée et persillée)	~ Chateaubriand gelatina di carne, burro e prezzemolo)	~ Chateaubriand (glasa de carne, mantequilla y perejil)
Cheese sauce	Käsesauce	~ Mornay	~ Mornay	~ Mornay

Sauces	Saucen	Sauces	Salse	Salsas
Chive sauce	Schnittlauchsauce	Sauce à la ciboulette	Salsa all'erba cipollina	Salsa de cebollino
Choron sauce (Béarnaise sauce blended with tomato purée)	Choron-Sauce (Béarner Sauce mit Tomatenpüree vermischt)	~ Choron (sauce béarnaise tomatée)	~ Choron (salsa bearnese al pomodoro)	Salsa Choron (salsa bearnesa con tomate)
Colbert sauce (maître d'hôtel butter blended with meat glaze)	Colbert-Sauce (Kräuterbutter mit Fleischglace vermischt)	~ Colbert (beurre maître d'hôtel additionné de glace de viande)	~ Colbert (burro maître d'hôtel con aggiunta di gelatina di carne)	~ Colbert (manteca maître d'hôtel con extracto de carne)
Cranberry sauce	Preiselbeersauce	~ aux airelles	~ di mirtilli	~ de arándanos
Cream sauce	Sahnesauce	~ à la crème	~ alla panna, ~ alla crema	~ a la crema
Cream sauce	Rahmsauce	~ à la crème	~ alla panna, ~ alla crema	~ a la crema
Creole sauce	Kreolische Sauce	~ créole	~ creola	~ criolla
Cumberland sauce (redcurrant jelly, shreds of orange and lemon rind, mustard and port)	Cumberland-Sauce (Johannisbeergelee, Senf, Streifen von Orangen- und Zitronenschalen, Portwein)	~ Cumberland (gelée de groseilles, zeste d'orange et de citron en julienne, moutarde, porto)	~ Cumberland (gelatina di ribes, senape, julienne di scorze d'arancio e limone, porto)	~ Cumberland (jalea de grosellas, mostaza, tiritas de cáscara de naranja y limón, oporto)
Curry sauce	Indische Sauce	~ à l'indienne	~ indiana, ~ al curry	~ india (al curry)
Curry sauce	Currysauce	~ au curry[3]	~ al curry	~ al curry
Devilled sauce (demiglace, white wine or vinegar, cayenne)	Teufelssauce (Demiglace, Weißwein oder Essig, Cayennepfeffer)	~ diable (demi-glace, vin blanc ou vinaigre, poivre de Cayenne)	~ alla diavola (demiglace, aceto o vino bianco, pepe di Caienna)	~ a la diabla (salsa española con vinagre y pimienta de Cayena)
Dill sauce	Dillsauce	~ à l'aneth	~ all'aneto	~ de eneldo
Egg sauce	Eiersauce	~ aux œufs	~ d'uovo	~ de huevos
Genevoise sauce (fish stock, red wine, anchovy butter)	Genfer Sauce[2] (Fischfond, Rotwein, Sardellenbutter)	~ genevoise (fumet de poisson, vin rouge, beurre d'anchois)	~ alla ginevrina (fondo di pesce, vino rosso, burro d'acciughe)	~ ginebrina (salsa de vino tinto con manteca de anchoas)
Green mayonnaise (with purée of herbs)	Grüne Mayonnaise (mit Kräuterpüree)	~ verte (mayonnaise à la purée d'herbes)	Maionese verde (con passato di erbe)	~ verde (mayonesa con puré de hierbas)
Gribiche sauce (tartar sauce with capers)	Gribiche-Sauce (Tatarensauce mit Kapern)	~ gribiche (sauce tartare aux câpres)	Salsa gribiche (salsa tartara con capperi)	~ gribiche (salsa tártara con alcaparras)

8

Sauces	Saucen	Sauces	Salse	Salsas
Hollandaise sauce (yolks of egg, melted butter, lemon juice)	Holländische Sauce (Eigelb, geschmolzene Butter, Zitronensaft)	Sauce hollandaise (émulsion de beurre et de jaunes d'œufs)	Salsa olandese (tuorli d'uovo, burro fuso, succo di limone)	Salsa holandesa (yemas de huevo, manteca fundida, zumo de limón
Horseradish sauce	Meerrettichsauce	~ raifort	~ di rafano	~ de rábano picante
Joinville sauce (white wine sauce with shrimp butter)	Joinville-Sauce (Weißweinsauce mit Garnelenbutter)	~ Joinville (sauce vin blanc avec beurre de crevettes)	~ Joinville (salsa di vino bianco con burro di gamberetti)	~ Joinville (salsa de vino blanco con manteca de cangrejos)
Juniper sauce	Wacholdersauce	~ au genièvre	~ al ginepro	~ de enebro
Lemon sauce	Zitronensauce	~ au citron	~ al limone	~ de limón
Lobster sauce	Hummersauce	~ homard	~ d'astice	~ de langosta
Lyonnaise sauce (onion sauce)	Lyoner Sauce (Zwiebelsauce)	~ lyonnaise (sauce aux oignons)	~ lionese (salsa di cipolle)	~ lionesa (salsa de cebollas)
Maître d'hôtel sauce (butter, parsley and lemon juice)	Maître-Sauce (Butter, Petersilie und Zitronensaft)	~ maître d'hôtel (beurre, persil et jus de citron)	~ alla maître d'hôtel (burro, prezzemolo, succo di limone)	~ mayordoma (mantequilla, perejil, zumo de limón)
Madeira sauce	Madeirasauce	~ Madère	~ al madera	~ Madera
Maltese sauce (Hollandaise sauce with juice of blood oranges)	Malteser Sauce (holländische Sauce mit Saft von Blutorangen)	~ maltaise (sauce hollandaise au jus d'oranges sanguines)	~ maltesa (salsa olandese all'arancia)	~ maltesa (salsa holandesa con zumo de naranjas sanguinas)
Marrow sauce	Marksauce	~ moelle	~ al midollo	~ de tuétano
Matelote sauce	Matrosensauce	Sauce marinière	Salsa alla marinara	Salsa a la marinera
Mayonnaise	Mayonnaise	~ mayonnaise	~ maionese	~ mayonesa, ~ mahonesa
Mint sauce	Minzsauce	~ menthe	~ di menta	~ de menta
Mornay sauce, cheese sauce	Mornay-Sauce (Béchamel mit geriebenem Käse)	~ Mornay (Béchamel au formage)	~ Mornay (besciamella al formaggio)	~ Mornay (bechamel con queso)
Mousseline sauce (Hollandaise sauce with whipped cream)	Mousseline-Sauce (holländische Sauce mit geschlagener Sahne)	~ mousseline (sauce hollandaise additionnée de créme fouettée)	~ mousseline (salsa olandese mescolata con panna montata)	~ muselina (salsa holandesa adicionada de nata batida)
Mushroom sauce	Champignonsauce	~ aux champignons	~ di funghi	~ de champiñones
Mustard sauce	Senfsauce	~ moutarde	~ di senape	~ de mostaza

Sauces	Saucen	Sauces	Salse	Salsas
Nantua sauce (béchamel with crayfish butter)	Nantua-Sauce (Béchamelsauce mit Krebsbutter)	Sauce Nantua (Béchamel et beurre d'écrevisses)	Salsa Nantua (besciamella e burro di gamberi)	Salsa Nantua (bechamel y manteca de cangrejos)
Orange sauce	Orangensauce	~ à l'orange	~ all'arancia	~ de naranjas
Paprika sauce	Paprikasauce	~ au paprika	~ alla paprica	~ de paprika
Parsley sauce	Petersiliensauce	~ persil	~ al prezzemolo	~ de perejil
Piquant sauce (with vinegar, gherkins, parsley)	Pikante Sauce (mit Essig, Petersilie, Essiggurken)	~ piquante (avec vinaigre, cornichons, persil)	~ piccante (con aceto, cetriolini, prezzemolo)	~ picante (con vinagre, pepinillos, perejil)
Poivrade sauce (with vinegar & pepper)	Pfeffersauce (mit Essig und Pfefferkörnern)	~ poivrade (avec vinaigre et poivre)	~ poivrade (con aceto e pepe)	~ poivrade (con vinagre y pimienta)
Port wine sauce	Portweinsauce	~ au porto	~ al porto	~ de Oporto
Ravigote sauce (vinaigrette with capers and fine herbs)	Ravigote-Sauce (Vinaigrette mit Kapern und feinen Kräutern)	~ ravigote (vinaigrette avec câpres et fines herbes)	~ ravigote (olio e aceto con capperi e un trito di erbe)	~ ravigote (vinagreta con alcaparras y finas hierbas)
Rémoulade sauce (mayonnaise with mustard, gherkins & capers)	Remouladensauce (Mayonnaise mit Senf, Kapern, Essiggurken)	Sauce rémoulade (mayonnaise avec moutarde, câpres et cornichons)	Salsa rémoulade (maionese con senape, capperi e cetriolini)	Salsa remolada (mayonesa con mostaza, alcaparras, pepinillos)
Red wine sauce	Rotweinsauce	~ vin rouge	~ di vino rosso	~ de vino tinto
Redcurrant sauce	Johannisbeersauce	~ aux groseilles (rouges)	~ di ribes	~ de grosellas
Robert sauce (onion, white wine, mustard)	Robert-Sauce (Zwiebel, Weißwein, Senf)	~ Robert (oignon, vin blanc moutarde)	~ Roberto (cipolla, vino bianco, senape)	~ Robert (cebolla, vino blanco, mostaza)
Sauce chasseur (mushrooms, white wine, tomato sauce)	Jägersauce (Champignons, Weißwein, Tomatensauce)	~ chasseur (champignons, vin blanc, sauce tomate)	~ alla cacciatora (funghi, vino bianco, salsa di pomodoro)	~ a la cazadora (champiñones, vino blanco, salsa de tomate)
Sauce financière (Madeira sauce flavoured with truffle)	Finanzmannsauce (Madeirasauce mit Trüffelfond)	~ financière (sauce madère à l'essence de truffes)	~ alla finanziera (salsa al madera con essenza di tartufi)	~ financiera (salsa madera aromatizada con trufas)
Sauce grand veneur (poivrade sauce with redcurrant jelly)	Grand-veneur Sauce (Pfeffersauce mit Johannisbeergelee)	~ grand-veneur[1] (sauce poivrade et gelée de groseilles)	~ grand-veneur (salsa poivrade con gelatina di ribes)	~ grand-veneur (salsa poivrade con jalea de grosellas)

Sauces	Saucen	Sauces	Salse	Salsas
Sauce normande (with wine sauce and fish stock)	Normannische Sauce (Weißweinsauce mit Fischfond)	Sauce normande (sauce vin blanc au fumet de poisson)	Salsa normanna (salsa di vino blanco con essenza di pesce)	Salsa normanda (salsa de vino blanco aromatizada con pescado)
Sauce suprême (chicken stock with cream	Suprême-Sauce (Geflügel-Rahmsauce)	~ suprême (velouté de volaille à la crème)	~ suprême (vellutata di pollo con panna)	~ suprema (salsa de ave con crema)
Shrimp sauce	Garnelensauce	~ aux crevettes	~ di gamberetti	~ de camarones
Smitane sauce, sour cream sauce	Saure Rahmsauce	~ smitane (avec crème aigre)	~ smitane (con panna acida)	~ smitane (salsa de crema agria)
Soubise sauce (onion purée with béchamel)	Soubise-Sauce (Zwiebel-püree mit Béchamel)	~ Soubise (ou coulis d'oignons)	~ Soubise (purè di cipolle con besciamella)	~ Soubise (bechamel con puré de cebollas)
Sweet-and-sour sauce	Süßsaure Sauce	~ aigre-douce	~ agrodolce	~ agridulce
Tartar sauce (mayonnaise of hard-boiled eggs with chives)	Tatarensauce (Mayonnaise aus hartgekochtem Eigelb mit Schnittlauch)	~ tartare (mayonnaise aux jaunes d'œufs durs)	~ tartara (maionese di uova sode con erba cipollina)	~ tártara (mayonesa de yemas de huevos duros con cebollino)
Tomato sauce	Tomatensauce	~ tomate	~ di pomodore	~ de tomate
Truffle sauce	Périgueux-Sauce	~ Périgueux (aux truffes)	~ Périgueux (con tartufi)	~ Périgueux (de trufas)
Truffle sauce	Trüffelsauce	Sauce Périgueux	Salsa di tartufi	Salsa de trufas
Turtle sauce (Madeira sauce with essence of herbs)	Schildkrötensauce (Madeirasauce mit Auszug von Kräutern)	~ tortue (sauce madère avec infusion d'herbes)	~ tortue (salsa madera con infusione di erbe)	~ tortue (salsa Madera con infusión de hierbas)
Tyrolean sauce	Tiroler Sauce	~ tyrolienne	~ tirolese	~ tirolesa
Venetian sauce (white wine sauce with purée of herbs)	Venezianische Sauce (Weißweinsauce mit Kräuterpüree)	~ vénitienne (sauce vin blanc avec purée d'herbes)	~ veneziana (salsa di vino bianco con passato di erbe)	~ veneciana (salsa de vino blanco con puré de hierbas)
Villeroi sauce (white sauce with essence of mushrooms)	Villeroi-Sauce (weiße Sauce mit Champignon-fond)	~ Villeroi (sauce allemande à l'essence de champignons)	~ Villeroi (salsa bianca con essenza di funghi)	~ Villeroi (salsa blanca aromatizada con champiñones)
Vinaigrette (sauce)	Vinaigrette	~ vinaigrette	~ vinaigrette	~ vinagreta
Vinaigrette sauce	Grüne Sauce	~ vinaigrette	~ verde	~ vinagreta
White sauce	Weiße Sauce	~ blanche	~ bianca	~ blanca
White wine sauce	Weißweinsauce	~ au vin blanc	~ di vino bianco	~ de vino blanco

Sauces	Saucen	Sauces	Salse	Salsas
Yoghurt sauce	Joghurt-Sauce	Sauce au yaourt	Salsa allo yogurt	Salsa de yogur
Zingara sauce (tomatoed sauce with strips of ham, ox-tongue, mushrooms)	Zigeuner-Sauce (Demi-glace mit Einlage von Champignons, Zunge und Schinken)	~ zingara (sauce tomatée avec julienne de jambon, langue, champignons)	~ alla zingara (demi-glace al pomodoro con filetti di prosciutto, lingua e funghi)	~ gitana (salsa española con tiritas de jamón, lengua, champiñones)

[1]) ou sauce ailloli.
[2]) Von Carême einst „génoise" (genuesische) genannt.
[3]) dite aussi sauce à l'indienne.
[4]) appelée aussi sauce venaison.

Butters	Buttermischungen	Beurres composés	Burri	Mantecas aromatizadas
Anchovy butter	Sardellenbutter	Beurre d'anchois	Burro d'acciughe	Manteca de anchoas
Black butter	Schwarze Butter	~ noir	~ nero	~ tostada, ~ negra
Brown butter	Nußbutter	~ noisette	~ nocciola	~ dorada
Brown butter	Braune Butter	Beurre noisette	Burro nocciola	Manteca dorada
Caviar butter	Kaviarbutter	~ de caviar	~ di caviale	~ de caviar
Colbert butter (maître d'hôtel butter mixed with meat-glaze and chopped tarragon)	Colbert-Butter (Kräuterbutter mit Fleischglace und gehacktem Estragon vermischt)	~ Colbert (beurre maître d'hôtel additionné de glace de viande et d'estragon haché)	~ Colbert (burro alla maître d'hôtel con gelatina di carne e dragoncello tritato)	~ Colbert (manteca maître d'hôtel con extracto de carne y estragón picado)
Crayfish butter	Krebsbutter	~ d' écrevisses	~ di gamberi	~ de cangrejos
Lobster butter	Hummerbutter	~ d' homard	~ d'astice	~ de bogavante
Maître d'hôtel butter[5] (with chopped parsley and lemon juice)	Kräuterbutter (Butter mit gehackter Petersilie und Zitronensaft)	~ maître d'hôtel (beurre avec persil haché et jus de citron)	~ alla maître d'hôtel (con prezzemolo trito e succo di limone)	~ maître d'hôtel (con perejil picado y zumo de limón)
Melted butter	Zerlassene Butter	~ fondu	~ fuso	~ derretida, ~ fundida
Mustard butter	Senfbutter	~ de moutarde	~ di senape	~ de mostaza
Salmon butter	Lachsbutter	~ de saumon fumé	~ di salmone	~ de salmón
Shrimp butter	Garnelenbutter	~ de crevettes	~ di gamberetti	~ de camarones
Shrimp butter	Krevettenbutter	~ de crevettes	~ di gamberetti	~ de camarones
Snail butter (butter mixed with shallots, garlic & parsley)	Schneckenbutter (Butter mit Schalotten, Knoblauch und Petersilie)	~ pour escargots (beurre pétri avec échalotes, ail et persil)	~ per lumache (burro misto con scalogno, aglio e prezzemolo)	~ para caracoles (mezclada con ajo, escaloñas y perejil)
Truffle butter	Trüffelbutter	~ de truffes	~ di tartufi	~ de trufas

[5]) or parsley butter.

Hors-d'œuvres	Vorspeisen	Hors-d'œuvres	Antipasti	Entremeses
Anchovy butter	Sardellenbutter	Beurre d'anchois	Burro d'acciughe	Manteca de anchoa
Anchovy canapés	Sardellenbrötchen	Canapés aux anchois	Canapè di acciughe	Canapés de anchoas
Anchovy fillets	Sardellenfilets	Filets d'anchois	Filetti d'acciuga	Filetes de anchoa
Anchovy-straws	Sardellenstäbchen	Allumettes aux anchois	Bastoncini d'acciughe	Barritas de anchoa
Angels-on-horseback (grilled oysters on toast)	Austernspießchen auf Toast	Brochettes d'huîtres sur toast	Spiedini d'ostriche su crostini	Broquetas de ostras sobre tostada
Assorted hors-d'œuvres	Gemischte Vorspeisen	Hors-d'œuvre variés	Antipasto assortito	Entremeses variados
Assorted sausages	Wurstplatte	Assiette de charcuterie	Salumi assortiti	Embutidos variados
Bacon	Speck (geräucherter)	Bacon, lard fumé	Pancetta affumicata	Tocino
Bear's ham	Bärenschinken	Jambon d'ours	Prosciutto d'orso	Jamón de oso
Bismarck herring	Bismarck-Hering	Hareng de la Baltique	Aringa marinata	Arenque marinado
Blinis (small buckwheat pancakes)	Blini (Hefeplinsen mit Buchweizenzusatz)	Blinis (petites crêpes au sarrasin)	Blini (frittatine con grano saraceno)	Blinis (crêpes pequeñas de trigo sarraceno)
Botargo (pressed caviar made of mullet roe)	Botarga (Preßkaviar aus Meeräscherogen)	Boutargue[6] (sorte de caviar d'œufs de mulet)	Bottarga (sorta di caviale di uova di muggine)	Botarga (embuchado de huevos de mújol)
Bouchées, patties	Pastetchen	Bouchées	Vol-au-vent	Pastelitos (de hojaldre)
Oyster patties	Austern-Pastetchen	~ aux huîtres	~ d'ostriche	~ de ostras
Bouchées à la reine	Königin-Pastetchen	~ à la reine	~ alla regina	~ a la reina
Buckling, bloater	Bückling	Buckling, hareng saur	Aringa affumicata	Arenque ahumado
Canapés	Canapés	Canapés	Canapè, tartine	Canapés
Caviar canapés	Kaviar-Canapés	~ au caviar	~ di caviale	~ de caviar
Anchovy canapés	Sardellen-Canapés	~ aux anchois	~ di acciughe	~ de anchoas
Caviar canapés	Kaviarbrötchen	Canapés au caviar	Canapè di caviale	Canapés de caviar
Caviar, caviare	Kaviar	Caviar	Caviale	Caviar
Cheese soufflé	Käse-Auflauf	Soufflé au fromage	Soufflé di formaggio	Soufflé de queso
Cheese-straws	Käsestangen	Allumettes au fromage	Bastoncini al formaggio	Barritas de queso
Chester-straws	Chesterstangen	Paillettes au chester	Bastoncini al chester	Barritas de chester
Chicken galantine	Geflügelgalantine	Galantine de volaille	Galantina di pollo	Galantina de ave
Chicken salad	Geflügelsalat	Salade de volaille	Insalata di pollo	Ensalada de ave
Chilled tomato juice	Eisgekühlter Tomatensaft	Jus de tomates glacé	Succo di pomodoro ghiacciato	Jugo de tomate helado

Hors-d'œuvres	Vorspeisen	Hors-d'œuvres	Antipasti	Entremeses
Cold eggs mayonnaise	Eier kalt mit Mayonnaise	Œufs durs mayonnaise	Uova sode con maionese	Huevos con mayonesa
Cold eggs in tartar sauce	~ kalt mit Tatarensauce	Œufs à la tartare	Uova alla tartara	~ fríos a la tártara
Cold meats, cold cuts	Aufschnitt	Charcuterie assortie[7])	Affettato misto	Fiambres surtidos
Cold meats, cold cuts	Kalte Platte	Viandes froides[8])	Piatto freddo	Fiambres surtidos
Crabmeat cocktail	Krabbencocktail	Cocktail de crabe	Cocktail di granchi	Cóctel de cangrejos
Crayfish cocktail	Krebsschwanz-Cocktail	Cocktail d'écrevisses	Cocktail di gamberi	Cóctel de cangrejos
Croquettes	Kroketten	Croquettes	Crocchette	Croquetas
Crudités (raw vegetables)	Rohkostplatte	Assiette de crudités	Crudità (verdure crude)	Verduras crudas
Eel in jelly	Aal in Gelee	Anguille à la gelée	Anguilla in gelatina	Anguila en gelatina
Fish salad	Fischsalat	Salade de poisson	Insalata di pesce	Ensalada de pescado
Fondue	Fondue (Käsefondue)	Fondue savoyarde	Fondue	Fondue a la suiza
Frankfurters	Frankfurter Würstchen	Saucisses de Francfort	Würstel	Salchichas de Francfort
Fruit cocktail, fruit cup	Früchtecocktail	Cocktail de fruits	Cocktail di frutta	Cóctel de frutas
Game pie, venison pie	Wildpastete	Pâté de gibier	Pâté di cacciagione	Pastel de caza
Gherkins	Gewürzgurken	Cornichons	Cetriolini sott'aceto	Pepinillos en vinagre
Goose-liver mousse	Gänseleber-Mousse	Mousse de foie gras	Mousse di fegato d'oca	Espuma de foie-gras
Green olives	Oliven (grüne)	Olives vertes	Olive verdi	Aceitunas verdes
Grisons air-dried beef	Bündner Fleisch	Viande des Grisons	Bresaola dei Grigioni	Cecina de los Grisones
Ham cornets, ham rolls	Schinken-Röllchen	Cornets de jambon	Cornetti di prosciutto	Rollos de jamón
Ham mousse	Schinken-Mousse	Mousse de jambon	Mousse di prosciutto	Espuma de jamón
Ham	Schinken	Jambon	Prosciutto	Jamón
Boiled ham	~ gekochter	~ cuit	~ cotto	~ en dulce, ~ cocido
Smoked ham	~ geräucherter	~ fumé	~ affumicato	~ serrano, ~ ahumado
Raw ham	~ roher	~ cru	~ crudo	~ natural, ~ crudo
Westphalian ham	~ westfälischer	~ de Westphalie	~ di Vestfalia	~ de Westfalia
Herring salad	Heringssalat	Salade de hareng	Insalata di aringhe	Ensalada de arenques
Herring fillets	Heringsfilets	Filets de hareng	Filetti d'aringa	Filetes de arenque
Hors-d'œuvres of fish	Fisch-Vorspeisen	Hors-d'œuvre de poissons	Antipasti di pesce	Entremeses de pescado
Iced grapefruit	Grapefruit, eisgekühlt	Grape-fruit frappé	Pompelmo ghiacciato	Pomelo helado
Iced melon	Melone, eisgekühlt	Melon frappé	Melone ghiacciato	Melón helado

Hors-d'œuvres	Vorspeisen	Hors-d'œuvres	Antipasti	Entremeses
Kipper (smoked herring)	Räucherhering	Hareng saur, hareng fumé	Aringa affumicata	Arenque ahumado
Lapwing eggs	Kiebitzeier	Œufs de vanneau	Uova di pavoncella	Huevos de avefría
Lobster boats	Hummer-Schiffchen	Barquettes d'homard	Barchette d'astice	Barquillas de bogavante
Lobster cocktail	Hummer-Cocktail	Cocktail d'homard	Cocktail d'astice	Cóctel de bogavante
Lobster mayonnaise	Hummer Mayonnaise	Mayonnaise d'homard	Maionese d'astice	Mayonesa de bogavante
Lobster salad	Hummer-Salat	Salade d'homard	Insalata d'astice	Ensalada de bogavante
Marinated artichokes	Artischocken, griechisch (marinierte Artisch.)	Artichauts à la grecque (artichauts marinés)	Carciofi alla greca (carciofi marinati)	Alcachofas a la griega (alcachofas marinadas)
Marinated tench	Marinierte Schleien	Escabèche de tanches	Tinche in carpione	Tencas en escabeche
Maatjes herring [9])	Matjeshering	Hareng vierge	Aringa giovane	Arenque joven
Meatless hors-d'œuvres	Fleischlose Vorspeisen	Hors d'œuvre maigres	Antipasti di magro	Entremeses de vigilia
Mixed pickles	Mixed Pickles	Mixed pickles	Sottaceti	Encurtidos
Mortadella	Mortadella	Mortadelle	Mortadella	Mortadela
Mushrooms on toast	Champignons auf Toast	Croûte aux champignons	Funghi sul crostone	Championes sobre tostada
Ox-muzzle salad	Ochsenmaulsalat	Museau de bœuf en salade	Insalata di muso di bue	Ensalada de lengua de buey
Oyster boats	Austern-Schiffchen	Barquettes d'huîtres	Barchette d'ostriche	Barquillas de ostras
Oyster bouchées	Austern-Pastetchen	Bouchées aux huîtres	Bocconcini d'ostriche	Pastelitos de ostras
Oyster cocktail	Austern-Cocktail	Cocktail d'huîtres	Cocktail d'ostriche	Cóctel de ostras
Oysters	Austern	Huîtres	Ostriche	Ostras
Pâté de foie gras	Gänseleber-Pastete	Pâté de foie gras	Pâté di fegato d'oca	Foie-gras (pasta de hígado de ganso)
Parfait de foie gras	Gänseleber-Parfait	Parfait de foie gras	Parfait di fegato d'oca	Parfait de foie-gras
Parma ham	Parmaschinken	Jambon de Parme	Prosciutto di Parma	Jamón de Parma
Parmesan en brochette	Parmesanspießchen	Brochettes de Parme	Spiedini di parmigiano	Parmesano en broqueta
Pickled onions	Silber- oder Perlzwiebeln	Petits oignons (au vinaigre)	Cipolline sott'aceto	Cebollitas en vinagre
Pressed caviar	Preßkaviar	Caviar pressé	Caviale pressato	Caviar aplastado
Quail's eggs	Wachteleier	Œufs de caille	Uova di quaglia	Huevos de codorniz
Quiche Lorraine (tart with bacon & cream)	Quiche lorraine (Lothringer Specktorte)	Quiche lorraine (tarte à la crème et au lard)	Quiche lorenese (torta con lardo e crema)	Tarta de Lorena (con tocino y crema)
Radish	Rettich	Radis (noir)	Rafano, ramolaccio	Rábano
Radishes	Radieschen	Radis (roses)	Ravanelli	Rabanitos

Hors-d'œuvres	Vorspeisen	Hors-d'œuvres	Antipasti	Entremeses
Ramekins (cheese tartlets)	Käsetörtchen	Ramequins	Tartelette al formaggio	Tartaletas de queso
Ripe olives, black olives	Oliven (schwarze)	Olives noires	Olive nere	Aceitunas negras
Rissoles (fried cakes with meat or fish stuffing)	Rissolen (gebackene Pasteten mit Füllung)	Rissoles (chaussons farcis, frits à grande friture)	Rissoles (crocchette di pasta con ripieno	Rissoles (croquetas de pasta con relleno)
~ with truffles	~ mit Trüffeln	~ aux truffes	Crocchette di tartufi	~ con trufas
Roebuck ham	Rehschinken	Jambon de chevreuil	Prosciutto di capriolo	Jamón de corzo
Rollmop (rolled herring)	Rollmops	Rollmops	Rollmops[10]	Rollmops[11])
Russian eggs (set on Russian salad)	Russische Eier (mit russischem Salat)	Œufs à la russe (dressés sur salade russe)	Uova alla russa (con insalata russa)	Huevos a la rusa (con ensalada rusa)
Salami	Salami	Salami	Salame	Salchichón
Hungarian salami	~ ungarische	Salami hongrois	Salame ungherese	~ húngaro
Salmon mayonnaise	Lachs-Mayonnaise	Mayonnaise de saumon	Maionese di salmone	Mayonesa de salmón
Salt ox-tongue	Pökelzunge	Langue écarlate	Lingua salmistrata	Lengua salada
Sandwich	Sandwich	Sandwich	Sandwich, panino	Emparedado, bocadillo
Cheese sandwich	Käsesandwich	~ au fromage	~ al formaggio	~ de queso
Ham sandwich	Schinkensandwich	~ au jambon	~ al prosciutto	~ de jamón
Sardines in oil	Ölsardinen	Sardines à l'huile	Sardine sott'olio	Sardinas en aceite
Sausage	Wurst	Saucisson	Salame; salsiccia	Embutido, salchichón
Scalloped chicken	Geflügel in Muschelschalen	Coquilles de volaille	Conchiglie di pollo	Conchas de ave
Scalloped fish	Fisch in Muschelschalen	Coquilles de poisson	Conchiglie di pesce	Conchas de pescado
Scampi cocktail	Scampi-Cocktail	Cocktail de langoustines	Cocktail di scampi	Cóctel de cigalas
Scotch woodcock (scrambled egg on anchovy toast)	Scotch woodcock (Rührei auf Sardellentoast)	Scotch woodcock, (œuf brouillé sur toast á l'anchois)	Scotch woodcock (uovo strapazzato su crostini all'acciuga)	Scotch woodcock (huevo revuelto sobre tostada de anchoa)
Seafood	Meeresfrüchte	Fruits de mer	Frutti di mare	Mariscos
Shellfish cocktail	Cocktail von Meeresfrüchten	Cocktail de fruits de mer	Cocktail di frutti di mare	Cóctel de mariscos
Shells à la financière	Ragoût fin in Muscheln	Coquilles à la financière	Conchiglie alla finanziera	Conchas a la financiera
Shrimp cocktail	Garnelen-Cocktail	Cocktail de crevettes	Cocktail di gamberetti	Cóctel de camarones
Shrimps	Krabben (Krevetten)	Crevettes (grises)	Gamberetti	Camarones

Hors-d'œuvres	Vorspeisen	Hors-d'œuvres	Antipasti	Entremeses
Shrimp salad	Garnelen-Salat	Salade de crevettes	Insalata di gamberetti	Ensalada de camarones
Smoked beef	Rauchfleisch	Bœuf fumé	Manzo affumicato	Carne ahumada, cecina
Smoked eel	Räucheraal	Anguille fumée	Anguilla affumicata	Anguila ahumada
Smoked goose-breast	Geräucherte Gänsebrust	Poitrine d'oie fumée	Petto d'oca affumicato	Pechuga de ganso ahumada
Smoked salmon	Räucherlachs	Saumon fumé	Salmone affumicato	Salmón ahumado
Smoked trout	Forelle, geräuchert	Truite fumée	Trota affumicata	Trucha ahumada
Snails	Schnecken	Escargots	Lumache	Caracoles
Stuffed eggs	Gefüllte Eier	Œufs durs farcis	Uova ripiene	Huevos rellenos
Stuffed olives	Gefüllte Oliven	Olives farcies	Olive farcite	Aceitunas rellenas
Swedish platter (marinated and smoked fish specialities)	Schwedenplatte (marinierte und geräucherte Fischspezialitäten)	Plat suédois (spécialités de poissons marinés et fumés)	Piatto svedese (specialità di pesce marinato e affumicato)	Plato sueco (surtido de pescados en escabeche y ahumados)
Sweetbread vol-au-vent	Kalbsmilch-Pastete	Vol-au-vent de ris de veau	Vol-au-vent con animelle	Vol-au-vent con mollejas
Tomato salad	Tomatensalat	Tomates à la vinaigrette	Pomodori in insalata	Tomates en ensalada
Tuna in olive oil	Thunfisch in Öl	Thon à l'huile	Tonno sott'olio	Atún en aceite
Variety of canapés	Verschiedene Canapés	Canapés divers	Canapè assortiti, tartine assortite	Canapés surtidos
Vol-au-vent	Blätterteigpastete	Vol-au-vent	Vol-au-vent	Vol-au-vent
~ à la financière (with chicken dumplings, cockscombs & kernels)	~ à la financière (mit Ragoût fin gefüllt)	~ à la financière (garni quenelles, crêtes et rognons de coq, olives)	~ alla finanziera (con chenelle, creste e rognoni di pollo)	~ a la financiera (con quenefas, crestas y riñones de gallo)
Welsh rarebit[12] (dish of melted cheese on toast)	Welsh Rarebit (Röstbrot mit heißem Käse belegt)	Welsh rarebit (fromage fondu sur toast)	Welsh rarebit (formaggio fuso su pane tostato)	Welsh rarebit (queso derretido sobre tostada)
York ham	Yorker Schinken	Jambon d'York	Prosciutto di York	Jamon de York

[6]) ou poutargue.
[7]) ou assiette anglaise.
[8]) ou assiette anglaise.
[9]) herring not fully developed.

[10]) aringa arrotolata e marinata.
[11]) arenque arrollado en escabeche.
[12]) or Welsh rabbit.

Soups	Suppen	Potages	Minestre	Sopas
Bagration soup (cream of veal soup with maca-roni)	Bagration-Suppe (Kalb-fleischsuppe mit Makkaroni-Einlage)	Potage Bagration (velouté de veau garni de tron-çons de macaroni)	Minestra Bagration (crema di vitello con maccheroncini)	Sopa Bagration (crema de ternera con trocitos de macarrones)
Barley soup	Gerstensuppe	Potage à l'orge	Minestra d'orzo	Sopa de cebada
Beer soup	Biersuppe	Soupe à la bière	Minestra di birra	~ de cerveza
Bird's nest soup	Schwalbennestersuppe	Potage aux nids d'hiron-delle	Brodo con nidi di rondine	Sopa con nidos de salangana
Bouillabaisse (French fish-soup with saffron)	Bouillabaisse (Fischsuppe mit Safran)	Bouillabaisse (soupe de poisson safranée)	Zuppa di pesce provenzale (con zafferano)	Bullabesa (potaje de pescado con azafrán)
Broth, bouillon, beef tea	Rindsuppe	Bouillon	Brodo	Caldo (de carne)
Broth, bouillon, beef tea	Bouillon	Bouillon	Brodo	Caldo
Bouillon with egg	~ mit Ei	~ à l'œuf	~ all'uovo	~ con huevo
Garnished bouillon	~ mit Einlage	~ garni	~ con pastina o riso o altro	~ guarnecido
Broth, bouillon, beef tea	Fleischbrühe	Bouillon	Brodo	Caldo
Bouillon with egg	~ mit Ei	~ à l'œuf	~ all'uovo	~ con huevo
Busecca (tripe and bean soup)	Busecca (Kuttelsuppe mit weißen Bohnen)	Busecca (gras-double de veau et haricots)	Busecca (zuppa di trippa e fagioli)	Busecca (sopa de callos con judias blancas)
Cabbage soup	Kohlsuppe	Soupe aux choux	Zuppa di cavoli	Sopa de coles
Calf's tail soup	Kalbsschwanzsuppe	Potage queue de veau	Brodo di coda di vitello	Sopa de rabo de ternera
Carmen soup (cream of rice coloured with tomato purée)	Carmen-Suppe (passierte Reissuppe mit Tomaten-mark gefärbt)	Velouté Carmen (velouté à la crème de riz tomatée)	Minestra Carmen (vellutata di riso al pomodoro)	Sopa Carmen (crema de arroz con tomate)
Chervil soup	Kerbelsuppe	Potage au cerfeuil	Zuppa di cerfoglio	Sopa de perifollo
Chicken gumbo	Gombosuppe mit Huhn	Potage de poulet aux gombos	Minestra di gombo e pollo	Sopa de gombo y ave
Chicken broth	Hühnerbrühe	Consommé de volaille	Brodo di pollo	Caldo de gallina
Clam chowder	Muschelsuppe	Soupe aux clams	Zuppa di vongole	Sopa de almejas
Clear rice soup	Reissuppe (klare)	Potage au riz	Riso in brodo	Sopa de arroz
Clear soup	Klare Suppe	Potage clair	Minestra chiara	Sopa clara
Cock-a-leekie (soup of chicken and leeks)	Schottische Hühnersuppe mit Lauch	Soupe au poulet et aux poireaux	Zuppa di pollo e porri	Sopa de pollo y puerros

19

Soups	Suppen	Potages	Minestre	Sopas
Cold consommé	Kalte Kraftbrühe	Consommé froid	Consommé freddo	Consomé frío
Cold fruit soup	Fruchtkaltschale	Potage froid aux fruits	Zuppa fredda di frutta	Sopa fría de fruta
Cold wine soup	Wein-Kaltschale	Potage froid au vin	Minestra fredda al vino	Sopa fría de vino
Condé soup (purée of red beans)	Bohnensuppe (rote)	Potage Condé (purée de haricots rouges)	Minestra Condé (passato di fagioli rossi)	~ Condé (puré de judías pintas)
Consommé Célestine (with shredded pancake)	Frittatensuppe	ConsomméCélestine(garni crêpe taillée en julienne)	Frittatine in brodo	Consomé Celestina (con una crêpe en tiritas)
Consommé, clear soup	Kraftbrühe	Consommé	Consommé[18]	Consomé, consumado
~ with profiteroles[13]	~ mit Backerbsen	~ aux profiteroles	~ con pasta reale	~ con profiteroles
~ Célestine (with shredded pancake)	~ Célestine (mit Pfannkuchenstreifen)	~ Célestine (garni crêpe taillée en julienne)	~ Celestina (frittatine in brodo)	~ Celestina (con una crêpe en tiritas)
Consommé with milt croûtons	Milzschnittensuppe	Potage aux croûtons de rate	Crostini di milza in brodo	Sopa con croûtons de bazo
Consommé with quenelles	Nockerlsuppe	Potage aux quenelles	Gnocchetti in brodo	Sopa con albondiguillas
Country style soup (vegetable soup)	Bauern-Suppe (Gemüsesuppe)	~ à la paysanne (potage aux légumes)	Zuppa alla contadina (zuppa di verdura)	~ campesina (sopa de verduras)
Crayfish cream soup[14]	Krebssuppe	Bisque d'écrevisses[15]	Crema di gamberi	Sopa de cangrejos
Cream of of asparagus soup	Spargelcremesuppe	Crème Argenteuil[16]	Crema d'asparagi	Crema de espárragos
Cream of barley soup	Gerstenschleimsuppe	Crème d'orge	Crema d'orzo	Crema de cebada
Cream of brain soup	Hirnsuppe	Crème de cervelle	Minestra di cervella	Sopa de sesos
Cream of carrot soup	Karottensuppe	Potage Crécy	Crema di carote	Sopa de zanahorias
Cream of celery soup	Selleriesuppe	Crème de céleri	Crema di sedani	Crema de apio
Cream of chicken soup	Königinsuppe	Potage à la reine	Crema di pollo	Sopa reina (crema de ave)
Cream of chicken soup	Geflügelcremesuppe	Crème de volaille[17]	Crema di pollo	Crema de ave
Cream of green pea soup	Erbsenpüreesuppe	Crème de petits pois	Crema di piselli	Sopa de guisantes
Cream of leek soup	Lauchcremesuppe	Crème de poireaux	Crema di porri	Crema de puerros
Cream of mushroom soup	Champignoncremesuppe	Crème de champignons	Crema di funghi	Crema de champiñones
Cream of rice soup	Reisschleimsuppe	Crème de riz	Crema di riso	Crema de arroz
Cream of spinach soup	Spinatcremesuppe	Crème d'épinards	Crema di spinaci	Crema de espinacas
Cream of vegetable soup	Gemüsecremesuppe	Crème de légumes	Crema di verdure	Crema de legumbres
Cream soup	Cremesuppe	Potage crème	Crema	Crema

Soups	Suppen	Potages	Minestre	Sopas
Cress soup	Kressesuppe	Potage au cresson	Minestra di crescione	Sopa de berros
Darblay soup (potato soup with shredded vegetables)	Darblay-Suppe (Kartoffelsuppe mit Gemüsestreifen)	Potage julienne Darblay (potage Parmentier garni julienne de légumes)	Minestra Darblay (minestra di patate con julienne di verdure)	Sopa Darblay (sopa de patatas con tiritas de verdura)
Double consommé	Doppelte Kraftbrühe	Consommé double	Consommé doppio	Consomé doble
Du Barry soup (cauliflower cream soup)	Blumenkohlsuppe	Crème Du Barry, crème de chou-fleur	Minestra Du Barry (crema di cavolfiori)	∼ Du Barry (crema de coliflor)
Eel soup	Aalsuppe	Potage à l'anguille	Minestra d'anguilla	Sopa de anguila
Fish soup	Fischsuppe	Soupe de poisson	Zuppa di pesce	Sopa de pescado
Game soup	Wildsuppe	Potage de gibier	Minestra di selvaggina	Sopa de venado
Game soup	Jägersuppe	Potage chasseur	Minestra dek cacciatore	Sopa del cazador
Garbanzo soup	Kichererbsensuppe	Potage aux pois chiches	Zuppa di ceci	Sopa de garbanzos
Gazpacho (soup of uncooked vegetables with vinegar & oil)	Gazpacho (kalte Suppe aus rohem Gemüse mit Öl und Essig)	Gaspacho (potage non cuit de légumes crus avec huile et vinaigre)	Gazpacho (minestra fredda di verdure crude con olio e aceto)	Gazpacho (sopa fría de legumbres crudos con aceite y vinagre)
Germiny soup (sorrel soup bound with egg-yolks & cream)	Germiny-Suppe (Sauerampfersuppe, stark mit Eigelb und Sahne legiert)	∼ Germiny (potage à l'oseille avec double liaison de crème et œufs)	Minestra Germiny (zuppa di acetosa, legata con molta panna e rossi d'uovo)	Sopa Germiny (sopa de acedera, ligada con mucha crema y yemas de huevo)
Goulash soup (highly seasoned soup of beef & potatoes)	Gulaschsuppe	∼ au goulash (potage très relevé avec dés de bœuf)	∼ di gulasch (minestra piccante con pezzetti di carne)	Sopa de gulasch (sopa picante con trozos de carne y patatas)
Gumbo (with okra pods)	Gombosuppe	Potage aux gombos	Minestra di gombo	Sopa de gombo
Haricot bean soup	Bohnensuppe (weiße)	∼ Faubonne (purée de haricots blancs)	∼ Faubonne (passato di fagioli bianchi)	∼ Faubonne (puré de judías blancas)
Julienne, vegetable soup	Juliennesuppe	Potage julienne	Minestra di verdura	∼ de hierbas, ∼ juliana
Kale	Kohlsuppe	Soupe aux choux	Zuppa di cavolo verde	Sopa de coles
Kangaroo-tail soup	Känguruhschwanzsuppe	Potage queue de kangourou	Brodo di coda di canguro	Sopa de rabo de canguro
Kidney Soup	Nierensuppe	Potage aux rognons	Minestra di rognone	Sopa de riñones
Lenten soup, soup maigre	Fastensuppe	Potage maigre	Minestra di magro	Sopa de vigilia[19])
Lentil soup	Linsensuppe	Potage Conti (ou Esaü)	Minestra di lenticchie	Sopa de lentejas

Soups	Suppen	Potages	Minestre	Sopas
Liver dumpling soup	Leberknödelsuppe	Potage aux boulettes de foie	Canederli di fegato in brodo	Sopa con albóndiga de hígado
Lobster soup, lobster bisque	Hummercremesuppe	Bisque d'homard	Minestra d'astice	Sopa de bogavante
Londonderry soup (consommé flavoured with Madeira, garnished w. diced calf's head)	Londonderry-Kraftbrühe (mit Madeira und Einlage von Kalbskopf in Würfeln)	Potage Londonderry (consommé au madère, garni tête de veau en dés)	Consommé Londonderry (brodo al madera con dadi di testina di vitello)	Sopa Londonderry (caldo al Madera con dados de cabeza de ternera)
Minestrone (thick vegetable soup with rice or pasta)	Minestrone (dicke Gemüsesuppe mit Reis- oder Teigwaren-Einlage)	Minestrone (potage aux légumes divers garni riz ou pâtes)	Minestrone (minestra di verdura con riso o pasta)	Minestrone (sopa de verduras con pasta o arroz)
Mulligatawny (soup) (chicken soup flavoured with curry)	Mulligatawny-Suppe (Currysuppe mit Huhn)	Potage mulligatawny (soupe de poulet au curry)	Minestra mulligatawny (minestra di pollo al curry)	Sopa mulligatawny (sopa de ave al curry)
Mussel soup	Muschelsuppe	Soupe aux moules	Zuppa di cozze	Sopa de mejillones
Noodle soup	Nudelsuppe	Potage aux pâtes	Pastina in brodo	Sopa de pastas
Noodle soup	Nudelsuppe (Eier-)	Potage aux nouilles	Taglierini in brodo	Sopa de tallarines
Noodle soup with chicken	~ mit Huhn	Poule au pot aux nouilles	Pollo e taglierini in brodo	~ de tallarines con ave
Oatmeal soup	Haferschleimsuppe	Crème d'avoine de requin	Crema d'avena	Crema de avena
Onion soup	Zwiebelsuppe	Soupe à l'oignon	Zuppa di cipolle	Sopa de cebolla
Baked onion soup	~ überbacken	Soupe gratinée	~ di cipolle gratinata	~ de cebolla gratinada
Oxtail soup	Ochsenschwanzsuppe (Oxtailsuppe)	Oxtail, potage queue de bœuf	Brodo di coda di bue	Sopa de rabo de buey
Pheasant consommé	Fasanen-Kraftbrühe	Consommé de faisan	Brodo di fagiano	Consomé de faisán
Philadelphia pepper pot	Philadelphier Kuttelsuppe (stark gepfeffert)	Potage aux tripes de Philadelphie (très épicé)	Zuppa Filadelfia (zuppa di trippa molto pepata)	Sopa de callos con pimienta
Portuguese soup (tomato soup)	Portugiesische Suppe (Tomatensuppe)	Potage à la portugaise (purée de tomates)	Minestra alla portoghese, minestra di pomodoro	Sopa portuguesa (sopa de tomate)
Potato soup	Kartoffelsuppe	Potage Parmentier	Minestra di patate	Sopa de patatas

Soups	Suppen	Potages	Minestre	Sopas
Pot-au-feu (broth with meat and vegetables)	Potaufeu (Eintopf aus Brühe, Fleisch u. Gemüse)	Pot-au-feu, petite marmite	Pot-au-feu (brodo con verdure e pezzi di lesso)	Pot-au-feu (cocido de carne de vaca)
Princess soup (cream of chicken soup with asparagus tips)	Prinzessin-Suppe (Geflügelcremesuppe mit Spargelspitzen)	Crème princesse (crème de volaille garnie de pointes d'asperges)	Cream principessa (crema di pollo con punte d'asparagi)	Sopa princesa (crema de ave con puntas de espárragos)
Pumpkin soup	Kürbissuppe	Soupe au potiron	Zuppa di zucca	Sopa de calabaza
Ravioli soup	Ravioli-Suppe	Potage aux ravioli	Ravioli in brodo	Sopa de ravioles
Turtle soup	Schildkrötensuppe	Potage tortue	Brodo di tartaruga	Sopa de tortuga
Mock-turtle soup	~ falsche	Potage fausse tortue	~ di finta tartaruga	~ de tortuga falsa
Turtle soup Lady Curzon (flavoured with curry & covered with whipped cream)	~ Lady Curzon (mit Curry gewürzt und mit überbräunter Schlagsahne bedeckt)	Potage tortue Lady Curzon (relevé au curry et couvert de crème fouettée)	~ di tartaruga Lady Curzon (condito con curry e coperto di panna montata)	~ de tortuga Lady Curzon (aromatizada con curry y cubierta de nata batida)
Rice and pea soup	Risi-Pisi (Risibisi)	Potage de riz aux petits pois	Risi e bisi	Sopa de arroz y guisante
Riced liver soup (liver mixture put through a ricer into boiled broth)	Leberreissuppe	~ au foie à la viennoise (consommé garni de petites nouilles de foie)	Passatelli di fegato (composto di fegato, passato dai buchi di uno stampo)	Sopa vienesa de hígado (caldo con fideos muy finos de hígado)
Royal soup (with diced egg custard)	Kraftbrühe mit Eierstich	Consommé royal (garni dés de royale)	Consommé reale (con dadini di crema reale)	Consomé real (con dados de crema real)
Vermicelli soup	~ mit Fadennudeln	~ au vermicelle	Vermicelli in brodo	~ con fideos
Consommé with liver quenelles	~ mit Lebernockerln	~ aux noques de foie	Gnocchetti di fegato in brodo	~ con albondiguillas de hígado
~ madrilène (tomatoed chicken broth)	~ Madrilène (mit Tomatenpüree)	~ madrilène (consommé de volaille tomaté)	Consommé alla madrilena (al pomodoro)	~ madrileño (consomé de ave con tomate)
~ with beef marrow	~ mit Mark	~ à la moelle	~ con midollo	~ con tuétano
~ with pasta or rice	~ mit Einlage	~ garni	~ con pastina o riso o altro	~ guarnecido
~ with marrow quenelles	~ mit Markklößchen	~ aux quenelles à la moelle	Gnocchetti di midollo in brodo	~ con albondiguillas de tuétano
Clear rice soup	~ mit Reiseinlage	Potage au riz	Riso in brodo	~ con arroz
Consommé in cup	~ in der Tasse	Consommé en tasse	Consommé in tazza	~ en taza
~ with pasta	~ mit Teigwaren	Potage aux pâtes	Pastina in brodo	Sopa de pastas

Soups	Suppen	Potages	Minestre	Sopas
Santé soup (potato purée with sorrel)	Gesundheitssuppe (Kartoffelsuppe mit Sauerampfer)	Potage santé (purée Parmentier à l'oseille)	Minestra santé (passato di patate con acetosa)	Sopa de la salud (puré de patatas con acedera)
Scotch broth (soup of mutton[20]) and pearl-barley)	Schottische Brühe (Suppe mit Hammelfleisch und Rollgerste)	Pot-au-feu écossais (soupe de mouton à l'orge)	Brodo scozzese (Zuppa di montone con orzo)	Caldo escocés (sopa de carnero con cebada)
Semolina dumpling soup	Grießnockerlsuppe	Potage aux quenelles de semoule	Gnocchetti di semolino in brodo	Sopa con albondiguillas de sémola
Semolina soup	Grießsuppe	~ à la semoule	Minestra di semolino	Sopa de sémola
Shark's fin soup	Haifischflossensuppe	Consommé aux nageoires	Zuppa di pinne di pesce	Sopa de aletas de tiburón
Snail soup	Schneckensuppe	Potage aux escargots	Zuppa di lumache	Sopa de caracoles
Sorrel soup	Sauerampfersuppe	Potage à l'oseille	Zuppa di acetosa	Sopa de acedera
Soup of the day	Tagessuppe	Potage du jour	Minestra del giorno	Sopa del dia
Spring vegetable soup	Frühlingssuppe	Potage printanier	Zuppa primaverile	Sopa de primavera
Tapioca soup	Tapiokasuppe	Potage au tapioca	Minestra di tapioca	Sopa de tapioca
Tomato soup	Tomatensuppe	Potage aux tomates	Minestra di pomodori	Sopa de tomate
Tyrolean dumpling soup	Knödelsuppe (Speck-)	Potage aux boulettes au lard	Canederli in brodo	Sopa con albóndiga de tocino
Vegetable broth	Gemüsebrühe	Bouillon de légumes	Brodo vegetale	Caldo de verduras
Vegetable soup	Gemüsesuppe	Potage aux légumes	Minestra di verdura	Sopa de verduras
Velvet soup (carrot purée with tapioca)	Samtsuppe (Karottenpüree mit Tapioka)	Potage velours (purée Crécy avec tapioca)	Minestra di carote e tapioca	Sopa de zanahorias y tapioca
Zuppa pavese (beef broth with slices of fried bread and an egg poached in it)	Zuppa pavese (Bouillon mit gerösteten Brotscheiben, darauf ein pochiertes Ei)	Zuppa pavese (consommé avec tranches de pain grillé et un œuf cassé dessus)	Zuppa alla pavese (brodo con fette di pane abbrustolito e sopra un uovo affogato)	Zuppa pavese (caldo con huevo y rebanadas de pan frito)

[13]) pea-sized balls of choux pastry.
[14]) or crayfish bisque.
[15]) ou coulis d'écrevisses.
[16]) ou crème d'asperges.

[17]) dite aussi potage à la reine.
[18]) o brodo ristretto.
[19]) o sopa de viernes.
[20]) or beef.

24

Eggs	Eierspeisen	Œufs	Uova	Huevos
Artichoke omelette	Eier mit Artischocken	Œufs aux fonds d'artichauts	Uova coi carciofi	Huevos de alcachofas
Asparagus omelette	Omelette mit Spargel-spitzen	Omelette aux pointes d'asperges	Omelette con punte d'asparagi	Tortilla con espárragos
Bacon and eggs	Eier mit Speck (Setzeier)	Œufs frits au bacon	Uova al bacon, uova con pancetta	Huevos al plato con tocino
Bacon omelette	Omelette mit Speck	Omelette au lard	Omelette con pancetta	Tortilla con tocino
Boiled eggs in tartar sauce	Eier mit Tatarensauce	Œufs froids à la tartare	Uova alla tartara	fríos a la tártara
Cheese omelette	Omelette nit Käse	Omelette au fromage	Omelette con formaggio	Tortilla de queso
Chicken-liver omelette	Omelette mit Geflügelleber	Omelette aux foies de volaille	Omelette con fegatini di pollo	Tortilla con higadillos
Creamed eggs en cocotte	Eier in Rahm	Œufs en cocotte à la crème	Uova alla panna	Huevos a la crema
Eggs en cocotte	Eier in Cocotte	Œufs en cocotte	Uova in cocotte	Huevos en cazuela
Egg mayonnaise	Eier mit Mayonnaise	Œufs durs à la maionese	Uova sode con maionese	fríos con mayonesa
Florentine omelette, spinach omelette	Omelette mit Spinat	Omelette à la florentine (aux épinards)	Omelette alla fiorentina, omelette con spinaci	Tortilla a la florentina, tortilla de espinacas
Fried eggs[21])	Spiegeleier (Setzeier)	Œufs sur le plat, œufs au plat, œufs au miroir	Uova al tegame, uova al piatto, uova al burro	Huevos estrellados, huevos al plato
Fried eggs (in deep fat)	Gebackene Eier	Œufs frits	Uova fritte	Huevos fritos
Fried eggs Bercy (with grilled sausage and tomato sauce)	Eier Bercy (Spiegeleier mit Bratwürstchen und Tomatensauce)	Œufs sur le plat Bercy (garnis d'une saucisse grillée, sauce tomate)	Uova al piatto Bercy (con una piccola salsiccia e salsa di pomodoro)	Huevos estrellados Bercy (con salchicha y salsa de tomate)
Fried eggs Meyerbeer (with grilled lamb's kidney & truffle sauce)	Eier Meyerberbeer (Setzeier mit gegrillter Lammniere und Trüffelsauce)	Œufs sur le plat Meerbeer (avec rognon grillé et sauce Périgueux)	Uova al tegame Meyerbeer (con rognone d'agnello e salsa di tartufi)	Huevos estrellados Meyer beer (con riñones y salsa de trufas)
Fried eggs Turbigo (with sausage)	Eier Turbigo (Spiegeleier mit Bratwürstchen)	Œufs sur le plat Turbigo (avec saucisse)	Uova al tegame Turbigo (con una salsiccia)	Huevos estrellados Turbigo (con salchicha)
Fried eggs with bacon	Eier auf amerikanische Art (Spiegeleier mit Speck)	Œufs frits à l'américaine (au bacon)	Uova all'americana (al tegame con bacon)	Huevos a la americana
Fried eggs with chicken livers	Eier türkisch (Spiegeleier mit Geflügelleber)	Œufs au plat à la turque (aux foies de volaille)	Uova al tegame alla turca (con fegatini)	Huevos estrellados a la turca (con higadillos)

Eggs	Eierspeisen	Œufs	Uofa	Huevos
Ham and eggs	Eier mit Schinken (Setzeier)	Oeufs frits[23]) au jambon	Uova al prosciutto	Huevos al plato con jamón
Ham omelette	Omelette mit Schinken	Omelette au jambon	Omelette con prosciutto	Tortilla con jamón
Hard-boiled eggs[22])	Hartgekochte Eier	Œufs durs	Uova sode	Huevos duros
Jellied eggs	Eier in Gelee	Œufs à la gelée	Uova in gelatina	Huevos en gelatina
Kidney omelette	Omelette mit Nieren	Omelette aux rognons	Omelette col rognone	Tortilla con riñones
Medium-boiled eggs	Weiche Eier (5–6 Min.)	Œufs mollets	Uova bazzotte	Huevos encerados, huevos blandos
Mushroom omelette	Omelette mit Pilzen	Omelette aux champignons	Omelette coi funghi	Tortilla con setas
Mushroom omelette	Omelette mit Champignons	Omelette aux champignons	Omelette coi funghi	Tortilla con champiñones
Mushroom omelette	Omelette nach Försterinart (mit Morcheln oder Pilzen)	Omelette à la forestière (aux morilles ou cèpes)	Omelette alla forestale (con spugnole o porcini)	Tortilla a la forestal (con setas)
Omelette, omelet	Omelette[23a])	Omelette	Omelette	Tortilla
Omelette	Eierkuchen	Omelette plate	Frittata	Tortilla española
Onion omelette	Omelette mit Zwiebeln	Omelette à la lyonnaise	Omelette con cipolle	Tortilla con cebolla
Peasant's omelette (omelette with sorrel, potato & bacon; not folded)	Omelette nach Bauernart (mit Speckwürfeln, Kartoffeln und Sauerampfer; nicht gerollt)	Omelette á la paysanne (omelette plate avec lardons, pommes de terre et oseille)	Omelette alla campagnola (non ripiegata, con lardo, patate e acetosa)	Tortilla a la campesina (tortilla española de patatas, acedera y tocino)
Plain omelette	Omelette natur	Omelette nature	Omelette semplice	Tortilla sencilla, Tortilla al natural
Poached eggs	Verlorene Eier	Œufs pochés	Uova affogate, uova in camicia	Huevos escalfados
Poached eggs au gratin	Gratinierte Eier	Œufs Mornay	Omelette con patate	Tortilla de patatas
Savoury omelette	Omelette mit Kräutern	Omelette aux fines herbes	Omelette verde (con erbe)	Tortilla con hierbas finas
Savoy omelette (cheese and potato omelette; not folded)	Omelette auf savoyische Art (mit Kartoffeln und Käse; nicht gerollt)	Omelette à la savoyarde (omelette plate avec gruyére et pommes)	Omelette alla savoiarda (non ripiegata, con patate e groviera)	Tortilla a la saboyarda (tortilla española con queso y patatas)
Scrambled eggs	Rühreier	Œufs brouillés	Uova strapazzate	Huevos revueltos

Eggs	Eierspeisen	Œufs	Uova	Huevos
Soft-boiled eggs	Weiche Eier (2–3 Min.)	Œufs à la coque	Uova alla coque, uova al guscio	Huevos pasados por agua[24])
Spanish omelette (flat omelette with onion, pimiento & tomato)	Omelette auf spanische Art (mit Tomaten und Paprika; nicht gerollt)	á l'espagnole (omelette plate avec tomates, oignons et piments)	Omelette alla spagnola (non ripiegata, con pomodori, cipolle e peperoni)	Tortilla a la española (con tomate, cebolla y pimiento morrón)
Stuffed eggs Chimay (eggs au gratin with mushroom stuffing)	Eier Chimay (gefüllte: überbackene Eier mit Champignonfülle)	Œufs farcis Chimay (œufs durs gratinés, farcis de champignons)	Uova ripiene alla Chimay (uova gratinate ripiene di funghi)	Huevos Chimay (huevos al gratén rellenos de champiñones)
Stuffed eggs	Gefüllte Eier	Œufs farcis	Uova ripiene	Huevos rellenos
Tomato omelette	Omelette mit Tomaten	Omelette à la portugaise	Omelette con pomodori	Tortilla con tomate

[21]) Am. sunny side up.
[22]) o huevos en cáscara.
[23]) auch das Omelett.
[23a]) on entend ici 'œufs frits' les œufs sur le plat.
[24]) o huevos en cáscara.

Fish and shellfish	Fische und Schaltiere	Poissons et crustacés	Pesci e crostacei	Pescados y crustáceos
Sea-fish	Seefisch	Poisson de mer	Pesce di mare	Pez marino
Freshwater fish	Süßwasserfisch	Poisson d'eau douce	Pesce d'acqua dolce	Pez de agua dulce
Abalones	Meerohren	Ormeaux	Orecchie di mare	Orejas de mar
Allice shad, shad	Alse, Maifisch	Alose	Cheppia, alosa	Sábalo, alosa
Anchovies	Sardellen	Anchois	Acciughe, alici	Boquerones
Angler-fish, frog-fish	Seeteufel	Lotte (de mer), baudroie	Rana pescatrice, coda di rospo	Rape, pejesapo
Broiled angler-fish	~ vom Rost	Lotte grillée	Coda di rospo alla griglia	Rape a la parrilla
Bar	Umber	Ombrine	Ombrina	Umbrina
Barbel	Barbe	Barbeau	Barbo, barbio	Barbo
Bass	Wolfsbarsch	Bar, loup (de mer)	Spigola, branzino	Lubina, róbalo
Boiled bass [naise	~ gekocht	Bar au court-bouillon	Spigola lessa	Lubina cocida
Cold bass with mayon-	~ mit Mayonnaise	Bar froid mayonnaise	~ lessa con maionese	~ fría con mayonesa
Bass meunière	~ nach Müllerinart	Bar meunière, bar au beurre rillé	~ alla mugnaia	~ a la molinera
Grilled bass	~ vom Rost		~ in gratella	~ a la parrilla
Bleaks	Silberfische	Ablettes	Alborelle	Albures
Fried bleaks	~ gebacken	Friture d'ablettes	Frittura di alborelle	Albures fritos
Bleaks	Ukeleie	Ablettes	Alborelle	Albures
Fried bleaks	~ gebacken	Friture d'ablettes	Alborelle fritte	Albures fritos
Bloaters	Bücklinge	Harengs saurs, craquelots	Aringhe affumicate	Arenques ahumados
Brandade of salt cod (purée of salt cod)	Stockfisch-Brandade (Stockfischpüree)	Brandade de morue (purée de morue)	Baccalà mantecato (crema di baccalà)	~ a la provenzal (puré de bacalao)
Bream	Brachsen	Brème	Abramide	Brema
Brill	Glattbutt	Barbue	Rombo liscio	Barbuda, rodaballo menor
Broiled sturgeon steak	Störschnitte vom Rost	Darne d'esturgeon grillée	Trancia di storione ai ferri	Esturión a la parrilla
Brook-trout, speckled trout	Bachsaibling	Omble, saumon de fontaine	Salmerino di fonte	Umbla
Brown trout, brook trout	Dachforelle	Truite de rivière	Trota di torrente	Trucha de río
Burbot, eel-pout	Aalquappe (Aalraupe), Trüsche	Lotte de rivière	Bottatrice	Lota

Fish and shellfish	Fische und Schaltiere	Poissons et crustacés	Pesci e crostacei	Pescados y crustáceos
Calamaries, squids	Kalmare	Calmars, encornets	Calamari	Calamares, chipirones
Fried calamaries	~ gebacken	Friture de calmars	~ fritti	~ fritos
Carp	Karpfen	Carpe	Carpa	Carpa
~ in beer sauce	~ in Bier	~ à la bière	~ alla birra	~ con cerveza
~ au bleu	~ blau	~ au bleu	~ al blu	~ al azul, ~ au bleu
Char, charr	Seesaibling	Omble, chevalier	Salmerino	Umbla
Chub	Döbel	Chevaine, chevesne	Cavedano	Cacho,
Cioppino (stew of	Cioppino (Fischragout	Cioppino (ragoût	Cioppino (stufato di	Cioppino (guiso de pes-
fish and shellfish	in Tomatensauce)	de poisson et de fruits de	pesce e frutti di	cado y mariscos
in tomato sauce		mer à la tomate)	mare al pomodoro)	al tomate)
Clam fritters	Muschelbeignets	Beignets de clams	Frittelle di vongole	Buñuelos de almejas
Clams, carpet shells	Venusmuscheln	Clovisses, palourdes	Vongole, arselle	Almejas
Venus clams	~ (warzige)	Praires	Tartufi di mare	Verigüetos, escupiñas
Clams	Clams, (Venus-)Muscheln	Clams, palourdes	Vongole [cabonaro	Almejas
Coalfish, pollack	Köhler	Lieu noir, charbonnier	Merlano nero, merluzzo	Faneca
Cockles	Herzmuscheln	Coques, bucardes	Cuori di mare	Berberechos
Cod, codfish	Kabeljau	Cabillaud	Merluzzo	Bacalao (fresco)
Fried cod	~ gebacken	~ frit	~ fritto	Bacalao frito
Cold cold with mayonnaise	~ mit Mayonnaise	~ froid mayonnaise	~ lesso con maionese	~ frío con mayonesa
Boiled cod with	~ mit Petersiliensauce	~ sauce persil	~ con salsa al prezzemolo	~ con salsa de perejil
parsley sauce				
Conger, conger eel	Meeraal	Congre	Grongo	Congrio
Crab	Taschenkrebs	Tourteau	Granciporro, granchio	Masera, pato
			paguro	
Crabs	Krabben	Crabes	Granchi	Cangrejos de mar, cám-
				baros
Crayfish	Krebse (Flußkrebse)	Écrevisses	Gamberi (di fiume)	Cangrejos de río
Swimming crayfish	~ in der Brühe	~ à la nage (servies dans	~ natanti (serviti nel brodo	Cangrejos nadando
(served in their broth)		leur cuisson)	di cottura)	(servidos en su caldo)
Crayfish pyramid	Krebspyramide	~ en buisson	~ in piramide	Pirámide de cangrejos

Fish and shellfish	Fische und Schaltiere	Poissons et crustacés	Pesci e crostacei	Pescados y crustáceos
Crucian	Karausche	Carassin	Carassio	Carasio
Cuttlefish	Tintenfische	Seiches	Seppie	Jibias
Dab	Kliesche	Limande	Limanda	Limanda
Date-shells	Meer-, Steindatteln	Dattes de mer	Datteri di mare	Dátiles de mar
Dentex	Zahnbrasse	Denté	Dentice	Dentón
Dorado, dolphin	Goldmakrele	Coriphène	Corifena, lampuga	Lampuga, dorado
Dory, John Dory	Heringskönig	Saint-pierre, dorée	Pesce San Pietro, sampietro	Pez de San Pedro, gallo
Dory, John Dory	Petersfisch	Saint-pierre, dorée	Pesce San Pietro, sampietro	Pez de San Pedro, gallo
Eel	Aal	Anguille	Anguilla	Anguila
Eel in dill sauce	~ in Dillsauce	~ à l'aneth	~ in salsa all'aneto	~ en salsa de enelgo
Fried eel	~ gebacken	~ frite	~ fritta	~ frita
Matelote of eel (eel stew)	~ auf Matrosenart	~ en matelote	~ alla marinara	~ a la marinera
Eel on the spit	~ vom Spieß	~ à la broche	~ allo spiedo	~ al asador
Elvers	Glasaale	Civelles, alevins d'anguille	Cieche, anguille giavani	Angulas
Fillets of hake	Seehechtfilets	Filets de colin	Filetti di nasello	Filetes de merluza
Fillets of sole	Seezungenfilets	Filets de sole	Filetti di sogliola	Filetes de lenguado
~ of sole Orly (deep-fried, served with tomato sauce)	~ Orly (gebacken und mit Tomatensauce angerichtet)	~ de sole Orly (filets frits servis avec sauce tomate)	~ di sogliola Orly (filetti fritti e serviti con salsa di pomodoro)	~ de lenguado Orly (filetes fritos con salsa de tomate)
Fillets of sole in white wine	Seezungenfilets in Weißwein	Filets de sole au vin blanc	Filetti di sogliola al vino bianco	Filetes de lenguado al vino blanco
Finnan haddock	Haddock (geräucherter Schellfisch)	Haddock (églefin fumé)	Haddock (eglefino affumicato)	Eglefino ahumado
Fish balls	Fischbuletten, Fischfrikadellen	Croquettes de poisson	Crocchette di pesce	Croquetas de pescado
Fish mayonnaise	Fischmayonnaise	Mayonnaise de poisson	Maionese di pesce	Mayonesa de pescado
Flounder	Flunder	Flet	Passera, pianuzza	Platija
Fried fish fillet	Fischfilet, gebacken	Filet de poisson frit	Filetto di pesce fritto	Filete de pescado frito
Fried rosefish fillet	Goldbarschfilet, gebacken	Filet de sébaste frit	Filetto di sebaste fritto	Filete de perca de mar frito

Fish and shellfish	Fische und Schaltiere	Poissons et crustacés	Pesci e crostacei	Pescados y crustáceos
Frog's legs	Froschschenkel	Grenouilles	Rane	Ranas
Fried frog's legs	~ gebacken	~ frites	Rane fritte	Ranas fritas
Frog's legs sauté	~ gebraten	~ sautées	Rane al burro	Ranas salteadas
Garfish, needlefish	Hornhecht	Orphie, aiguille de mer	Aguglia	Aguja
Gilthead	Goldbrasse	Daurade, dorade royale	Orata	Dorada
Goby	Meergrundel	Gobie	Ghiozzo	Gobio, pez del diablo
Grayling	Äsche	Ombre	Temolo	Tímalo
Greater weever	Drachenfisch	Vive	Trachino, pesce ragno	Peje araña
Greater weever	Petermännchen	Vive	Pesce ragno, trachino	Peje araña
Grey mullet	Meeräsche	Mulet, muge	Cefalo, muggine	Mujol, cabezudo
Broiled grey mullet	~ gegrillt	Mulet grillé	Cefalo ai ferri	Mujol a la parrilla
Gudgeons	Gründlinge	Gaujons	Gobioni, ghiozzi di fiume	Gobios
Gurnard, gurnet	Knurrhahn	Grondin	Pesce cappone[25]	Rubio, gallina de mar
(fresh) Haddock	Schellfisch	Églefin, aiglefin	Eglefino	Eglefino
Haddock smoked	Haddock (geräucherter Schellfisch)	Haddock (aiglefin fumé)	Haddock (eglefino affumicato)	Eglefino ahumado
Hake	Seehecht	Colin, merlu	Nasello, merhuzzo	Merluza
Hake meunière	~ in Butter gebraten	Colin meunière	Nasello al burro	~ a la molinera
Poached hake	~ pochiert	Colin poché	Nasello lesso	~ cocida
Halibut	Heilbutt	Flétan	Ippoglosso, halibut	Halibut, hipogloso
Broiled halibut	~ vom Rost	Flétan grillé	~ ai ferri	Halibut a la parrilla
Hard clams	Venusmuscheln	Clams, palourdes	Vongole	Almejas
Herring	Hering	Hareng	Aringa	Arenque [beche
Marinated herring	~ mariniert	~ mariné	~ marinata	~ marinado, ~ en esca-
Kedgeree (dish of rice, fish and hard-boiled eggs)	Kedgeree (Reisgericht mit Fisch und harten Eiern)	Kedgeree (riz garni de poisson et d'œufs durs)	Kedgeree (riso con pesce e fettine di nouva sode)	Kedgeree (carroz con pescado y huevos duros)
Lake-trout	Seeforelle	Truite de lac	Trota di lago	Trucha de lago
Grilled lake-trout	~ vom Grill	Truite de lac grillée	~ di lago alla griglia	~ de lago a la parrilla
Lamprey	Neunauge	Lamproie	Lampreda	Lamprea

Fish and shellfish	Fische und Schaltiere	Poissons et crustacés	Pesci e crostacei	Pescados y crustáceos
Limpets	Napfschnecken	Patelles	Patelle	Lapas
Ling	Leng	Lingue	Molva	Molva
Loach	Schmerle	Loche	Cobite	Locha
Loach	Steinbeißer	Loche de rivière	Cobite	Locha
Lobster	Hummer	Homard	Astice	Bogavante
Lobster, American style (in rich tomato sauce)	~ auf amerikanische Art (in Tomatensauce)	~ à l'américaine (sauté aux tomates)	~ all'americana (in salsa di pomodoro e cognac)	~ a la americana (en salsa de tomate)
Lobster in aspic	~ in Aspik	Aspic d'homard	~ in gelatina	~ en gelatina
Lobster flambé	~ flambiert	Homard flambé	~ alla fiamma	~ flameado
Lobster thermidor (lobster meat baked in lobster shell)	~ Thermidor (Hummerfleisch in der Schale überbacken)	Homard thermidor (escalopes gratinées dans la carapace)	~ alla termidoro (fette d'astice gratinate nella corazza)	~ Termidor (carne de bogavante gratinada en el caparazón)
Lobster mayonnaise	Hummer-Mayonnaise	Mayonnaise d'homard	Maionese d'astice	Mayonesa de bogavante
Mackerel	Makrele	Maquereau	Sgombro, scombro	Caballa (Am. macarela)
~ en papillote	~ en Papillote	~ en papillote	~ al cartoccio	~ en papillote
~ with black butter	~ mit schwarzer Butter	~ au beurre noir	~ al burro nero	~ con mantequilla tostada
Miller's thumbs, bullheads	Kaulköpfe (Groppen)	Chabots	Scazzoni, magnaroni	Cotos
Mirror carp	Spiegelkarpfen	Carpe miroir	Carpa a specchio	Carpa de espejo
Mixed fried fish	Fischfritüre	Friture de poissons	Frittura di pesce	Fritura de pescado
Moray	Muräne	Murène	Murena	Morena, murena
Mussels	Miesmuscheln	Moules	Cozze, mitili	Mejillones
~ au gratin	~ gratiniert	~ au gratin	Cozze gratinate	~ al gratén
~ à la marinière (in white wine)	~ nach Matrosenart (in Weißwein)	~ à la marinière (au vin blanc)	Cozze alla marinara (al vino bianco)	~ a la marinera (al vino blanco)
Octopus	Krake, (Seepolyp)	Poulpe, pieuvre	Polpo	Pulpo
Ormers, see abalones Pompano[26])	Gabelmakrele	Liche	Leccia stella	Palomete blanca
Oysters	Austern	Huîtres	Ustriche	Ostras
Fried oysters	~ gebacken	~ frites	~ fritte	~ fritas
Oysters Mornay	~ gratiniert	~ Mornay, ~ au gratin	~ gratinate	~ al gratén

32

Fish and shellfish	Fische und Schaltiere	Poissons et crustacés	Pesci e crostacei	Pescados y crustáceos
Perch	Barsch	Perche	Pesce persico	Perca
Perch au bleu	~ blau	~ au bleu	Pesce persico al blu	Perca al azul
Periwinkles	Strandschnecken	Bigorneaux	Littorine	Bígaros
Piddocks	Bohrmuscheln	Pholades	Foladi	Barrenas
Pike	Hecht	Brochet	Luccio	Lucio
Roast pike	~ gebraten	Brochet rôti	Luccio arrosto	Lucio asado
Pike balls	Hechtklößchen	Quenelles de brochet	Polpettine di luccio	Albóndigas de lucio
Pike-perch fillets	Zanderfilets	Filets de sandre	Filetti di lucioperca	Filetes de lucioperca
Pike-perch, zander	Zander	Sandre	Lucioperca[27], sandra	Lucioperca
Pike-perch au bleu	~ blau	~ au bleu	Lucioperca al blu	~ au bleu, ~ al azul
Stuffed pike-perch	~ gefüllt	~ farci	~ farcita	~ rellena
Grilled pike-perch	~ vom Rost	~ grillé	~ alla griglia	~ a la parrilla
Pike-perch au gratin	~ überbacken	~ au gratin	~ al gratin	~ al gratén
Pilchards, sardines	Sardinen	Sardines	Sardine, sarde	Sardinas
Plaice	Scholle	Carrelet, plie	Platessa, passera	Platija
Porbeagle	Heringshai (Kalbfisch)	Lamie, taupe	Smeriglio	Marrajo
Potted char	Saibling, eingemacht	Conserve d'omble cheva-lier en pot	Pâté di salmerino	Conserva de umbla
Prawns	Hummerkrabben	Gambas, crevettes rouges	Gamberi imperiali	Gambas; langostinos
Quahogs	Venusmuscheln	Clams, palourdes	Vongole	Almejas
Rainbow trout	Regenbogenforelle	Truite arc-en-ciel	Trota arcobaleno	Trucha arco iris
Razor shells, razor clams	Scheidenmuscheln	Couteaux	Cannolicchi, cannelli	Navajas
Rosefish, red perch	Goldbarsch	Sébaste, rascasse du Nord	Sebaste, scorfano di fondale	Perae de mar
Red mullet	Meerbarbe	Rouget, rouget barbet	Triglia (di fango)	Salmonete (barbo de mar)
Red mullet en papillote	~ en Papillote	Rouget en papillote	~ al cartoccio	~ en papillote
Grilled red mullet	~ vom Rost	Rouget grillé	~ in gratella	~ emparrillado
Surmullet, red mullet	~ (Streifenbarbe)	Rouget de roche, surmulet	Triglia di scoglio	Salmonete de roca
Rhine salmon	Rheinsalm	Saumon du Rhin	Salmone del Reno	Salmón del Rin
Roach	Plötze (Rotauge)	Gardon	Leucisco	Bermejuela
Rockling, sea loach	Seequappe	Loche de mer, motelle	Motella	Motela

Fish and shellfish	Fische und Schaltiere	Poissons et crustacés	Pesci e crostacei	Pescados y crustáceos
Rolled sole fillets	Seezungenröllchen	Paupiettes de sole	Involtini di sogliola	Popietas de lenguado
Salmon cutlet	Lachskotelett	Côtelette de saumon	Costoletta di salmone	Chuleta de salmón
Salmon medallion	Lachsmedaillon	Médaillon de saumon	Medaglione di salmone	Medallón de salmón
Salmon trout, sea trout	Lachsforelle	Truite saumonée, truite de mer	Trota salmonata, trota marina	Trucha de mar
Salmon	Lachs	Saumon	Salmone	Salmón
Boiled salmon	~ gekocht	~ au court-bouillon	~ lesso	~ cocido
Broiled salmon steak	~ vom Rost	~ grillé	~ ai ferri	~ emparrillado
Salt cod, stockfish	Stockfisch	Morue	Baccalà, stoccafisso	Bacalao
Salt cod in cream	~ in Rahmsauce	~ à la crème	Baccalà alla crema	~ a la crema
Salt cod in tomato sauce	~ in Tomatensauce	~ sautée aux tomates	Baccalà in umido	~ en salsa de tomate
Scallops	Jakobsmuscheln	Coquilles Saint-Jacques	Conchiglie dei pellegrini, ventagli	Conchas de peregrino, vieiras
Scallops[28])	Kammuscheln	Pétoncles, peignes	Pettini, canestrelli	Vieiras
Scampi, Norway lobsters, Dublin (Bay) prawns	Scampi	Langoustines, scampi	Scampi	Cigalas
Curried scampi	~ mit Curry	Langoustines au curry	Scampi al curry	Cigalas al curry
Fried scampi	~ gebacken	Langoustines frites	Scampi fritti	Cigalas fritas
Sea-bream	Meerbrasse	Pageot, pagel, pageau	Pagello	Pagel, besugo
Sea-fish	Seefisch	Poisson de mer	Pesce di mare	Pez marino
Seafood	Meeresfrüchte	Fruits de mer	Frutti di mare	Mariscos
Sea-urchins	Seeigel	Oursins, châtaignes de mer	Ricci di mare	Erizos de mar
Shad roe	Maifischrogen	Œufs d'alose	Uova di cheppia	Huevas de sábalo
Sheat-fish	Wels (Waller)	Glane, silure glane	Siluro	Siluro
Shellfish, see seafood				
Shore crabs, green crabs	Strandkrabben	Crabes	Granchi	Cámbaros, cangrejos de mar
Shrimp creole	Garnelen auf kreolische Art	Crevettes à la créole	Gamberetti alla creola	Camarones a la criolla

Fish and shellfish	Fische und Schaltiere	Poissons et crustacés	Pesci e crostacei	Pescados y crustáceos
Shrimp jambalaya (dish of rice with shrimp, chicken, ham, tomato)	Jambelaye von Garnelen (Reisgericht mit Garnelen, Huhn, Schinken, Tomaten)	Jambelaye de crevettes (plat de riz garni de crevettes, jambon, poulet, tomates)	Jambelaye di gamberetti (riso misto a prosciutto, gamberetti, pollo, pomodiri)	Jambolaye de camarones (arroz con pollo, camarones, jamón, tomates)
Shrimps	Garnelen	Crevettes	Gamberetti	Camarones, quisquillas
Curried shrimps	~ in Currysauce	Crevettes au curry	Gamberetti al curry	Camarones al curry
Prawns	~ (Stein-)	Crevettes roses	Gamberetti rosa	Gambas
Skate, ray	Rochen	Raie	Razza	Raya
Boiled with caper sauce	~ mit Kapernsauce	~ sauce aux câpres	~ con salsa di capperi	~ con alcaparras
Skate with black butter	~ mit schwarzer Butter	~ au beurre noir	~ al burro nero	~ con mantequilla negra
Smelt	Stint	Éperlan	Sperlano, eperlano	Eperlano
Smelt en brochette	Stint-Spießchen	Éperlans en brochettes	Spiedini di sperlani	Broquetas de eperlanos
Smoked fillets of trout	Forellenfilets, geräuchert	Filets de truite fumés	Filetti di trota affumicati	Filetes de trucha ahumados
Smooth dogfish	Glatthai	Émissole	Palombo	Musola
Snails	Schnecken	Escargots	Lumache	Caracoles
Soft (shell) clams	Sandmuscheln	Clams, palourdes	Vongole	Almejas
Soft-shell crabs	Weichschalige Strandkrabben	Crabes mous (en mue)	Mollecche	Cámbaros mollares
Sole	Seezunge	Sole	Sogliola	Lenguado
Sole Colbert (breaded, fried, filled with parsley butter)	~ Colbert (paniert, gebacken und mit Kräuterbutter gefüllt)	~ Colbert (panée, frite fourrée de beurre maître d'hôtel)	~ Colbert (panata, fritta e farcita di burro maître d'hôtel)	~ Colbert (lenguado frito relleno de manteca maître d'hôtel)
Fried sole	~ gebacken	~ frite	~ fritta	~ frito
Grilled sole	~ gegrillt	~ grillée	~ alla griglia	~ a la parrilla
Sole Mornay	~ Mornay	~ Mornay (au gratin)	~ Mornay (al gratin)	~ Mornay (al graten)
Sole meunière	~ nach Müllerinart	~ meunière (au beurre)	~ alla mugnaia	~ a la molinera
Spider-crabs	Meerspinnen	Araignées de mer	Grancevole	Centollos, centollos
Spiny dogfish	Dornhai	Aiguillat	Spinarolo	Galludo
Spiny lobster medallions	Langustenmedaillons	Médaillons de langouste	Medaglioni di aragosta	Medallones de langosta

Fish and shellfish	Fische und Schaltiere	Poissons et crustacés	Pesci e crostacei	Pescados y crustáceos
Spiny lobster[29]	Languste	Langouste	Aragosta	Langosta
Spiny lobster en bellevue (lobster meat in jelly)	~ Bellevue (Schwanz-scheiben in Gelee)	~ à la parisienne[30] (escalopes à la gelée)	~ in bella vista (fette di aragosta in gelatina)	~ a la parisiense (rodajas en gelatina)
Crawfish with mayonnaise	~ mit Mayonnaise	~ à la mayonnaise	~ con maionese	~ con mayonesa
Sprats	Sprotten	Sprats	Spratti, sarde	Espadines
Smoked sprats	~ (Kieler)	~ fumés de Kiel	~ affumicati	~ ahumados de Kiel
Squills, mantis shrimps	Heuschreckenkrebse	Squilles	Canocchie, pannocchie	Galeras
Sterlet	Sterlet	Sterlet	Sterletto, sterlatto	Esturión esterlete
Sturgeon	Stör	Esturgeon	Storione	Esturión
Surmullet, red mullet	Streifenbarbe	Rouget de roche, surmulet	Triglia di scoglio	Salmonete de roca
Swordfish	Schwertfisch	Espadon	Pesce spada	Pez espada
Tench	Schleie	Tanche	Tinca	Tenca
~ au bleu	~ blau	~ au bleu	~ al blu	~ au bleu
~ au gratin	~ überbacken	~ gratinée	~ gratinata	~ al gratén
Terrine of fish	Fischterrine	Terrine de poisson	Terrina di pesce	Terrina de pescado
Trout	Forelle	Truite	Trota	Trucha
Trout au bleu	~ blau	~ au bleu	~ al blu	~ al azul, ~ au bleu
Fried trout	~ gebacken	~ frite	~ fritta	~ frita
Trout meunière	~ gebraten	~ au beurre, ~ meunière	~ al burro	~ a la molinera
Stuffed trout	~ gefüllt	~ farcie	~ ripiena	~ rellena
Trout in jelly	~ in Gelee	~ en gelée	~ in gelatina	~ en gelatina
Trout amandine	~ mit Mandeln	~ aux amandes	~ con le mandorle	~ con almendras
Trout meunière	~ nach Müllerinart	~ meunière	~ alla mugnaia	~ a la molinera
Trout in red wine	~ in Rotwein	~ au vin rouge	~ al vino rosso	~ al vino tinto
Trout from the fish-tank	Zuchtforellen	Truites d'élevage	Trote di vivaio	Truchas de vivero
Turtle	Schildkröte	Tortue	Tartaruga	Tortuga
Whitebait	Weißfische	Blanchailles	Bianchetti, gianchetti	Chanquetes
Fried whitebait	~ gebacken	Friture de blanchailles	Frittura di bianchetti	Fritura de chanquetes

Fish and shellfish	Fische und Schaltiere	Poissons et crustacés	Pesci e crostacei	Pescados y crustáceos
Whitefish	Blaufelchen	Corégone	Coregono azzurro	Farra, corégono
Whitefish	Renke	Corégone, lavaret	Coregono, lavarello	Corégono, farra
Whitefish	Maräne	Marène, corégone	Marena, coregono	Corégono
Whitefish	Sandfelchen	Féra	Coregono bianco	Farra
Whitefish	Felchen	Corégone	Coregono, lavarello	Corégono, farra
Whiting	Merlan	Merlan	Merlano, merlango	Pescadilla, merlan
Fried whiting	~ gebacken	~ frit	~ fritto	Pescadilla frita
Whiting in white wine	~ in Weißwein	~ au vin blanc	~ al vino bianco	Pescadilla al vino blanco
Wrasse	Lippfisch	Vieille, labre	Tordo, labro	Labro, tordo de mar
Tuna(-fish), tunny(-fish)	Thunfisch	Thon	Tonno	Atún
Braised tuna with mushrooms	~ gedünstet mit Champignons	~ braisé aux champignons	~ in umido coi funghi	~ estofado con champiñones
Broiled tuna-fish	~ vom Rost	~ grillé	~ ai ferri	~ a la parrilla
Turbot	Steinbutt	Turbot	Rombo	Rodaballo
Poached turbot sauce hollandaise	~ gekocht mit holländischer Sauce	~ poché sauce hollandaise	Rombo lesso con salsa olandese	~ cocido con salsa holandesa
Braised turbot	~ geschmort	~ braisé	Rombo brasato	~ estofado
Grilled turbot	~ vom Rost	~ grillé	Rombo in gratella	~ a la parrilla
Turbot in white wine	~ in Weißwein	~ au vin blanc	Rombo al vino bianco	~ al vino bianco

[25]) o gallinella.
[26]) fish of the family Carandigae.
[27]) o lucioperca.
[28]) or comb shells.
[29]) or also crawfish and rock lobster.
[30]) ou langouste en bellevue.

Meat	Fleisch	Viandes	Carni	Carnes
Beef	Rindfleisch	Bœuf	Manzo	Vaca, buey
Lamb	Lammfleisch	Agneau	Agnello	Cordero
Mutton	Hammelfleisch	Mouton	Montone, castrato	Carnero
Pork	Schweinefleisch	Porc	Maiale	Cerdo
Spring lamb, baby lamb	Milchlamm	Agneau de lait	Agnello di latte	Cordero lechal
Sucking-pig	Spanferkel	Cochon de lait, porcelet	Maialino di latte	Lechón, cochinillo de leche
Veal	Kalbfleisch	Veau	Vitello	Ternera

Meat dishes	Fleischgerichte	Plats de viande	Piatti di carne	Platos de carne
Beef olives	Rinderrouladen	Paupiettes de bœuf	Involtini di manzo	Popietas de vaca
Beef roulade	Rinderrouladen	Paupiettes de bœuf	Involtini di manzo	Popietas de vaca
Beef stew, ragout of beef	Rinderragout	Estouffade (de bœuf)[31])	Stufato di manzo	Estofado de vaca
Beef Stroganoff (beef stew in sour cream)	Filetgulasch Stroganow (in saurer Sahne)	Sauté de bœuf Stroganov (à la crème aigre)	Manzo alla Stroganov (con panna acida)	Vaca Stroganov (estofado en crema agria)
Beefsteak, steak	Beefsteak	Bifteck, steak	Bistecca	Bistec
Beefsteak with a fried egg	~ mit Setzei	~ à cheval (avec un œuf au plat dessus)	~ alla Bismarck (con un uova sopra)	Bistec a caballo (con un huevo al plato)
Black pudding	Blutwurst	Boudin noir	Sanguinaccio	Morcilla
Boiled beef	Gekochtes Rindfleisch, Suppenfleisch	Bœuf bouilli	Manzo lesso, bollito	Carne del cocido
Boiled pig's trotters	Schweinsfüße, gekocht	Pieds de porc bouillis	Piedini di maiale lessi	Pies de cerdo hervidos
Boiled pork with horse-radish	Krenfleisch	Porc bouilli au raifort	Maiale lesso con rafano	Cerdo hervido con rábano
Braised beef, pot-roast	Schmorbraten	Bœuf braisé	Manzo brasato	Estofado de buey
Breast of beef	Rinderbrust	Poitrine de bœuf	Petto di manzo	Pecho de vaca

Meat dishes	Fleischgerichte	Plats de viande	Piatti di carne	Platos de carne
Bubble and squeak (cabbage, potato and sometimes meat fried together)	Bubble and squeak (Kohl, Kartoffeln und manchmal Fleisch zusammen aufgebraten)	Bubble and squeak (choux et pommes de terre sautés, parfois avec de la viande)	Bubble and squeak (cavoli, patate e talvolta carne rosolati assieme)	Bubble and squeak (coles, patatas y a veces carne, salteados juntos)
Burgundy beef stew (stewed in red wine with mushrooms and small onions)	Rindfleisch auf Burgunder Art (in Rotwein mit Zwiebelchen und Champignons geschmort)	Bœuf bourguignon (sauté au vin rouge avec champignons et petits oignons)	Bue alla borgognona (brasato nel vino rosso con funghi e cipolline)	Vaca a la borgoñona (estofado al vino tinto con cebollitas y champiñones)
Boiled beef	~ gekocht	Bouilli, bœuf bouilli	Bollito, manzo lesso	Carne del cocido
Beef à la mode (braised with carrots, onions and calf's foot)	~ auf modische Art (mit Karotten und Kalbsfuß geschmort)	Bœuf à la mode (braisé avec carottes et pied de veau)	Manzo alla moda (brasato con carote, cipolline e piede di vitello)	Vaca a la moda (braseada con zanahorias y pies de ternera)
Calf's brains (pl)	Kalbshirn	Cervelle de veau	Cervello di vitello	Sesos de ternera
Fried calf's brains	~ gebacken	Cervelle frite	Cervello fritto	~ fritos
Brains fried in butter	~ gebraten	~ de veau meunière	Cervello al burro	~ salteados
Brains with black butter	~ mit schwarzer Butter	Cervelle au beurre noir	Cervello al burro nero	~ con mantequilla negra
Calf's brains with egg	Hirn mit Ei	Cervelle de veau à l'œuf	Cervello di vitello all'uovo	Sesos con huevo
Fried calf's brains	~ gebacken	Cervelle frite	Cervello fritto	Sesos fritos
Calf's ears	Kalbsohren	Oreilles de veau	Orecchi di vitello	Orejas de ternera
Calf's gristle	Kalbsbrustknorpel	Tendrons de veau	Tenerume di vitello	Ternillas de ternera
Braised calf's gristle	~ geschmort	~ de veau braisés	~ di vitello brasato	Ternillas braseadas
Calf's head in vinaigrette sauce	Kalbskopf in grüner Sauce	Tête de veau à la vinaigrette	Testina di vitello in salsa verde	Cabeza de ternera a la vinagreta
Calf's head in vinaigrette sauce	Kalbskopf ~ gebacken	Tête de veau ~ de veau frite	Testina di vitello ~ di vitello fritta	Cabeza de ternera ~ de ternera frita

Meat dishes	Fleischgerichte	Plats de viande	Piatti di carne	Platos de carne
Calf's kidney	Kalbsniere	Rognon de veau	Rognone di vitello	Riñones de ternera
Calf's kidney flambé	~ flambiert	~ de veau flambé	Rognone alla fiamma	~ de ternera flameados
Grilled calf's kidney	~ gegrillt	~ de veau grillé	~ di vitello alla griglia	~ asados a la parrilla
Kidney in Madeira sauce	~ in Madeirasauce	~ de veau au Madère	~ di vitello al madera	~ de ternera al Madera
Calf's kidney sauté	~ sautiert	~ de veau sauté	~ di vitello saltato	~ de ternera salteados
Calf's kidney Turbigo (garnished with mushrooms and sausage)	~ Turbigo (mit Champignons und Bratwürstchen)	~ de veau Turbigo (garni de champignons et d'une saucisse)	~ alla Turbigo (guarnito di funghi e di una salsiccia)	~ de ternera Turbigo (con champiñones y salchicha)
Calf's kidney in white wine	~ in Weißweinsauce	~ de veau au vin blanc	~ al vino bianco	~ en vino blanco
Calf's lights	Kalbslunge	Mou de veau	Polmone di vitello	Bofes de ternera
Calf's liver, Tyrolean style (fried liver in sour cream sauce)	Tiroler Leber (Kalbsleberscheiben in Sauerrahmsauce)	Foie de veau à la tyrolienne (sauté, nappé sauce crème aigre)	Fegato di vitello alla tirolese (in salsa di panna acida)	Hígado de ternera a la tirolesa (en salsa de crema agria)
Calf's liver	Kalbsleber	Foie de veau	Fegato di vitello	Hígado de ternera
Calf's liver with apples	~ nach Berliner Art (mit Äpfeln)	~ à la berlinoise (aux pommes fruits)	~ di vitello alla berlinese (con mele)	~ de ternera a la berlinesa (con manzanas)
Calf's liver and bacon	~ auf englische Art (mit Speckscheiben)	~ de veau à l'anglaise (sauté au bacon)	~ all'inglese (con fettine di pancetta)	~ de ternera a la inglesa (con tocino)
Fried calf's liver	~ gebacken	~ de veau frit	~ di vitello fritto	~ de ternera frito
Calf's liver sauté	~ gebraten	~ de veau sauté	~ di vitello al burro	~ de ternera salteado
Calf's liver en brochette	~ am Spießchen	Brochettes de foie de veau	Spiedini di fegato	Hígado de ternera en broqueta
Calf's sweetbreads	Kalbsbries	Ris de veau	Animelle di vitello	Mollejas[33]) de ternera
~ sweetbreads with mushrooms	~ mit Champignons	~ de veau aux champignons	Animelle coi funghi	~ de ternera con champiñones
Sweetbreads with peas	~ mit Erbsen	~ de veau Clamart	Animelle coi piselli	~ con guisantes
Calf's tongue	Kalbszunge	Langue de veau	Lingua di vitello	Lengua de ternera

Meat dishes	Fleischgerichte	Plats de viande	Piatti di carne	Platos de carne
Carpaccio (thin slices of raw beef seasoned with oil and Parmesan)	Carpaccio (rohe Filetscheiben mit Öl und Parmesan)	Carpaccio (tranches très minces de bœuf ou servies avec huíle et parmesan)	Carpaccio (fette fottili di filetto crudo condite con olio e parmigiano)	Carpaccio (lonjas de solomillo crudo con aceite y parmesano)
Charcoal-grilled meats	kohlengrill Fleisch vom Holz-	[bois Grillades au feu de	Carni alla brace	Carnes asadas a la brasa
Chateaubriand (double thick fillet steak)	Chateaubriand (doppelt dickes Filetsteak)	Chateaubriand (ou châteaubriant)	Chateaubriand (bistecca doppia di filetto)	Chateaubriand (filete doble de solomillo)
Chilli con carne (chilli-flavoured stew of minced beef and beans)	Chili con carne (mit Chillies gewürztes Fleischragout mit Bohnen)	Chili con carne (ragoût de bœuf haché au piment et aux haricots)	Chili con carne (stufato di manzo tritato e fagioli al peperoncino)	Chile con carne (estofado de vaca con guindilla y judías)
Chopped veal in cream	Geschnetzeltes (Kalbfleisch in Rahm)	Émincé de veau zurichoise	Vitello alla zurighese	Lonjas de ternera a la crema
Cold meats, cold cuts	Kalte Platte	Viandes froides[32])	Piatto freddo	Fiambres
Cornish pasty Cottage pie, see shepherd's pie	Fleischpastete	Petit pâté en croûte	Pâté di carne in crosta	Pastel de carne
Crown roast of lamb	Gebratener Lammkranz	Couronne d'agneau rôtie	Corona d'agnello arrosto	Corona de cordero asada
Double sirloin steak	Doppeltes Entrecote	Entrecôte double	Costata doppia	Entrecote doble
Escalope of veal chasseur	Jäger-Schnitzel	Escalope de veau chasseur	Scaloppina alla cacciatora	Escalope a la cazadora
Escalope of veal Cordon bleu (filled with ham & cheese)	Cordon bleu (Kalbsschnitzel mit Schinken-Käsefüllung)	Escalope de veau Cordon bleu (farcie de jambon et de fromage)	Scaloppina Cordon bleu (farcita di prosciutto e formaggio)	Escalope Cordon bleu (rellena de jamón y queso)
Escalope of veal Holstein (with a fried egg and anchovy fillets)	Holstein-Schnitzel (mit Setzei und Sardellen-filets)	Escalope de veau Holstein (garnie œuf poêlé et filets d'anchois)	Scaloppina alla Holstein (con filetti d'acciuga e un uovo al piatto)	Escalope Holstein (con un huevo al plato y filetes de anchoas)
Escalope of veal in cream	Sahneschnitzel	Escalope de veau à la crème	Scaloppina di vitello alla panna	Escalope de ternera a la crema
Escalope of veal, Parisienne (dipped in beaten egg & fried)	Pariser Schnitzel (in verquirltes Ei getaucht und gebacken)	Escalope de veau à la parisienne (panée à l'œuf et frite)	Scaloppina alla parigina (passata nell'uovo sbattuto e fritta)	~ de ternera a la parisiense (pasada en huevo batido y frita)

Meat dishes	Fleischgerichte	Plats de viande	Piatti di carne	Platos de carne
Escalope of veal sauté	Naturschnitzel	Escalope de veau sautée	Scaloppina di vitello al burro	Escalope de ternera salteada
Escalope of veal with paprika	Paprika-Schnitzel	Escalope de veau au paprika	Scaloppina di vitello alla paprica	Escalope de ternera con pimentón
Escalope of veal	Kalbsschnitzel	Escalope de veau	Scaloppina di vitello	Escalope de ternera
Veal escalope chasseur (with mushrooms)	~ nach Jägerart (mit Champignons)	~ de veau chasseur (aux champignons)	~ di vitello alla cacciatora (con funghi)	~ de ternera a la cazadora (con champiñones)
Breaded escalope of veal	~ paniert	~ de veau panée	~ di vitello impanata	~ de ternera empanada
Creamed escalope of veal	~ in Rahm	~ de veau à la crème	~ di vitello alla panna	~ de ternera a la crema
Escalope of veal, gipsy-style (with strips of ham, tongue and mushrooms)	Zigeuner-Schnitzel (mit feinen Schinkenstreifen, Zunge und Champignons)	Escalope de veau zingara (garnie de julienne de jambon, langue et champignons)	Scaloppina di vitello alla zingara (con filetti di prosciutto, lingua e funghi)	Escalope de ternera a la gitana (con tiritas de jamón, lengua y champiñones)
Fillet of beef Wellington (baked in pastry)	Rinderfilet Wellington (in Blätterteig)	Filet de bœuf Wellington (en croûte de feuilletage)	Filetto di manzo Wellington (in involucro di pasta sfoglia)	Solomillo Wellington (envuelto en pasta de hojaldre)
Fillet of beef, tenderloin	Rinderfilet	Filet de bœuf	Filetto di manzo	Solomillo
Fillet of beef with mixed vegetables	~ nach Gärtnerinart (mit Gemüse)	~ de bœuf à la jardinière (aux légumes)	~ di manzo alla giardiniera (con verdure)	~ a la jardinera (con legumbres)
Roast fillet of beef	~ gebraten	~ de bœuf rôti	~ di manzo arrosto	~ asado
Fillet of beef in Madeira	~ in Madeirasauce	~ de bœuf au Madère	~ di manzo al madera	~ al Madera
Fillet of beef Portuguese (with stuffed tomatoes)	~ auf portugiesische Art (mit Tomaten)	~ de bœuf portugaise (aux tomates farcies)	~ di manzo alla portoghese (con pomodori)	~ a la portuguesa (con tomates rellenos)
Fillet steak	Filetsteak	Filet grillé	Bistecca di filetto	Filete de solomillo asado
Fillet of veal	Kalbsfilet	Filet de veau	Filetto di vitello	Filete de ternera
Larded fillet of veal	~ gespickt	Filet de veau piqué	~ di vitello lardellato	~ de ternera mechado
Flemish stew (slices of beef stewed in beer)	Flämische Karbonaden (Rinderschnitzel in Bier geschmort)	Carbonnades à la flamande (tranches de bœuf braisées à la bière)	Brasato alla fiamminga (fette di bue brasate nella birra)	Carbonada flamenca (bistecs braseados en cerveza)

Meat dishes	Fleischgerichte	Plats de viande	Piatti di carne	Platos de carne
Fondue bourguignonne	Fleischfondue	Fondue bourguignonne	Fondue bourguignonne	Fondue borgoñón
Frankfurters	Frankfurter Würstchen	Saucisses de Francfort	Würstel	Salchichas de Francfort
Fricandeau of veal[34]	Kalbs-Frikandeau[35]	Fricandeau de veau	Fricandò di vitello	Fricandó de ternera
Fricassee of lamb	Lamm-Frikassee	Fricassée d'agneau	Fricassea d'agnello	Fricasé de cordero
Fricassee of veal	Kalbs-Frikassee	Fricassée de veau	Fricassea di vitello	Fricasé de ternera
Fricasseed veal	Eingemachtes Kalbfleisch	Blanquette de veau	Fricassea di vitello	Fricasé de ternera
Fried calf's feet	Kalbsfüße, gebacken	Pieds de veau frits	Piedi di vitello fritti	Pies de ternera fritos
Grilled calf's feet	~ vom Rost	Pieds de veau grillés	~ di vitello in gratella	~ de ternera a la parrilla
Galantine of veal	Kalbfleischgalantine	Galantine de veau	Galantina di vitello	Galantina de ternera
Garnished sauerkraut	Sauerkraut, garniert	Choucroute à l'alsacienne	Crauti all'alsaziana	Chucruta a la alsaciana
Goulash of pork	Schweinsgulasch	Goulash de porc	Gulasch di maiale	Gulash de cerdo
Grenadines (braised larded slices of veal)	Grenadins (gespickte Kalbsschnitzel)	Grenadins de veau (escalopes piquées)	Grenadine (scaloppine lardellate)	Escalopes mechadas
Grilled calf's heart	Kalbsherz vom Rost	Cœur de veau grillé	Cuore di vitello ai ferri	Corazón de ternera a la parrilla
Grilled meats, grills	Grilladen	Grillades	Carni alla griglia	Carnes a la parrilla
Grilled steak	Grill-Steak	Steak grillé	Bistecca ai ferri	Bistec a la parrilla
Grilled steak	Rostbraten (auf dem Rost)	Bifteck grillé	Bistecca ai ferri	Bistec a la parrilla
Grilled sausages	Bratwürste vom Grill	Saucisses grillées	Salsicce ai ferri	Salchichas a la parrilla
Haggis (sheep's offal boiled in the animal's stomach)	Haggis (Innereien vom Schaf in Schafsmagen gekocht)	Haggis (fressure de brebis bouillie dans la parse de l'animal)	Haggis (frattaglie di pecora bollite nello stomaco dell'animale)	Haggis (asaduras de oveja cocidas en lo estómago del animal)
Ham medallions	Schinkenmedaillons	Médaillons de jambon	Medaglioni di prosciutto	Medallones de jamón
Ham steak	Schinkensteak	Steak de jambon	Bistecca di prosciutto	Bistec de jamón
Ham	Schinken	Jambon	Prosciutto	Jamón
~ in jelly	~ in Gelee	~ en gelée	~ in gelatina	~ en gelatina
~ in Madeira sauce	~ in Madeirasauce	~ braisé au Madère	~ al madera	~ con salsa Madera
~ with sauerkraut	~ mit Sauerkraut	~ à la choucroute	~ con crauti	~ con chucruta
~ with spinach	~ mit Spinat	~ aux épinards	~ con spinaci	~ con espinacas
~ baked in pastry	~ in Teigkruste	~ en croûte	~ in crosta	~ envuelto en pasta

Meat dishes	Fleischgerichte	Plats de viande	Piatti di carne	Platos de carne
Hamburger	Deutsches Beefsteak	Hamburger	Hamburger	Hamburguesa
Hamburger	Hamburger (Frikadelle, Hacksteak)	Hamburger	Hamburger (polpetta in forma di medaglione)	Hamburguesa (bistec de picadillo)
Hash calf's lights	Lungen-Haschee	Hachis de mou de veau	Polmone di vitello tritato	Bofes de ternera picados
Hotpot	Eintopf	Potée	Piatto unico	Plato único; puchero
Hotpot (stew of mutton and potato)	Hammelragout mit Kartoffeln	Ragoût de mouton aux pommes	Stufato di montone e patate	Estofado de carnero y patatas
Hungarian goulash	Gulasch, ungarisch	Goulash à la hongroise	Gulasch all'ungherese	Gulash húngaro
Irish stew (mutton stew with onion & potato)	Irish Stew (Eintopf aus Hammelfleisch)	Irish stew (ragoût de mouton)	Irish stew (spezzatino di montone)	Irish stew (estafado de carnero)
Jellied pork cutlet	Sülzkotelett	Côte de porc en gelée	Braciola di maiale in gelatina	Chuleta de cerdo en gelatina
Kebabs, shashliks (meat on skewers)	Schaschliks (Hammelspießchen)	Kebabs, chachliks (brochettes de mouton)	Spiedini di montone	Broquetas de cordero
Kid	Zicklein	Chevreau, cabri	Capretto	Cabrito
Kidneys en brochette	Nierenspießchen	Rognons en brochettes	Spiedini di rognone	Riñones en broqueta
Knuckle of pork (salted)	Eisbein	Jarret de porc (salé)	Zampetto di maiale (salato)	Jarrete de cerdo (salado)
~ of pork with sauerkraut	~ mit Sauerkraut	~ de porc à la choucroute	~ di maiale con crauti	~ de cerdo con chucruta
Knuckle of pork	Schweinshaxe	Jarret de porc	Zampetto di maiale	Jarrete de cerdo
Roast knuckle of pork	~ gebraten	Jarret de porc rôti	~ di maiale arrosto	~ de cerdo asado
Knuckle of veal; shin of veal	Kalbshaxe, Kalbsstelze	Jarret de veau	Stinco di vitello	Jarrete de ternera
Lamb cutlet, lamb chop	Lammkotelett	Côtelette d'agneau	Costoletta d'agnello	Chuleta de cordero
Breaded lamb cutlet	~ gebacken	~ d'agneau panée	~ d'agnello impanata	~ de cordero empanada
Grilled lamb cutlet	~ vom Rost	~ d'agneau grillée	~ d'agnello alla griglia	~ de cordero a la parrilla
Lamb noisettes	Lammnüßchen	Noisettes d'agneau	Medaglioni d'agnello	Medallones de cordero
Lamb pluck	Beuschel von Lamm	Fressure d'agneau	Coratella d'agnello	Asadura de cordero
Lamb stew	Lammragout	Sauté d'agneau	Spezzatino d'agnello	Estofado de cordero
Lamb stew with spring vegetables	~ auf Frühlingsart (mit jungem Gemüse)	~ d'agneau printanier (aux primeurs)	~ d'agnello primaverile (con verdure novelle)	~ de cordero primaveral (con verduras)
Lamb's sweetbreads	Lammbries	Ris d'agneau	Animelle d'agnello	Mollejas de cordero

Meat dishes	Fleischgerichte	Plats de viande	Piatti di carne	Platos de carne
Leg of mutton, gigot	Hammelkeule	Gigot de mouton	Cosciotto di montone	Pierna de carnero
Roast leg of mutton with onions & potatoes	~ nach Bäckerinart (mit Kartoffeln und Zwiebeln im Backofen gebraten)	~ de mouton boulangère (rôti avec pommes de terre et oignons)	~ di montone alla fornaia (cotto in forno con patate e cipolle)	~ de carnero a la panadera (asada con patatas y cebollas)
Braised leg of mutton	~ geschmort	~ de mouton braisé	~ di montone brasato	~ de carnero braseada
Leg of pork	Schweinskeule	Cuisse de porc	Cosciotto di maiale	Pierna de cerdo
Leg of veal	Kalbskeule, -schlegel	Cuisseau de veau	Coscia di vitello	Pierna de ternera
Liverwurst, liver sausage	Leberwurst	Boudin de foie	Salsiccia di fegato	Embutido de hígado
Loin de veal	Nierenbraten (Kalbs-)	Longe de veau	Lombata di vitello	Solomillo de ternera
Loin of pork	Schweinsfilet	Filet de porc	Filetto di maiale	Lomo de cerdo
Loin of veal	Kalbsnierenbraten	Longe de veau	Lombata di vitello	Solomillo de ternera
Meat-filled cabbage rolls	Kohl-Rouladen	Paupiettes de choux	Involtini di cavolo	Popietas de coles
Meatballs in savoury sauce	Königsberger Klopse	Boulettes de bœuf sauce piquante	Polpette di carne in salsa piccante	Albóndigas de carne en salsa picante
Meatballs, meat croquettes	Buletten	Fricadelles, boulettes	Polpette di carne	Albóndigas
Meatballs, meat croquettes	Frikadellen	Fricadelles, boulettes	Polpette di carne	Albóndigas
Meatballs	Fleischklöße	Boulettes, fricadelles	Polpette di carne	Albóndigas de carne
Meatloaf	Hackbraten	Pain de bœuf	Polpettone	Pastel casero
Medallion of veal	Kalbsmedaillon	Médaillon de veau	Medaglione di vitello	Medallón de ternera
~ with mushrooms	~ mit Champignons	~ aux champignons	~ con funghi	~ con champiñones
Mixed grill	Mixed grill	Mixed grill	Grigliata mista	Parrillada mixta
Mutton cutlet	Hammelkotelett	Côtelette de mouton	Costoletta di montone	Chuleta de carnero
Mutton stew	Hammelragout	Navarin, ragoût de mouton	Spezzatino di montone	Estofado de carnero
Olives	Rouladen	Paupiettes	Involtini	Popietas
Ossobuco (braised section of veal knuckle)	Ossobuco (Kalbshaxe in Scheiben gedünstet)	Osso-buco (rouelle de jarret de veau braisée)	Ossobuco (garretto di vitello col midollo cotto in umido)	Ossobuco (rodaja braseada de jarrete de ternera)
Ox-tongue	Ochsenzunge	Langue de bœuf	Lingua di bue	Lengua de vaca
Braised ox-tongue	~ geschmort	~ de bœuf braisée	~ di bue brasata	~ de vaca braseada
Ox-tongue in Madeira	~ in Madeira	~ de bœuf au Madère	~ di bue al madera	~ de vaca al Madera
Oxtail	Ochsenschwanz	Queue de bœuf	Coda di bue	Rabo de vaca

Meat dishes	Fleischgerichte	Plats de viande	Piatti di carne	Platos de carne
Pepper-steak	Pfeffersteak	Steak au poivre	Bistecca al pepe	Bistec con pimienta
Piccata (slice of veal fried in butter with parsley and lemon)	Piccata (Naturschnitzel mit Petersilie und Zitrone)	Piccata (escalope de veau sautée au persil et au citron)	Piccata (fettina di vitello al burro con prezzemolo e limone)	Piccata (escalope con perejil y zumo de limón)
Pig's ears	Schweinsohren	Oreilles de porc	Orecchi di maiale	Orejas de cerdo
Pig's ears with peas	~ mit Erbsenbrei	~ de porc à la purée de pois	~ di maiale con piselli	~ de cerdo con guisantes
Pork cutlet, pork chop	Schweinskotelett	Côte de porc	Costoletta di maiale[36])	Chuleta de cerdo
Breaded pork cutlet	~ gebacken	~ de porc panée	~ di maiale impanata	~ de cerdo empanada
Grilled pork cutlet	~ gegrillt	~ de porc grillée	~ di maiale ai ferri	~ de cerdo a la parrilla
Pork chop in paprika sauce	~ in Paprikasauce	~ de porc au paprika	~ di maiale alla paprica	~ de cerdo al pimentón
Pork goulash with sauerkraut	Szegediner Gulasch	Goulash de porc à la choucroute	Gulasch di maiale con crauti	Gulash de cerdo con chucruta
Pork liver	Schweinsleber	Foie de porc	Fegato di maiale	Hígado de cerdo
Prime boiled beef	Tafelspitz	Bœuf bouilli	Bollito, manzo lesso	Carne del cocido
Ragout of oxtail	Ochsenschwanz-Ragout	~ de bœuf en ragoût	Coda di bue in umido	~ de vaca en estofado
Ragout of tongue	Kalbszungen-Ragout	Langue de veau en ragoût	Lingua di vitello in umido	Lengua estofada
Ragout of tongue	Zungenragout	Langue de bœuf en ragoût	Lingua di bue in umido	Lengua de vaca en estofado
Ribs of pork	Schweinskarree	Carré de porc	Carré di maiale	Carré de cerdo
Ribs of pork with sauerkraut	~ mit Sauerkraut	Carré de porc à la choucroute	Carré di maiale con crauti	Carré de cerdo con chucruta
Roast beef	Rinderbraten[37])	Rôti de bœuf	Arrosto di manzo	Asado de vaca
Roast fillet of beef	Lungenbraten	Filet de bœuf rôti	Filetto di manzo arrosto	Solomillo asado
Roast kid	Kitzbraten	Chevreau rôti	Capretto arrosto	Cabrito asado
Roast lamb	Lammbraten	Rôti d'agneau	Arrosta d'agnello	Asado de cordero
Roast leg of lamb	Lammkeule, gebraten	Gigot d'agneau rôti	Cosciotto d'agnello arrosto	Pierna de cordero asada
Roast loin of veal	Kalbsnuß, gebraten	Noix de veau rôtie	Noce di vitello arrosto	Nuez de ternera asada
Braised loin of veal	~ geschmort	~ de veau braisée	~ di vitello brasata	~ de ternera braseada
Jellied loin of veal	~ gesülzt	~ de veau en gelée	~ di vitello in gelatina	~ de ternera en gelatina
Roast mutton	Hammelbraten	Rôti de mouton	Arrosto di montone	Asado de carnero

Meat dishes	Fleischgerichte	Plats de viande	Piatti di carne	Platos de carne
Roast pork	Schweinsbraten	Rôti de porc	Arrosto di maiale	Asado de cerdo
Roast saddle of lamb	Lammrücken, gebraten	Selle d'agneau rôtie	Sella d'agnello arrosto	Silla de cordero asada
Roast sirloin (of beef)	Rippenstück, gebraten	Contrefilet rôti	Controfiletto arrosto	Contrafilete asado
Roast sirloin (of beef)	Lendenbraten	Aloyau rôti	Lombata di bue arrosto	Solomillo asado
Roast sirloin	Roastbeef	Rosbif	Roastbeef	Rosbif
Roast stuffed suckling pig	Spanferkel, gefüllt	Porcelet farci rôti	Maialino di latte farcito	Cochinillo relleno asado
Roast veal	Kalbsbraten	Rôti de veau	Arrosto di vitello	Asado de ternera
Cold roast veal	~ kalt	Rôti de veau froid	Arrosto freddo	~ de ternera frío
Rolled roast veal	Rollbraten	Roulade de veau	Rollè di vitello	Asado arrollado
Rump-steak	Rumpsteak[38])	Rumsteak, rumpsteak	Bistecca di manzo	Bistec de vaca
Saddle of mutton	Hammelrücken	Selle de mouton	Sella di montone	Silla de carnero
Saddle of veal Orlov (braised sliced saddle browned in hot oven with onion purée)	Kalbsrücken Prinz Orlow (braisiert, in Scheiben geschnitten und mit Zwiebelmus glaciert)	Selle de veau Orlov (braisée, escalopée, glacée au four avec une purée Soubise)	Sella di vitello Orlov (brasata, affettata e glassata al forno con purè di cipolle)	Silla de ternera Orlov (braseada, tajada en lonjas y glaseada al horno con puré de cebollas)
Saddle of veal	Kalbsrücken	Selle de veau	Sella di vitello	Silla de ternera
Saddle of veal chartreuse (with vegetables cooked in moulds)	~ nach Kartäuser Art (mit Gemüsen, in Becherformen gekocht)	~ de veau à la chartreuse (garnie de chartreuse et de légumes)	~ di vitello alla certosina (con verdure cotte in uno stampo)	~ de ternera a la cartuja (con verduras cocidas en un molde)
Salt ox-tongue	Pökelzunge	Langue écarlate	Lingua salmistrata	Lengua salada
Salt ribs of pork	Pökelkarree	Carré de porc salé	Carré di maiale salato	Costillar de cerdo salado
Pot roast (braised beef, previously marinated in vinegar)	Sauerbraten (in Essigbeize vorbehandelter Schmorbraten)	Bœuf braisé à l'aigre (bœuf mariné au vinaigre et braisé)	Manzo brasato all'agro (manzo marinato nell'aceto e brasato)	Sauerbraten (estofado de vaca con vinagre)
Sausages with cabbage	Würstchen mit Kohl	Saucisses aux choux	Salsicce coi cavoli	Salchichas con coles
~ in white wine	~ in Weißwein	~ au vin blanc	~ al vino bianco	~ al vino blanco
Schlachtplatte (fresh sausages, boiled pork meat and sauerkraut)	Schlachtplatte (frische Würste, Wellfleisch, Sauerkraut)	Schlachtplatte (saucisses fraîches, viande de porc bouillie, choucroute)	Schlachtplatte (salsicce fresche, carne di maiale lessa, crauti)	Schlachtplatte (embuchados frescos, carne de cerdo cocida, chucruta)

Meat dishes	Fleischgerichte	Plats de viande	Piatti di carne	Platos de carne
Shepherd's pie (minced meat topped with mashed potato)	Hirtenpastete (Kartoffelpüree auf Hackfleisch)	Hachis parmentier (Gratin de viande hachée et de purée de pommes)	Pasticcio del pastore (gratin di carne tritata e di purè di patate)	Pastel del pastor (picadillo cubrierto de puré de patatas y gratinado)
Shoulder of lamb	Lammschulter	Épaule d'agneau	Spalla d'agnello	Espaldilla de cordero
Roast shoulder of lamb with onions and potatoes	~ nach Bäckerinart (mit Kartoffeln im Backofen gebraten)	~ d'agneau boulangère (cuite au four sur pommes boulangère)	~ d'agnello alla fornaia (cotta in forno con patate e cipolle)	~ de cordero a la panadera (asada al horno con patatas)
Shoulder of pork	Schweinsschulter	Épaule de porc	Spalla di maiale	Espaldilla de cerdo
Sirloin steak with fried onions	Wiener Rostbraten	Entrecôte à la viennoise (aux oignons)	Bistecca di manzo con cipolle	Bistec de vaca con cebollas
Sirloin steak, entrecôte	Entrecote	Entrecôte	Costata di manzo	Entrecote
Grilled sirloin steak with parsley butter	~ vom Grill mit Kräuterbutter	~ grillée maître d'hôtel	~ alla griglia con burro maître d'hôtel	~ a la mayordoma (con manteca maître d'hôtel
Sirloin steak with cress	~ mit Kresse	~ vert pré (au cresson)	~ con crescione	~ con berros
Sirloin steak lyonnaise (with fried onions)	Entrecote nach Lyoner Art (mitZwiebeln)	Entrecôte à la lyonnaise (aux oignons)	Costata di manzo alla lionese (con cipolle)	Entrecote a la lionesa (concebollas)
Minute sirloin steak	~ minute	~ minute	~ al minuto	~ al minuto
Sirloin steak Mirabeau (with anchovy fillets & olives)	~ Mirabeau (mit Sardellenfilets und Oliven)	~ Mirabeau (garnie de filets d'anchois et olives)	~ Mirabeau (con filetti d'acciuga e olive)	~ Mirabeau (con filetes de anchoas y aceitunas)
Tyrolean sirloin steak (with tomatoes & fried onion rings)	~ nach Tiroler Art (mit Tomaten und Zwiebelringen garniert)	~ tyrolienne (garnie de tomates et rondelles d'oignons frits)	~ alla tirolese (guarnita di pomodori e di cipolle fritte)	~ a la tirolesa (con tomates y cebollas fritas)
Sirloin steak in red wine sauce	~ nach Weinhändlerart (in Rotweinsauce)	~ marchand de vin (au vin rouge)	~ al vino rosso	~ a la vinatera (con salsa de vino tinto)
Smoked beef	Rauchfleisch	Bœuf fumé	Manzo affumicato	Carne de vaca ahumada
Smoked loin of pork	Selchkarree	Carré de porc fumé	Carré di maiale affumicato	Carré de cerdo ahumado
Smoked ox-tongue	Räucherzunge	Langue de bœuf fumée	Lingua affumicata	Lengua de vaca ahumada

Meat dishes	Fleischgerichte	Plats de viande	Piatti di carne	Platos de carne
Smoked spare-rib	Kasseler (Rippespeer)	Côte de porc fumée	Braciola di maiale affumicata	Chuleta de cerdo ahumada
Sour calf's lights	Wiener Beuschel (Saure Lunge)	Mou de veau à l'aigre	Polmone di vitello all'agro	Bofes de ternera a la vienesa
Sour calf's liver	Saure Leber	Foie de veau à l'aigre	Fegato di vitello all'agro	Hígado en salsa agria
Spit-roasted meat	Spießbraten	Rôti à la broche	Arrosto allo spiedo	Carne al asador
Steak and kidney pie	Steak- und Nierenpastete	Pâté de bœuf et de rognon en croûte	Pâté di manzo e di rognone in crosta	Pastel de bistec y de riñon
Stewed steak	Schmorsteak	Steak étuvé, stew-steak	Bistecca brasata	Bistec braseado
Stuffed breast of lamb	Lammbrust, gefüllt	Poitrine d'agneau farcie	Petto d'agnello farcito	Pecho de cordero relleno
Stuffed breast of veal	Kalbsbrust gefüllt	Poitrine de veau farcie	Petto di vitello farcito	Pecho de ternera relleno
Stuffed shoulder of veal	Kalbsschulter, gefüllt	Épaule de veau farcie	Spalla di vitello ripiena	Espaldilla de ternera rellena
Tartar steak (raw minced steak topped with egg)	Tatarbeefsteak (rohes Hacksteak mit Eigelb)	Steak tartare (steak cru haché avec un jaune d'œuf dessus)	Bistecca alla tartara (bistecca di carne cruda tritata con uova sopra)	Bistec a la tartara (bistec de picadillo crudo con encima un huevo)
Terrine of veal	Kalbfleischterrine	Terrine de veau	Terrina di vitello	Terrina de ternera
Toad-in-the-hole (sausages baked in batter)	Würstchen in Teig	Saucisses en pâte	Salsicce nella pastella	Salchichas en pasta
Tournedos (tenderloin steak)	Lendenschnitte[39])	Tournedos (médaillon de filet de bœuf)	Tournedos (medaglione di filetto di bue)	Tournedós (medallón de solomillo)
Tournedos, arlésienne (with aubergine, onions and tomatoes)	~ auf arlesische Art (mit Eierfrüchten, Zwiebeln, Tomaten)	~ à l'arlésienne (garni d'aubergines, oignons et tomates)	~ all'arlesiana (guarnito di melanzane, cipolle e pomodori)	~ a la arlesiana (con berenjenas, cebollas y tomates)
Tournedos Clamart (with artichoke bottoms filled with peas)	~ Clamart (mit erbsengefüllten Artischockenböden)	~ Clamart (aux fonds d'artichauts remplis de pois)	~ Clamart (con fondi di carciofo, riempiti di piselli)	~ Clamart (con guisantes sobre fondos de alcachofas)
Tournedos for gourmets (with goose liver)	~ nach Feinschmeckerart (mit Gänseleber)	~ des gourmets (fourré escalope de foie gras)	~ del buongustaio (con fegato d'oca)	~ de los gastrónomos (con foie-gras)

Meat dishes	Fleischgerichte	Plats de viande	Piatti di carne	Platos de carne
Grilled tournedos	~ vom Grill	~ grillé	~ alla griglia	~ a la parrilla
Grilled tournedos sauce béarnaise	~ vom Grill mit Béarner Sauce	~ béarnaise	~ alla bearnese (con salsa bearnese)	~ a la bearnesa (con salsa bearnesa)
Tournedos Helder (with tomatoes & Parisienne potatoes)	~ Helder (mit Tomaten und Pariser Kartoffeln garniert)	~ Helder (aux tomates concassées et pommes parisienne)	~ Helder (guarnito di pomodori e di patate alla parigina)	~ Helder (con tomates y patatas a la parisiense)
~ in Madeira sauce	~ in Madeirasauce	~ sauté au Madère	~ al madera	~ al Madera
~ mascotte (with quartered artichokes & potatoes)	~ Mascotte (mit geviertelten Artischocken, Kartoffeln und Trüffeln)	~ mascotte (aux quartiers d'artichauts, pommes et truffes)	~ mascotte (con spicchi di carciofo, patate e tartufi)	~ mascotte (con fondos de alcachofas, patatas y trufas)
~ Masséna (with artichoke bottoms and marrow. Truffle sauce)	~ Masséna (mit Artischockenböden und Rindermark)	~ Masséna (aux fonds d'artichauts et moelle. Sauce Périgueux)	~ Massena (con fondi di carciofo e midollo. Salsa di tartufi)	~ Masséna (con fondos de alcachofas y tuétano)
Tournedos Portuguese (with tomatoes)	~ auf portugiesische Art (mit Tomaten)	~ à la portugaise (aux tomates)	~ alla portoghese (guarnito di pomodori)	~ a la portuguesa (con tomate)
~ Rossini (with slice of goose liver & truffles Madeira sauce)	~ Rossini (mit Gänseleberscheibe und Trüffeln, Madeirasauce)	~ Rossini (garni de foie gras et lames de truffes. Sauce madère)	~ Rossini (con fegato d'oca e fettine di tartufo. Salsa al madera)	~ Rossini (con lonja de foie-gras, trufas y salsa Madera)
Tournedos Henry IV (a: chipped potatoes, sauce béarnaise; b: artichoke bottoms, noisette potatoes)	Lendenschnitte Heinrich IV. (a: Pommes frites, Béarner Sauce; b: Artischockenböden, Nußkartoffeln)	Tournedos Henri IV (a: pommes pont-neuf, sauce béarnaise; b: fonds d'artichauts, pommes noisettes)	Tournedos Enrico IV (a: patate fritte, salsa bearnese; b: fondi di carciofo, patate nocciola)	Tournedos Enriquo IV (a: con patatas fritas y salsa bearnesa; b: con fondos de alcachofas rellenos de patatas)
Tripe	Kaldaunen, Kutteln	Tripes[41] (pl)	Trippa	Callos, tripas
Tripe and onions	Kutteln mit Zwiebeln	Tripes aux orignons	Trippa con cipolle	Callos con cebolla
Veal balls	Kalbsfrikadellen	Fricadelles de veau	Polpette di vitello	Albóndigas de ternera

Meat dishes	Fleischgerichte	Plats de viande	Piatti di carne	Platos de carne
Veal cutlet	Kalbskotelett	Côte de veau	Costoletta di vitello	Chuleta de ternera
Veal cutlet in jelly	~ Bellevue (in Gelee)	~ de veau en bellevue (en gelée)	~ di vitello in bella vista (in gelatina)	~ de ternera en bella vista (en gelatina)
Veal cutlet Milanese (breaded cutlet)	~ nach Mailänder Art (paniertes Kotelett)	~ de veau milanaise (côte de veau panée)	~ alla milanese (costoletta impanata)	~ a la milanesa (chuleta empanada)
Veal cutlet sauté	~ natur	~ de veau sautée	~ di vitello al burro	~ de ternera salteada
Breaded veal cutlet	~ paniert	~ de veau panée	~ di vitello impanata	~ de ternera empanada
Veal cutlet en papillote	~ en Papillote	~ de veau en papillote	~ di vitello al cartoccio	~ en papillote
Veal cutlet Pojarski (minced veal cutlet)	~ Pojarski (gehacktes Kotelett)	~ de veau Pojarski (côte de veau hachée)	~ di vitello Pojarski (costoletta tritata)	~ de ternera Pojarski (chuleta de picadillo)
Grilled veal cutlet	~ vom Rost	~ de veau grillée	~ di vitello ai ferri	~ a la parrilla
Veal goulash	Kalbsgulasch	Goulash de veau	Gulasch di vitello	Gulash de ternera
Veal pie	Kalbfleischpastete	Pâté de veau	Pâté di vitello	Pastel de ternera
Veal roulade[40]	Kalbsrouladen	Paupiettes de veau	Involtini di vitello	Popietas de ternera
Veal steak	Kalbssteak	Steak de veau	Bistecca di vitello	Bistec de ternera
Veal stew	Kalbsragout	Sauté de veau	Spezzatino di vitello	Estofado de ternera
Veal stew with spring vegetables	~ auf Frühlingsart (mit jungem Gemüse)	~ de veau printanier (aux primeurs)	~ di vitello primaverile (con verdure novelle)	~ de ternera primaveral (con verduras)
Veal stew, hunter's style (with mushrooms and tomatoes)	~ nach Jägerart (mit Champignons und Tomaten)	~ de veau chasseur (aux champignons et tomates)	~ di vitello alla cacciatora (con funghi e pomodori)	~ de ternera a la cazadora (con champiñones y tomates)
Veal stew Marengo (with tomatoes and mushrooms)	Kalbsragout Marengo (mit Tomaten, Champignons und Weißwein)	Sauté de veau Marengo (aux tomates et aux champignons)	Spezzatino di vitello Marengo (con pomodori e funghi)	Estofado de ternera Marengo (con tomates y champiñones)
White sausages	Weißwürste	Boudins blancs	Salsicce di vitello	Salchichas de ternera
Wiener schnitzel[42] (breaded veal slice)	Wiener Schnitzel (paniertes Kalbsschnitzel)	Escalope de veau viennoise (escalope panée)	Cotoletta alla milanese (scaloppina di vitello impanata)	Escalope a la vienesa (escalope de ternera empanada)
Yorkshire pudding (baked batter pudding)	Yorkshire Pudding (Pfannkuchenteig im Ofen gebacken)	Yorkshire pudding (Galette épaisse de pâte à crêpe cuite au four)	Yorkshire pudding (pastella da crêpe cotta al forno)	Yorkshire pudding (pasta de harima, huevo y leche corida al homo)

Meat dishes	Fleischgerichte	Plats de viande	Piatti di carne	Platos de carne
Zampone (pork sausage wrapped in the skin of a pig's trotter)	Zampone (Wurst in der Haut eines ganzen Schweinsfußes)	Zampone (saucisson enveloppé dans la peau d'un pied de porc)	Zampone (salame insaccato nella zampa del maiale)	Zampone (embutido en la piel de la pata entera de cerdo)
~ with lentils	~ mit Linsen	~ aux lentilles	~ con lenticchie	~ con lentejas
~ with sauerkraut	~ mit Sauerkraut	~ à la choucroute	~ con crauti	~ con chucruta

[31]) ou ragoût de bœuf.
[32]) o lechecillas de ternera.
[33]) ou assiette anglaise.
[34]) slice of braised larded veal.
[35]) Schnitte von gespickter Kalbsnuß.
[36]) o braciola di maiale.
[37]) auch Rindsbraten, Rindsbrust usw. (bes. südd., österr.).
[38]) in Deutschland bezeichnet oft das Rumpsteak ein Entrecôte (simple).
[39]) runde Schnitte aus dem Filet im Gewichte von 100–120 g.
[40]) slices of veal rolled up with stuffing & stewed.
[41]) ou gras-double (sing.).
[42]) or Vienna schnitzel.

Poultry	Geflügel	Volaille	Pollame	Aves
Breast of chicken[43]	Hühnerbrustfilet	Suprêmes de volaille[45]	Petti di pollo[46]	Supremas de pollo[47]
~ of chicken Maryland (with corn fritters & fried bananas)	~ Maryland (mit kleinen Maisbeignets und gebratenen Bananen)	~ de volaille Maryland (aux beignets de maïs et bananes frites)	Petti di pollo Maryland (con frittelle di mais e banane fritte)	~ de pollo Maryland (con galletas de maíz y plátanos fritos)
~ of chicken with salted ox-tongue	~ mit Pökelzunge	~ de volaille à l'écarlate	Petti di pollo con lingua salmistrata	~ de pollo con lengua salada
~ of chicken in cream	~ in Sahne	~ de volaille à la crème	Petti di pollo alla panna	~ de pollo a la crema
Breast of turkey (or turkey fillets)	Puterbrustfilet	Suprêmes de dinde (ou filets de dinde)	Petti di tacchino (o filetti di tacchino)	Pechuga de pavo
Capon	Kapaun	Chapon	Cappone	Capón
Roast truffled capon	~ getrüffelt	Chapon truffé rôti	~ arrosto tartufato	~ asado trufado
Chaud-froid of chicken[44]	Geflügel-Chaudfroid	Chaud-froid de volaille	Chaud-froid di pollo	Chaud-froid de pollo
Chicken à la King (in cream sauce with mushrooms and sherry)	Hühnchen nach Königsart (in Rahmsauce mit Champignons und Sherry)	Poulet à la royale (en sauce crème avec champignons et xérès)	Pollo alla reale (in salsa di panna con funghi e sherry)	Pollo a la real (en salsa de crema con champiñones y jerez)
Chicken baked in pastry	Hahn in Teigkruste	Coq en pâte	Pollo in crosta	Pollo vestido
Grilled chicken with bacon	Huhn	Poulet	Pollo	Pollo
bacon	~ auf amerikanische Art (vom Rost, mit Speck)	~ grillé à l'américaine (au bacon)	~ alla griglia all'americana (con bacon)	~ a la americana (a la parrilla con tocino)
Jellied chicken	~ in Aspik	~ en gelée	~ in gelatina	~ en gelatina
Boned stuffed chicken	~ ausgebeint und gefüllt	~ désossé et farci	~ disossato ripieno	~ deshuesado y relleno
Chicken in champagne	~ in Champagnerwein	~ au champagne	~ allo champagne	~ al champaña
Roast chicken	~ gebraten	~ rôti	~ arrosto	~ asado
Roast stuffed chicken	~ gefüllt	~ farci rôti	~ ripieno arrosto	~ relleno asado
Grilled chicken	~ gegrillt	~ grillé	~ alla griglia	~ a la parrilla
Boiled chicken	~ gekocht	~ bouilli	~ lesso	~ cocido
Chicken, hunter's style (with mushrooms)	~ nach Jägerart (mit Champignons)	~ sauté chasseur (aux champignons)	~ alla cacciatora (con funghi)	~ a la cazadora (con champiñones)
Casserole of chicken	~ in der Kasserolle	~ en cocotte	~ in casseruola	~ en cacerola

Poultry	Geflügel	Volaille	Pollame	Aves
Chicken Marengo (with mushrooms & tomatoes)	Huhn Marengo (sautiert mit Champignons und Tomaten)	Poulet Marengo (avec champignons et tomates)	Pollo alla Marengo (con funghi e pomodori)	Pollo a la Marengo (en salsa de tomate con champiñones)
~ with mayonnaise	~ mit Mayonnaise	~ froid mayonnaise	~ con maionese	~ con mayonesa
Chicken with paprika	~ mit Paprika	~ sauté au paprika	~ alla paprica	~ con pimentón
Chicken in cream sauce	~ in Rahmsauce	~ sauté à la crème	~ alla panna	~ a la crema
Chicken creole (with rice, tomatoes and green peppers)	Hühnchen auf Kreolische Art (mit Reis, Tomaten, Paprikaschoten)	Poulet à la créole (au riz avec tomates et poivron)	Pollo alla creola (con riso, pomodori e peperoni)	Pollo a la criolla (con arroz, tomates y pimientos)
Chicken croquettes	Geflügelkroketten	Croquettes de volaille	Crocchette di pollo	Croquetas de ave
Chicken curry	Curryhuhn	Curry de poulet	~ al curry	~ al curry
Chicken cutlet	Geflügelkotelett	Côtelette de volaille	Costoletta di pollo	Chuleta de pollo
Chicken fricassee	Hühner-Frikassee	Fricassée de poulet	Fricassea di pollo	Fricasé de pollo
Chicken jambalaya	Jambeya von Huhn	Jambelage de poulet	Jambelaye di pollo	Jambalaya de pollo
Chicken livers	Geflügelleber	Foies de volaille	Fegatini (di pollo)	Higadillos de ave
Chicken livers en brochette	~ am Spießchen	Brochettes de foies de volaille	Spiedini di fegatini	~ de ave en broqueta
Chicken mayonnaise	Hühnermayonnaise	Mayonnaise de volaille	Maionese di pollo	Mayonesa de pollo
Chicken mousse	Geflügel-Mousse	Mousse de volaille	Mousse di pollo	Espuma de ave
Chicken pie	Hühnerpastete	Pâté de poulet	Pâté di pollo	Pastel de ave
Chicken pilau	Hühnerpilaf	Pilaf de volaille	Pilaf di pollo	Pilav de pollo
Chicken with paprika	Paprika-Huhn	Poulet sauté au paprika	Pollo alla paprica	Pollo con pimentón
Duck	Ente	Canard[48])	Anitra, anatra	Pato
Roast duck	~ gebraten	Caneton rôti	~ arrosto	~ asado
Roast stuffed duckling	~ gefüllt	Caneton farci	~ ripiena	~ relleno
Duckling	~ , junge	Caneton	~ novella	~ joven
Duckling with turnips	~ mit Mairübchen	Caneton aux navets	~ con le rape	~ con nabos
Braised duck with olives	~ mit Oliven	Caneton aux olives	~ con le olive	~ con aceitunas
Duckling with oranges	~ mit Orangen	Caneton à l'orange	~ all'arancia	~ a la naranja
Pressed duck	~ in der Presse	Caneton à la presse	~ al torchio	~ a la sangre
Duckling with red cabbage	~ mit Rotkohl	Caneton aux choux rouges	~ con cavoli rossi	~ con col lombarda

Poultry	Geflügel	Volaille	Pollame	Aves
Escalope of turkey	Puterschnitzel	Escalope de dinde	Scaloppina di tacchino	Escalope de pavo
Fried spring chicken	Wiener Backhendl	Poulet frit à la viennoise	Pollastrino fritto	Pollo frito a la vienesa
Fried spring chicken	Backhähnchen	Poulet de grain frit	Pollo fritto	Pollo frito
Galantine of chicken	Geflügel-Galantine	Galantine de volaille	Galantina di pollo	Galantina de pollo
Giblets	Geflügelklein	Abatis	Rigaglie di pollo	Menudillos
Goose	Gans	Oie	Oca	Ganso
Braised goose with sauerkraut	~ auf elsässische Art (mit Sauerkraut)	~ à l'alsacienne (à la choucroute)	~ all'alsaziana (con crauti)	~ a la alsaciana (con chucruta)
Roast goose with apple sauce	~ auf englische Art (mit Apfelmus)	~ à l'anglaise (rôtie, sauce aux pommes)	~ arrosto all'inglese (con salsa di mele)	~ asado a la inglesa (con puré de manzanas)
Roast goose	~ gebraten	~ rôtie	~ arrosto	~ asado
Goose giblets	Gänseklein	Abatis d'oie	Rigaglie d'oca	Menudillos de ganso
Goose liver	Gänseleber	Foie gras	Fegato d'oca	Hígado de ganso
Grilled chicken	Grillhähnchen	Poulet grillé	Pollo alla griglia	Pollo emparrillado
Grilled chicken	Huhn vom Rost	Poulet grillé	Pollo alla griglia	Pollo a la parrilla
Chicken sauté	~ sautiert	~ sauté	~ sauté	~ salteado, ~ guisado
Spring chicken on the spit	~ vom Spieß	~ de grain à la broche	~ allo spiedo	~ al asador
Devilled spring chicken (grilled chicken)	~ nach Teufelsart (vom Grill)	~ grillé à la diable (sauce diable à part)	~ alla diavola (cotto in gratella)	~ a la diabla (asado a la parrilla)
Guinea-fowl, guinea-hen	Perlhuhn	Pintade	Faraona	Pintada[49])
Roast guinea-fowl	~ gebraten	~ rôtie	Faraona arrosto	~ asada
Guinea-hen en papillote	~ en Papillote	~ en papillote	Faraona al cartoccio	~ en papillote
Guinea-hen in cream	~ in Rahmsauce	~ à la crème	Faraona alla panna	~ a la crema
Hamburg poussins	Hamburger Stubenküken	Poussins de Hambourg	Pulcini di Amburgo	Polluelos de Hamburgo
Hen	Henne	Poule	Gallina	Gallina
Leg of chicken	Hühnerkeule	Cuisse de poulet	Coscia di pollo	Muslo de pollo
Maryland fried chicken (garnished with fried bacon)	Backhähnchen Maryland (mit gebratenem Speck garniert)	Poulet frit Maryland (garni de tranches frites de bacon)	Pollo fritto Maryland (con fettine di pancetta fritte)	Pollo frito Maryland (con lonjas fritas de tocino)
Pâté de foie gras	Gänseleber-Pastete	Pâté de foie gras	Pâté di fegato d'oca	Foie-gras[50])

Poultry	Geflügel	Volaille	Pollame	Aves
Parfait de foie gras	Gänseleber-Parfait	Parfait de foie gras	Parfait di fegato d'oca	Parfait de foie-gras
Pigeon	Taube	Pigeon (junge	Piccione	Pichón
(young pigeon: squab		Taube: pigeonneau)		
Roast stuffed squab	~ gefüllt	Pigeonneau farci	~ farcito	~ relleno
Grilled squab	~ vom Grill	~ à la crapaudine	~ in gratella	~ asado a la parrilla
Pigeon sauté	~ sautiert	~ à la minute	~ al minuto	~ al minuto
Pigeon on the spit	~ vom Spieß	~ rôti à la broche	~ allo spiedo	~ al asador
Pigeon pie	Taubenpastete	Pâté de pigeons	Pâté di piccione	Pastel de pichón
Poulard, poularde	Poularde	Poularde	Pollastra	Pularda
Poulard with tarragon	~ mit Estragon	~ à l'estragon	~ al dragoncello	~ con estragón
Boiled poulard	~ gekocht	~ pochée	~ lessa	~ cocida
Truffled poulard	~ getrüffelt	~ truffée	~ tartufata	~ trufada
Poulard with rice	~ mit Reis	~ au riz	~ col riso	~ con arroz
~ Suvorov (stuffed with	~ Suworow (mit Gänse-	~ Souvarov (farcie de	~ Suvarov (ripiena di	~ Suvarov (rellena de
goose liver & truffles)	leber und Trüffeln)	foie gras et truffes)	fegato d'oca e tartufi)	foie-gras y trufas)
Poussin	Küken	Poussin	Pulcino	Polluelo
Grilled poussin	~ vom Rost	~ grillé	Pulcino alla griglia	~ asado a la parrilla
Fried poussin	~ auf Wiener Art	~ frit à la viennoise	Pulcino fritto	~ frito a la vienesa
Roast chicken	Brathähnchen	~ rôti	~ arrosto	~ asado
Spring chicken on the spit	~ vom Spieß	~ de grain à la broche	~ allo spiedo	~ al asador
Roast turkey	Puterbraten	Dinde rôtie	Tacchino arrosto	Pavo asado
Salmi of guinea-hen	Perlhuhnragout	Pintade en salmis	Faraona in salmis	Pintada en salmorejo
Spring chicken	Hähnchen	Poulet nouveau	Pollastrino, pollo novello	Pollo joven
Stuffed winglets	Hühnerflügel, gefüllt	Ailerons farcis	Alette di pollo ripiene	Alones rellenos
Terrine de foie gras	Gänseleber-Terrine	Terrine de foie gras	Terrina di fegato d'oca	Terrina de foie-gras
Turkey	Truthahn	Dinde	Tacchino	Pavo
Roast stuffed turkey	~ gefüllt	~ farcie rôtie	~ ripieno arrosto	~ relleno
Boiled turkey	~ gekocht	~ pochée	~ lesso	~ cocido
Braised turkey	~ geschmort	~ braisée	~ brasato	~ braseado
Truffled turkey	~ getrüffelt	~ truffée	~ tartufato	~ trufado

Poultry	Geflügel	Volaille	Pollame	Aves
Young turkey Roast turkey with chestnut dressing	junger Truthahn ~ mit Maronen gefüllt	Dindonneau Dinde farcie aux marrons	Tacchinotto Tacchino ripieno di marroni	Pavo joven, pavipollo Pavo relleno de castañas

[43]) or chicken fillets.
[44]) filleted poultry served in jelly.
[45]) ou filets de volaille.
[46]) o suprême di pollo.
[47]) o pechuga de pollo.
[48]) auf den Speisekarten fast immer „caneton" = junge Ente.
[49]) o gallina de Guinea.
[50]) pasta de hígado de ganso.

Game	Wildbret	Gibier	Selvaggina	Caza
Bald coot, water-hen	Bläßhuhn	Foulque noire	Folaga	Foja, gallina de agua
Beccafico	Feigendrosseln	Becfigues	Beccafichi	Papafigos
Black-cock, heath-cock	Spielhahn	Coq des bois	Fagiano di monte	Grigallo
Black grouse, heath-cock	Birkhahn	Coq des bois	Fagiano di monte	Grigallo
Blackbirds	Amseln	Merles	Merli	Mirlos
Breast of partridge	Rebhuhnbrüstchen	Suprêmes de perdreau	Petti di pernice	Pechuga de perdiz
Breast of pheasant	Fasanenbrüstchen	Suprêmes de faisan	Petti di fagiano	Pechuga de faisán
~ of pheasant in cream	~ in Rahm	~ de faisan à la crème	~ di fagiano alla crema	~ de faisán a la crema
Breast of woodcock	Schnepfenbrüstchen	Suprêmes de bécasse	Petti di beccaccia	Supremas de becada
Grilled quails	Wachteln vom Rost	Cailles grillées	Quaglie alla griglia	Codornices a la parrilla
Minute quails	~ auf schnellste Art	~ à la minute, ~ sautées	~ al minuto	~ al minuto
Quails on the spit	~ vom Spieß	~ à la broche	~ allo spiedo	~ al asador
Quails Sovorov (stuffed with goose liver & truffles)	~ Suworow (mit Gänse-leber und Trüffeln gefüllt)	~ Souvarov (farcies de foie gras et truffes)	~ Suvarov (ripiene di fegato d'oca e tartufi)	~ Suvarov (rellenas de foie-gras y trufas)
Quails roasted in vine leaves	~ in Weinblättern gebraten	~ aux feuilles de vigne	~ in veste verde (av-volte in foglia di vite)	~ asadas en hojas de vid
Quails with grapes	~ nach Winzerart (mit Weinbeeren)	~ à la vigneronne (aux raisins)	~ alla vignaiola (con l'uva)	~ a la viñadora (con granos de uva)
Capercailzie, wood-grouse	Auerhahn	Coq de bruyère	Gallo cedrone	Gallo silvestre, urogallo
Chamois	Gemse	Chamois	Camoscio	Gamuza
Coot, bald coot	Wasserhuhn	Foulque noire	Folaga	Foja, gallina de agua
Deer, stag	Hirsch	Cerf	Cervo	Ciervo, venado
Elk	Elch, Elentier	Élan	Alce	Anta, alce
Escalope of venison	Rehschnitzel	Escalope de chevreuil	Scaloppina di capriolo	Escalope de corzo
Escalope of venison with mushrooms	~ mit Champignons	~ de chevreuil aux champignons	Scaloppina di capriolo con funghi	~ de corzo con champi-ñones
Fallow-deer	Damhirsch	Daim	Daino	Gamo
Fillets of hare	Hasenfilets	Filets de lièvre	Filetti di lepre	Filetes de liebre
Fillets of venison	Rehfilets	Filets de chevreuil	Filetti di capriolo	Filetes de corzo
Game pie, venison pie	Wildpastete	Pâté de gibier	Pâté di cacciagione	Pastel de caza

Game	Wildbret	Gibier	Selvaggina	Caza
Hare pie	Hasenpastete	Pâté de lièvre	Pâté di lepre	Pastel de liebre
Hare	Hase	Lièvre	Lepre	Liebre
Haunch of venison[51]	Rehkeule	Cuissot de chevreuil[53]	Cosciotto di capriolo	Pernil de corzo
~ of venison with cream	~ in Rahmsauce	~ de chevreuil à la crème	~ di capriolo alla panna	~ de corzo a la crema
Haunch of wild boar[52]	Wildschweinskeule	Cuissot de sanglier	Cosciotto di cinghiale	Pernil de jabalí
Haunch of wild boar in sweet-and-sour sauce	~ süß-sauer	Cuissot de sanglier à l'aigre-doux	Cosciotto di cinghiale in agrodolce	~ de jabalí en agridulce
Hazel grouse, hazel hen	Haselhuhn	Gelinotte	Francolino di monte	Bonasa
Hunter's brochette	Jagdspießchen	Brochette du chasseur	Spiedino di caccia	Broquetas de caza
Jugged chamois	Gemsenpfeffer	Civet de chamois	Camoscio in salmì	Gamuza en salmorejo
Jugged hare	Hasenpfeffer	Civet de lièvre	Lepre in salmì	Liebre en salmorejo
Jugged rabbit	Kaninchen-Pfeffer	Lapin en civet	~ in salmì	~ en salmorejo
Jugged venison	Rehpfeffer	Civet de chevreuil	Capriolo in salmì	Salmorejo de corzo
Jugged wild boar	Wildschweinpfeffer	Sanglier en civet	Cinghiale in salmì	Civet de jabalí
Lapwing, peewit, pewit	Kiebitz	Vanneau	Pavoncella, vanello	Avefría
Larks	Lerchen	Alouettes, mauviettes	Allodole	Alondras
Medallions of pheasant	Fasanenmedaillons	Médaillons de faisan	Medaglioni di fagiano	Medallones de faisán
Medallions of venison	Rehmedaillons	Médaillons de chevreuil	Medalgioni di capriolo	Medallones de corzo
~ of venison, hunter's style (with mushrooms & tomatoes)	~ nach Jägerart (mit Champignons und Tomaten)	~ de chevreuil chasseur (aux champignons et tomates)	~ di capriolo alla cacciatora (con funghi e pomodori)	~ de corzo a la cazadora (con champiñones y tomates)
Medallions of venison with chestnuts	~ mit Maronenpüree	~ de chevreuil à la purée de marrons	~ di capriolo con marroni	~ de corzo con puré de castañas
Moorfowl, see red grouse moorhen, Water-hen	Teichhuhn	Poule d'eau	Gallinella d'acqua	Polla de agua, rascón

Game	Wildbret	Gibier	Selvaggina	Caza
Partridge	Rebhuhn	Perdreau (perdrix)	Pernice, starna	Perdiz
Roast partridge on toast	~ gebraten auf Röstbrot	Perdreau rôti sur canapé	~ arrosto sul crostone	~ asada sobre tostada
Partridge with cabbage	~ mit Kohl	~ aux choux	~ con cavoli	~ con coles
Partridge with apples	~ auf normannische Art (mit Äpfeln)	~ à la normande (aux pommes reinettes)	~ alla normana (con mele)	~ a la normanda (con manzanas)
Partridge in cream	~ in Rahmsauce	~ à la crème	~ alla crema	~ a la crema
Pheasant pie	Fasanenpastete	Pâté de faisan	Pâté di fagiano	Pastel de faisán
Pheasant	Fasan	Faisan	Fagiano	Faisán
Roast pheasant	~ gebraten	~ rôti	~ arrosto	~ asado
Roast truffled pheasant	~ getrüffelt	~ truffé	~ tartufato	~ trufado
Casserole of pheasant	~ in der Kasserolle	~ en cocotte	~ in casseruola	~ en cacerola
Pheasant with sauer-kraut	~ mit Sauerkraut	~ à la choucroute	~ con crauti	~ con chucruta
Ptarmigan, white grouse	Schneehuhn	Perdrix des neiges, poule des neiges	Pernice bianca	Perdiz blanca
Quails	Wachteln	Cailles	Quaglie	Codornices
Roast quails	~ gebraten	~ rôties	~ arrosto	~ asadas
Quail casserole	~ in der Kasserolle	~ en cocotte	~ in casseruola	~ en cacerola
Quails in nests	~ im Nest	~ au nid	~ nel nido	~ en los nidos
Quails with rice	~ mit Reis	~ au riz	~ al riso	~ con arroz
Quails with risotto	Wachtel-Risotto	Risotto de cailles	Risotto con le quaglie	~ con arroz
Rabbit fricassee	Kaninchen-Frikassee	Blanquette de lapin	~ in fricassea	~ en salsa blanca
Rabbit	Kaninchen	Lapin, lapereau	Coniglio	Conejo
Fried rabbit	~ gebacken	Lapereau frit	~ fritto	~ frito
Roast rabbit	~ gebraten	Lapin rôti	~ arrosto	~ asado
Rabbit ragout	Kaninchenragout	Ragoût de lapin, lapin sauté	~ in umido	~ en estofado
Ragout of hare	Hasenragout	Ragoût de lièvre	Lepre in umido	Estofado de liebre
Red grouse	Schottisches Moorschnee-huhn	Grouse (lagopède d'Écosse)	Lagopode, pernice bianca di Scozia	Perdiz blanca de Escocia
Reindeer steak	Rentiersteak	Steak de renne	Bistecca di renna	Bistec de reno
Reindeer	Rentier	Renne	Renna	Reno

Game	Wildbret	Gibier	Selvaggina	Caza
Roast hare	Hasenbraten	Lièvre rôti	Lepre arrosto	Asado de liebre
Roast ortolans	Ortolane, gebraten	Ortolans rôtis	Ortolani arrosti	Hortelanos asados
Roast venison	Rehbraten	Chevreuil rôti	Capriolo arrosto	Corzo asado
Roast venison	Hirschbraten	Cerf rôti	Cervo arrosto	Asado de venado
Roast wild boar	Wildschweinbraten	Sanglier rôti	Arrosto di cinghiale	Asado de jabalí
Roe(buck), venison	Reh	Chevreuil	Capriolo	Corzo
Saddle of hare	Hasenrücken	Râble de lièvre	Lombo di lepre	Lomo de liebre
~ of hare with juniper	~ mit Wacholdersauce	~ de lièvre au genièvre	~ di lepre al ginepro	~ de liebre al enebro
Saddle of venison	Rehziemer	Cimier de chevreuil	Sella di capriolo	Silla de corzo
Saddle of venison	Rehrücken	Selle de chevreuil	Sella di capriolo	Lomo de corzo
~ of venison with mushrooms	~ nach Försterinart (mit Pilzen)	~ de chevreuil forestière (aux champignons)	~ di capriolo alla forestale (con funghi)	~ de corzo con setas
Larded saddle of venison	~ gespickt	~ de chevreuil piquée	~ di capriolo lardellata	~ de corzo mechado
Saddle of venison with cherries	~ mit Kirschen	~ de chevreuil aux cerises	~ di capriolo con cillegie	~ de corzo con cerezas
Saddle of venison with fried bananas	Rehrücken nach Kreolenart (mit gebratenen Bananen)	Selle de chevreuil à la créole (aux bananes)	Sella di capriolo alla creola (guarnita di banane)	Lomo de corzo a la criolla (con plátanos)
Saddle of young wild boar	Frischlingsrücken	Selle de marcassin	Sella di cinghialetto	Lomo de jabato
Salmi of pheasant	Salmi von Fasan	Salmis de faisan	Fagiano in salmì	Salmorejo de faisán
Salmi of partridges	~ von Rebhühnern	Salmis de perdreaux	Pernice in salmì	~ de perdiz
Salmi of woodcock	~ von Schnepfen	Salmis de bécasses	Beccaccia in salmì	~ de becada
Salmi of wild duck	~ von Wildente	Canard sauvage en salmis	Anitra selvatica in salmì	~ de pato silvestre
Snipe	Sumpfschnepfe	Bécassine	Beccaccino	Becacina
Snipe	Bekassine	Bécassine	Beccaccino	Becacina
Grilled snipe	~ vom Rost	~ grillée	~ alla griglia	~ a la parrilla
Teal	Krickente (Kriekente)	Sarcelle	Alzavola	Cerceta

Game	Wildbret	Gibier	Selvaggina	Caza
Thrushes, fieldfares	Drosseln	Grives	Tordi	Tordos
~ à la bonne femme (with diced bacon and croûtons)	~ nach Hausfrauenart (mit Speckwürfeln und Croûtons)	~ à la bonne femme (aux lardons et croûtons)	~ alla bonne femme (con lardo e crostini)	~ a la bonne femme (con tocino y trocitos de pan frito)
~ on the spit	~ am Spieß gebraten	~ à la broche	~ allo spiedo	~ al asador
~ with juniper sauce	~ mit Wacholdersauce	~ au genièvre	~ al ginepro	~ con enebro
Venison cutlet	Rehkotelett	Côtelette de chevreuil	Costoletta di capriolo	Chuleta de corzo
Venison cutlet Conti (with lentil purée)	~ Conti (mit Linsen- püree)	~ de chevreuil Conti (aux lentilles)	~ di capriolo Conti (con purè di lenticchie)	~ de corzo Conti (con puré de lentejas)
Venison cutlet with mushrooms	Rehkotelett mit Pilzen	Côtelette de chevreuil aux champignons	Costoletta di capriolo ai funghi	Chuleta de corzo con setas
Venison cutlet St. Hu- bert (with mush- rooms and poivrade sauce)	~ St. Hubertus (mit Champignons und Pfeffersauce)	~ de chevreuil Saint- Hubert (avec champignons et sauce poivrade)	~ di capriolo Sant'Uberto (con funghi e salsa poivrade)	~ de corzo San Huberto (con champiñones y salsa poivrade)
Venison noisettes	Rehnüßchen	Noisettes de chevreuil	Medaglioni di capriolo	Medallones de corzo
Venison pie	Rehpastete	Pâté de chevreuil	Pâté di capriolo	Pastel de corzo
Venison ragout	Rehragout	Ragoût de chevreuil[54]	Capriolo in umido	Corzo guisado
Venison steak	Hirschsteak	Steak de cerf	Bistecca di cervo	Bistec de venado
Venison steak	Rehsteak	Steak de chevreuil	Bistecca di capriolo	Bistec de corzo
Water hen, see moorhen				
Wild boar	Wildschwein	Sanglier	Cinghiale	Jabalí
Wild duck, mallard	Wildente	Canard sauvage	Anitra selvatica[55]	Pato silvestre
Wild duck with oranges	~ mit Orangen	~ sauvage à la bigarade	~ selvatica all'arancia	~ silvestre con naranjas
Wild rabbit	Wildkaninchen	Lapin de garenne	Coniglio selvatico	Conejo silvestre
Woodcock pie	Schnepfenpastete	Pâté de bécasses	Pâté di beccaccia	Pastel de becada
Woodcock	Schnepfe	Bécasse	Beccaccia	Becada, chocha
Woodcock flambó	~ flambiert	~ flambée	~ alla fiamma	Becada flameada
Roast woodcock on toast	~ gebraten auf Röstbrot	~ rôtie sur canapé	~ arrosto sul crostone	~ asada sobre canapé
Grilled woodcock	~ gegrillt	~ grillée	~ alla griglia	~ a la parrilla

Game	Wildbret	Gibier	Selvaggina	Caza
Woodpigeon, ring-dove	Ringeltaube	Palombe	Colombaccio, palombo	Paloma torcaz
Stuffed woodpigeon	~ gefüllt	Palombe farcie	Colombaccio ripieno	Paloma torcaz rellena
Young wild boar	Frischling	Marcassin	Cinghialetto	Jabato

[51]) or leg of venison.
[52]) or leg of wild boar.
[53]) dit aussi gigue de chevreuil.
[54]) ou sauté de chevreuil.
[55])o germano reale.

Vegetables	Gemüse	Légumes	Verdure	Verduras
Artichoke bottoms	Artischockenböden	Fonds d'artichaut	Fondi di carciofo	Fondos de alcachofas
Stuffed artichoke bottoms	~ gefüllt	~ d'artichaut farcis	~ di carciofo ripieni	~ de alcachofas rellenos
Artichokes	Artischocken	Artichauts	Carciofi	Alcachofas
Fried artichokes	~ gebacken	~ frits	~ fritti	~ fritas
Artichokes with tartar sauce	~ mit Tatarensauce	~ sauce tartare	~ con salsa tartara	~ con salsa tártara
Asparagus tips	Spargelspitzen	Pointes d'asperges	Punte d'asparagi	Puntas de espárragos
Asparagus tips in cream	~ in Rahmsauce	~ d'asperges à la crème	~ d'asparagi alla panna	~ de espárragos a la crema
Asparagus	Spargel	Asperges	Asparagi	Espárragos
~ with a fried egg	~ auf Mailänder Art (mit Spiegelei)	~ à la milanaise (garnies œuf poêlé)	~ alla milanese (con un uovo al burro)	~ a la milanesa (con huevo al plato)
~ with fried breadcrumbs	~ auf polnische Art (mit Butterbröseln)	~ à la polonaise (à la mie de pain frite)	~ alla polacca (con pan grattato rosolato)	~ a la polaca (con pan rallado frito)
~ au gratin	~ überbacken	~ au gratin	~ gratinati	~ al gratén
~ vinaigrette sauce	~ mit Vinaigrette	~ à la vinaigrette[57])	~ all'olio	~ con vinagreta
~ with melted butter	~ mit zerlassener Butter	~ au beurre fondu	~ al burro fuso	~ con manteca fundida
Assorted vegetables	Gemüseplatte	Légumes variés	Verdure assortite	Legumbres variadas
Assorted vegetables with fried egg	~ mit Ei	~ variés à l'œuf	Verdure assortite con uovo al tegame	Legumbres variadas con huevo al plato
Aubergines, eggplant	Auberginen	Aubergines	Melanzane	Berenjenas
Fried aubergines	~ gebacken	~ frites	~ fritte	~ fritas
Baked stuffed eggplant	~ gefüllt	~ farcies	~ ripiene	~ rellenas
Beans and bacon	Speckbohnen	Haricots blancs au lard	Fagioli al lardo	Judías blancas con tocino
Beetroots, red beets	Rote Rüben	Betteraves	Barbabietole	Remolachas
Belgian endives[56])	Chicorée	Endives	Indivia belga	Endibia de Bruselas
Braised Belgian endives	~ gedünstet	Endives braisées	Indivia belga brasata	~ de Bruselas braseada
~ in cream	~ in Rahm	Endives à la crème	Indivia belga alla crema	~ de Bruselas a la crema
Black salsify, scorzonera	Schwarzwurzeln	Salsifis, scorsonères	Scorzonera	Escorzoneras[58])
Fried black salsify	~ gebacken	Salsifis frits	~ fritta	~ fritas
Sautéed black salsify	~ in Butter	~ sautés	~ al burro	~ salteadas

Vegetables	Gemüse	Légumes	Verdure	Verduras
Boston baked beans (with salt pork and molasses)	Bostoner Bohnen (mit Speck und Melasse im Ofen geschmort)	Haricots à la bostonienne (cuits au four avec petit salí et mélasse)	Fagioli al forno alla bostoniana (con pancetta e melassa)	Judías al estilo de Boston (cocidos al horno con tocino y melaza)
Broad beans	Saubohnen, Puffbohnen	Fèves	Fave	Habas
Broccoli	Spargelkohl, Brokkoli	Brocolis	Broccoli	Brécoles, bróculis
Brunswick asparagus	Braunschweiger Spargel	Asperges de Brunswick	Asparagi di Brunswick	Espárragos de Brunswick
Brussels sprouts	Rosenkohl	Choux de Bruxelles	Cavoletti di Bruxelles	Coles de Bruselas
Sautéed Brussels sprouts	~ in Butter	~ de Bruxelles sautés	~ di Bruxelles al burro	~ de Bruselas salteadas
Buttered French beans	Butter-Bohnen	Haricots verts au beurre	Fagiolini al burro	Judías verdes salteadas
Buttered green peas	Butter Erbsen	Petits pois au beurre	Piselli al burro	Guisantes salteados
Buttered leaf-spinach	Blattspinat	Épinards à l'anglaise[59])	Spinaci al burro	Espinacas a la inglesa
Cabbage	Kohl	Chou	Cavolo	Col
Cardoons	Kardonen	Cardons	Cardi, cardoni	Cardos
~ in cream	~ in Rahmsauce	~ à la crème	Cardi alla crema	~ a la crema
~ with marrow sauce	~ mit Rindermark	~ à la moelle	Cardi al midollo	~ con tuétano
Carrots	Karotten	Carottes	Carote	Zanahorias
Glazed carrots	~ glaciert	~ glacées	~ glassate	~ glaseadas
Carrots in cream	~ in Rahmsauce	~ à la crème	~ alla panna	~ a la crema
Cauliflower	Blumenkohl	Chou-fleur	Cavolfiore	Coliflor
Sautéed cauliflower	~ in Butter	~ sauté au beurre	~ al burro	~ salteada
Boiled cauliflower	~ auf englische Art	~ à l'anglaise	~ lessato	~ a la inglesa
Cauliflower cheese	~ gratiniert	~ Mornay (au gratin)	~ al gratin	~ al gratén
Cauliflower with fried breadcrumbs	~ auf polnische Art (mit Butterbröseln)	~ à la polonaise (à la mie de pain frite)	~ alla polacca (con pan grattato rosolato)	~ a la polaca (con pan rallado frito)
Cauliflower pudding	Blumenkohlauflauf	Pain[60]) de chou-fleur	Sformato di cavolfiore	Budín de coliflor
Celery	Sellerie	Céleris	Sedani	Apio
Braised celery	~ gedünstet	~ braisés	~ brasati	~ estofado
Celery au gratin	~ gratiniert mit Parmesan	~ au parmesan gratinés	~ al gratin	~ al gratén
Celery in gravy	~ in Jus	~ au jus	~ al sugo di carne	~ con jugo de carne
Creamed celery	~ in Rahmsauce	~ à la crème	~ alla besciamella	~ a la crema

Vegetables	Gemüse	Légumes	Verdure	Verduras
Celeriac	Knollensellerie	Céleri-rave	Sedano rapa	Apio-nabo
Chanterelles	Pfifferling	Girolles, chanterelles	Gallinacci, finferli	Rebozuelos
Chanterelles	Eierschwämme	Girolles, chanterelles	Gallinacci, cantarelli	Rebozuelos
(Swiss) chards, spinach beets	Mangold	Blettes, bettes, poirées	Bietole	Acelgas
Buttered chard	~ in Butter	Blettes au beurre	Bietole al burro	~ salteadas
Chestnuts	Maronen	Marrons	Marroni	Castañas
Chick-peas	Kichererbsen	Pois chiches	Ceci	Garbanzos
Corn on the cob, sweet corn	Maiskolben	Maïs en épis	Pannocchia di granturco	Mazorca de maíz
Courgettes, zucchini(s)[61]	Zucchini	Courgettes	Zucchini, zucchine	Calabacines
Fried courgettes	~ gebacken	~ frites	Zucchini fritti	~ fritos
Baked stuffed courgettes	~ gefüllt	~ farcies	~ ripieni	~ rellenos
Creamed horseradish	Meerrettichsahne	~ à la crème	Rafano alla panna	~ picante a la crema
Cress, watercress	Kresse	Cresson	Crescione	Berro
Crudités (raw vegetables)	Rohkostplatte	Assiette de crudités	Crudità (verdure crude)	Plato de legumbres crudos
Cucumbers	Gurken	Concombres	Cetrioli	Pepinos
Stuffed cucumbers	~ gefüllt	Concombres farcis	Cetrioli ripieni	~ rellenos
Early vegetables	Frühgemüse	Primeurs	Primizie	Primicias
Endive	Endivie	Chicorée frisée	Indivia riccia	Endibia, escarola
Fennel, Florence fennel	Fenchel(knollen)	Fenouils	Finocchi	Hinojo
Fried fennel	~ gebacken	~ frits	~ fritti	~ frito
Fennel au gratin	~ gratiniert	~ au gratin	~ gratinati	~ al gratén
French beans, string beans	Prinzessbohnen	Haricots verts	Fagiolini	Judías verdes
French beans[62])	Bohnen, grüne	Haricots verts	Fagiolini	Judías verdes
Buttered French beans	~ in Butter	~ verts au beurre	~ al burro	~ verdes salteadas
French beans in cream	~ in Rahmsauce	~ verts à la crème	~ alla besciamella	~ verdes a la crema
Red beans	~ , rote	~ rouges	Fagioli rossi	~ pintas
White beans, haricot beans	~ , woiße	~ blancs	Fagioli bianchi	~ blancas
Gherkins	Cornichons	Cornichons	Cetriolini sott'aceto	Pepinillos

Vegetables	Gemüse	Légumes	Verdure	Verduras
Green peas	Erbsen	Petits pois	Piselli	Guisantes
Buttered green peas	~ in Butter	~ pois au beurre	~ al burro	~ con mantequilla
Green peas, French style (stewed with small onions & lettuce)	~ auf französische Art (mit Zwiebelchen und Kopfsalat gedünstet)	~ pois à la française (cuits avec petits oignons et laitue)	~ alla francese (stufati con cipolline e lattuga)	~ à la francesa (cocidos con lechuga y cebollitas)
Peas in potato nests	~ im Nestchen	~ pois au nid	Nidi di patate con piselli	~ en nidos de patatas
Minted peas	~ mit Pfefferminze	~ pois à la menthe	Piselli alla menta	~ con menta
Green peas with bacon	~ mit Speck	~ pois au lard	Piselli con la pancetta	~ con tocino
Gumbo	Gombos, Okras	Gombos	Gombi	Gombos
Hop sprouts	Hopfensprossen	Jets de houblon	Cime di luppolo	Retoños de lúpulo
Horseradish	Kren	Raifort	Cren, rafano	Rábano picante
Horseradish	Meerrettich	Raifort	Rafano, cren	Rábano picante
Japanese artichokes	Knollenziest	Crosnes	Tuberi del Giappone	Stachys
~ artichokes sauté	~ sautiert	~ sautés	~ del Giappone al burro	~ salteados
Jerusalem artichokes	Topinamburs	Topinambours	Topinamburi	Patacas[63])
Kale	Blattkohl	Chou vert	Cavolo verde	Col verde
Kale	Grünkohl	Chou vert	Cavole verde	Col verde
Kohlrabi, turnip cabbage	Kohlrabi	Chou-rave (pl. choux-raves)	Cavolo rapa	Colinabo
Leek	Lauch	Poireaux	Porri	Puerros
Leek	Porree	Poireaux	Porri	Puerros
Leek au gratin	~ überbacken	~ au gratin	Porri gratinati	Puerros gratinados
Lentils with bacon	Specklinsen	Lentilles au lard	Lenticchie al lardo	Lentejas con tocino
Lentils	Linsen	Lentilles	Lenticchie	Lentejas
Lettuce	Kopfsalat	Laitues	Lattughe	Lechugas
Braised lettuce in gravy	~ gedünstet	~ braisées au jus	~ brasate al sugo	Lechugas al jugo
Lima beans	Limabohnen, Mondbohnen	Haricots de Lima	Fagioli di Lima	Judías
Okra, see gumbo				
Mixed vegetables	Mischgemüse	Macédoine de légumes	Macedonia di verdure	Macedonia de legumbres

Vegetables	Gemüse	Légumes	Verdure	Verduras
Morels	Morcheln	Morilles	Spugnole, morchelle	Morillas, cagarrias
Mushroom caps	Steinpilzköpfe	Chapeaux de cèpes	Cappelle di porcini	Sombreros de setas
Grilled mushroom caps	~ grilliert	~ de cèpes grillés	~ di porcini alla griglia	~ de setas a la parrilla
Mushrooms, ceps	Steinpilze	Cèpes	Porcini, funghi porcini	Rodellones
Mushrooms Bordelaise	~ auf Bordelaiser Art	~ à la bordelaise	~ alla bordolese	~ a la bordelesa
Mushrooms, Provençal style (sautéed in oil with garlic)	~ auf provenzalische Art (mit Knoblauch in Öl geröstet)	~ à la provençale (sautés à l'huile avec ail et persil)	~ alla provenzale (funghi porcini trifolati)	~ a la provenzal (salteados en aceite con ajo y perejil)
~ au gratin	~ überbacken	~ au gratin	~ gratinati	~ al gratén
Mushrooms, champignons	Champignons	Champignons (de Paris[64])	Funghi (coltivati), champignons	Champiñones
Stuffed mushrooms	~ gefüllt	~ farcis	Funghi ripieni	~ rellenos
Grilled mushrooms	~ gegrillt	~ grillés	Funghi in gratella	~ a la parrilla
Creamed mushrooms	~ in Rahmsauce	~ à la crème	Funghi alla crema	~ a la crema
Mushrooms sauté	~ sautiert	~ sautés	Funghi al burro	~ salteados
Mushrooms	Kaiserlinge (Kaiserpilze)	Oronges	Ovoli	Oronjas
Mushrooms	Maipilze (Mairitterlinge)	Mousserons	Funghi prugnoli	Mucerones, mojardones
Mushrooms	Pilze	Champignons	Funghi	Setas, hongos
Nettles	Brennessel	Ortie	Ortica	Ortiga
Onions	Zwiebeln	Oignons	Cipolle	Cebollas
Fried onion rings	~ gebacken	~ frits	~ fritte	~ fritas
Stuffed onions	~ gefüllt	~ farcis	~ ripiene	~ rellenas
Braised onions	~ geschmort	~ braisés	~ stufate	~ estofadas
Glazed onions	~ glaciert	~ glacés	~ glassate	~ glaseadas
Parsnip	Pastinake	Panais	Pastinaca	Chirivías
Pease-pudding	Erbsenpüree	Purée de pois cassés	Passato di piselli	Puré de guisantes
(Green) peppers, pimientos	Paprikaschoten	Poivrons, piments	Peperoni	Pimientos
Stuffed green peppers	~ gefüllt	Poivrons farcis	Peperoni ripieni	~ rellenos
Pineapple sauerkraut	Ananaskraut	Choucroute à l'ananas	Crauti all'ananas	Chucruta con piña
Pumpkin, squash, gourd	Kürbis	Potiron, courge	Zucca	Calabaza

Vegetables	Gemüse	Légumes	Verdure	Verduras
Purée	Püree	Purée	Purè, purea	Puré
Mushroom purée	~ von Champignons	~ de champignons	Purè di funghi	~ de champiñones
Purée of peas	~ von Erbsen	~ Saint-Germain	~ di piselli	~ de guisantes
Lentil purée	~ von Linsen	~ Ésaü	~ di lenticchie	~ de lentejas
Chestnut purée	~ von Maronen	~ de marrons	~ di marroni	~ de castañas
White bean purée	~ von weißen Bohnen	~ soissonnaise	~ di fagioli bianchi	~ de judías blancas
Mashed turnips	~ von weißen Rüben	~ de navets	~ di rape	~ de nabos
Onion purée	~ von Zwiebeln	~ Soubise	~ di cipolle	~ de cebollas
Purslane	Portulak	Pourpier	Portulaca	Verdolaga
Radish	Rettich	Radis (noir)	Rafano, ramolaccio	Rábano
Radishes	Radieschen	Radis roses	Ravanelli	Rabanitos
Ratatouille niçoise (Provençal stew of vegetables)	Ratatouille niçoise (provenzalisches Gemüseragout)	Ratatouille niçoise (ragoût de légumes variés)	Peperonata nizzarda (con zucchini, pomodori, melanzane, peperoni)	Ratatouille niçoise (estofado de verduras variadas)
Red cabbage	Rotkohl	Chou rouge	Cavolo rosso	Lombarda
Red cabbage, Flemish style (with apples)	~ auf flämische Art (mit Äpfeln)	~ (rouge à la flamande aux pommes fruits)	~ rosso alla fiamminga (con mele)	Lombarda a la flamenca (con manzanas)
Red cabbage with chestnuts	~ mit Maronen	~ rouge à la limousine (aux marrons)	~ rosso alla limosina (con marroni)	Lombarda a la lemosina (con castañas)
Red chicory	Radicchio	Trévise, chicorée rouge	Radicchio di Treviso	Achicoria de Treviso
Rocket	Rauke	Roquette	Ruchetta, rucola	Ruca
Sauerkraut	Sauerkraut	Choucroute	Crauti (pl)	Chucruta
Garnished sauerkraut	~ garniert	~ à l'alsacienne	Crauti all'alsaziana	~ a la alsaciana
Savoy cabbage	Wirsing	Chou de Milan	Verza	Berza
Sorrel	Sauerampfer	Oseille	Acetosa, acetosella	Acedera
Spinach purée	Spinatpüree	Purée d'épinards	Spinaci passati	Puré de espinacas
Spinach	Spinat	Épinards	Spinaci	Espinacas
Buttered leaf-spinach	~ (Blattspinat)	~ à l'anglaise[65])	~ al burro	~ a la inglesa
Creamed spinach	~ mit Rahm	~ à la crème	~ alla crema	~ a la crema
Spinach with fried egg	~ mit Spiegelei	~ à l'œuf	~ all'uovo	~ con huevo
Spinach pudding	Spinat-Auflauf	Pain d'épinards	Sformato di spinaci	Budín de espinacas

Vegetables	Gemüse	Légumes	Verdure	Verduras
Stewed cucumbers	Gurkengemüse	Concombres étuvés	Cetrioli stufati	~ estofados
Stuffed cabbage	Kohlrouladen	Paupiettes de choux	Involtini di cavolo	Popietas de coles
Succotash (maize and beans boiled together)	Succotash (Eintopf aus Mais und Bohnen)	Succotash (mélange de maïs et de haricots bouillis)	Succotash (granturco e fagioli bolliti insieme)	Succotash (mezcla de maíz y de judías cocidos juntos)
Swedes, Swedish turnips	Kohlrüben	Navets, rutabagas	Rape	Nabos
Sweet potatoes, batatas	Bataten	Patates douces	Patate americane, batate	Batatas, boniatos
Tomatoes	Tomaten	Tomates	Pomodori	Tomates
Baked stuffed tomatoes	~ gefüllt	~ farcies	~ ripieni	~ rellenos
Rice-stuffed tomatoes	~ mit Reis gefüllt	~ farcies de riz	~ ripieni di riso	~ rellenos de arroz
Grilled tomatoes	~ gegrillt	~ grillées	~ alla griglia	~ a la parrilla
Baked tomatoes Provençal (baked tomatoes filled with breadcrumbs & garlic)	~ auf provenzalische Art (mit Bröseln und Knoblauch gratinierte Tomaten)	~ à la provençale (tomates gratinées, farcies mie de pain, ail et persil haché)	~ alla provenzale (pomodori gratinati ripieni di pangrattato e aglio)	~ a la provenzal (tomates al gratén rellenos de miga de pan y ajo)
Tomatoes au gratin	~ überbacken	~ au gratin	~ gratinati	~ al gratén
Truffles	Trüffeln	Truffes	Tartufi	Trufas
~ baked in ashes	~ in der Asche gebraten	~ sous la cendre	~ sotto la cenere	~ asadas en las brasas
~ in a napkin	~ in der Serviette	~ à la serviette	~ in salvietta	~ en servilleta
Turnips	Mairüben	Navets	Rape	Nabas
Turnips	Weiße Rüben	Navets	Rape	Nabas
Vegetables in season	Gemüse der Jahreszeit	Légumes de saison	Verdure di stagione	Legumbres del tiempo
White beans	Weiße Bohnen	Haricots blancs	Fagioli bianchi	Judías blancas
White cabbage	Weißkohl (Weißkraut)	Chou blanc	Cavolo bianco	Repollo
Braised cabbage	~ gedünstet	~ blanc braisé	~ brasato	~ estofado
Stuffed cabbage	~ gefüllt	~ blanc farci	~ ripieno	~ relleno

[56]) or witloof (chicory).
[57]) dites aussi asperges à l'huile.
[58]) también salsifíes negros o de España.
[59]) ou épinards en branches.

[60]) ou gâteau de chou-fleur.
[61]) or vegetable marrow, Am. marrow squash and summer squash.
[62]) Am. string beans.

[63]) llamadas también cotufas y aguaturmias.
[64]) ou champignons de couche.
[65]) ou épinards en branches.

Potatoes	Kartoffeln	Pommes de terres	Patate	Patatas
Bacon potatoes	Speckkartoffeln	Pommes au lard	Patate al lardo	Patatas con tocino
Baked jacket potatoes[66] (baked in their skins)	Kartoffeln, in der Schale gebraten	Pommes au four (cuites telles quelles)	Patate al forno in camicia	Patatas asadas al horno (sin pelar)
Boiled potatoes	Salzkartoffeln	~ à l'anglaise, ~ nature	~ lesse	~ al vapor, ~ cocidas
Bouillon potatoes	Bouillon-Kartoffeln	~ au bouillon	~ cotte nel brodo	~ caldosas
Boulangère potatoes (baked with onions)	Bäckerin-Kartoffeln (mit Zwiebeln gebraten)	~ boulangère (cuites au four avec oignons)	~ alla fornaia (cotte in forno con cipolle)	~ a la panadera (asadas al horno con cebolla)
Caraway potatoes	Kümmelkartoffeln	~ au cumin	Patate al comino	Patatas al comino
Château potatoes (olive-shaped fried potatoes)	Schloßkartoffeln (oliven-förmig geschnitten und in Butter gebraten)	~ château (tournées en grosses olives et sautées au beurre)	~ château (tagliate in forma di grosse olive e rosolate nel burro)	~ castillo (patatas sal-teadas en forma de gruesas aceitunas)
(Potato) chips	Chips	~ chips	Patatine, patate chips	~ chips
Creamed potatoes	Rahmkartoffeln	~ à la créme	Patate alla panna	~ a la crema
Croquette potatoes amandine	Berny-Kartoffeln (Kartoffelkroketten mit Mandeln paniert)	~ Berny (pommes cro-quettes aux amandes)	~ Berny (crocchette di patate involte in mandorle)	~ Berny (croquetas empanadas con almendras)
Dauphine potatoes (potato croquettes)	Dauphine-Kartoffeln (Kartoffelkroketten)	~ dauphine (croquettes en forme de boulette)	~ alla dauphine (croc-chette di patate)	~ a la delfina (croquetas en forma de tapón)
Dill potatoes	Dillkartoffeln	~ à l'aneth	~ all'aneto	~ con eneldo
Duchesse potatoes (cro-quette potatoes browned in the oven)	Duchesse-Kartoffeln (Kartoffelkroketten im Backofen gebraten)	~ duchesse (pommes croquettes cuites au four)	~ duchesse (crocchette di patate cotte in forno)	~ a la duquesa (croquetas cocidas al horno)
Fondant potatoes	Schmelzkartoffeln	~ fondantes	~ fondenti	~ fundientes
Lattice French fried potatoes	Waffelkartoffeln	~ gaufrettes	~ fritte	~ fritas (en forma de barquillos)
Lorette potatoes (potato croquettes)	Lorette-Kartoffeln (Kartoffelkroketten)	~ Lorette (pommes cro-quettes au fromage)	~ Lorette (crocchette di patate al formaggio)	~ Lorette (croquetas de patatas)
Lyonnaise potatoes (fried with onions)	Lyoner Kartoffeln (mit Zwiebeln gebraten)	~ à la lyonnaise (sautées aux oignons)	~ alla lionese (rosolate con cipolle)	~ a la lionesa (salteadas con cebolla)

Potatoes	Kartoffeln	Pommes de terres	Patate	Patatas
Macaire potatoes (potato cake fried in butter)	Macaire-Kartoffeln (Kartoffelkuchen in der Pfanne gebräunt)	Pommes Macaire (galette de pommes rissolée à la poêle)	Patate Macaire (tortino di patate rosolato in padella)	Patatas Macaire (pastel de patatas dorado en mantequilla)
Maître d'hôtel potatoes (creamed potatoes with parsley)	Maître-Kartoffeln (Rahmkartoffeln mit Petersilie) [Kartoffeln	~ maître d'hôtel (pommes à la crème avec persil)	~ alla maître d'hôtel (patate alla panna con prezzemolo)	~ a la maître d'hôtel (patatas con crema y perejil)
Mashed potatoes	Kartoffelpüree	Pommes en purée	Purè di patate	Puré de patatas
Mashed potatoes	Kartoffelbrei	Pommes en purée	Purè di patate	Puré de patatas
Mousseline potatoes (mashed potatoes with whipped cream)	Schaumkartoffeln (Kartoffelpüree mit Schlagsahne vermischt)	Pommes mousseline[68]) (purée de pommes à la crème)	Patate mousseline (purè di patate con panna montata)	Patatas mousseline (puré de patatas adicionado de nata batida)
New potatoes	Neue Kartoffeln	~ nouvelles	~ novelle	~ nuevas
Noisette potatoes (nut-shaped fried potatoes)	Nußkartoffeln (haselnußgroße Bratkartoffeln)	~ noisettes (pommes rissolées en forme de noisette)	~ nocciola (patate rosolate in forma di nocciola)	~ salteadas (en forma de avellana)
Parisienne potatoes (noisette potatoes rolled in meat-glaze)	Pariser Kartoffeln (Nuß-Kartoffeln in Fleischglace gerollt)	~ à la parisienne (pommes noisettes à la glace de viande)	~ alla parigina (patate nocciola al sugo di carne)	~ a la parisiense (patatas salteadas al jugo de carne)
Parmentier potatoes (cube-shaped potatoes fried in butter)	Parmentier-Kartoffeln (gebratene Kartoffelwürfel)	~ Parmentier (pommes en gros dés, sautées au beurre)	~ Parmentier (patate a dadi rosolate nel burro)	~ Parmentier (patatas salteadas en forma de dado)
Parsley potatoes	Petersilienkartoffeln	Pommes persillées	Patate al prezzemolo	Patatas al perejil
Pont-Neuf potatoes (French-fried potato strips)	Pont-Neuf-Kartoffeln (gebackene Kartoffelstäbchen)	~ pont-neuf (pommes frites en bâtonnets)	~ Pont-Neuf (patate fritte a bastoncini)	~ Pont-Neuf (patatas fritas en forma de bastoncillos)
Potato cakes	Kartoffelpuffer	Galettes de pommes	Frittelle di patate	Tortillas de patatas
Potato chips	Kartoffelchips	Pommes chips	Patatine, patate chips	Patatas chips
Potato oroquottoo[67])	Kartoffelkroketten	Pommes (en) croquettes	Crocchette di patate	Croquetas de patatas
Potato dumplings	Kartoffelklößchen	Gnocchi de pommes	Gnocchi di patate	Noqui de patatas
Potato nests	Kartoffelnestchen	Nids de pommes paille	Nidi di patate	Nidos de patatas
Potato soufflé	Kartoffelauflauf	Soufflé de pommes	Soufflé di patate	Soufflé de patatas

Potatoes	Kartoffeln	Pommes de terres	Patate	Patatas
Potato straws[69]	Strohkartoffeln	Pommes paille	Patate fritte	Patatas paja
Potatoes Anna (sliced potatoes cake-shaped and baked in a special casserole)	Anna-Kartoffeln (Kartoffelscheiben fladenförmig in einer Kasserolle überbacken)	Pommes Anna (galette de pommes de terre)	Patate Anna (tortino di patate al forno)	Patatas Ana (pastel hecho de rodajas de patatas y mantequilla)
Potatoes au gratin	Überbackene Kartoffeln	Pommes au gratin	~ gratinate	Patatas al gratén
Potatoes in their jackets, jacket potatoes	Pellkartoffeln (Kartoffeln in der Schale)	~ en robe des champs[72]	~ in camicia	~ (cocidas) con piel
Roast potatoes, baked potatoes	Geröstete Kartoffeln	~ rôties	~ arrostite, ~ arrosto	~ asadas
Roast potatoes	Röstkartoffeln	~ rôties	~ arrosto, ~ arrostite	~ asadas
Rosemary potatoes	Rosmarinkartoffeln	~ au romarin	~ al rosmarino	~ al romero
Saratoga chips, see potato chips				
Sauté potatoes	Schwenkkartoffeln	~ sautées	~ saltate	~ salteadas
Sauté potatoes, fried potatoes	Bratkartoffeln	~ sautées, ~ rissolées	~ saltate, ~ rosolate	~ salteadas
Savoy potatoes (potatoes gratinated with broth & cheese)	Savoyer Kartoffelgratin (mit Käse und Bouillon überbacken)	Gratin savoyard (gratin de pommes au bouillon et fromage)	~ alla savoiarda (gratinate con brodo e formaggio)	~ a la saboyarda (gratinadas con caldo y queso)
Shoestring potatoes	Streichholzkartoffeln	Pommes allumettes	Patate fritte (a forma di fiammifero)	Patatas cerilla
Shoestring potatoes	Pommes allumettes	~ allumettes	~ fritte	~ cerilla
Potato croquettes[70]	~ croquettes	~ croquettes	Crocchette di patate	Croquetas de patatas
French fried potatoes[71]	~ frites	~ frites	Patate fritte	Patatas fritas
Soufflé potatoes (sliced potatoes fried twice in deep fat)	~ soufflées (zweimal in heißem Fett gebacken)	~ soufflées (pommes frites, replongées dans la friture)	~ soffiate (fritte, quindi rituffate in una seconda frittura)	~ soufflées (patatas fritas dos veces)
Steamed potatoes	Dampfkartoffeln	~ vapeur	Patate al vapore	~ al vapor
Stewed potatoes	Schmorkartoffeln	~ à l'étuvée	~ in umido	~ guisadas

Potatoes	Kartoffeln	Pommes de terres	Patate	Patatas
Stuffed potatoes	Gefüllte Kartoffeln	~ farcies	~ ripiene	~ rellenas
Surprise potatoes	Überraschungskartoffeln	~ en surprise	~ a sorpresa	~ a sorpresa
Sweet potatoes[73]	Süßkartoffeln	Patates douces	Patate americane, batate	Batatas, boniatos
Voisin potatoes (cake of potato, butter and cheese)	Voisin-Kartoffeln (Kartoffeltörtchen mit Butter und Käse)	Pommes Voisin (galette de pommes au beurre et fromage)	~ Voisin (tortino di patate, burro e formaggio)	Patatas Voisin (pastel hecho de patatas, mantequilla y queso)

[66] or potatoes baked in their jackets.
[67] or croquette potatoes.
[68] ou mousse Parmentier.
[69] or straw potatoes.
[70] or croquette potatoes.
[71] or (potato) chips, Am. french fries.
[72] ou pommes en chemise.
[73] also batatas or Spanish potatoes.

Farinaceous dishes	Teigwaren und Reis	Pâtes et riz	Pasta e riso	Pastas italianas, arroz
Bacon dumplings	Speckknödel	Boulettes au lard	Canederli	Albóndigas con tocino
Bread dumplings	Semmelknödel	Boulettes de pain	Canederli di pane	Albóndigas de pan
Buttered rice	Butterreis	Riz au blanc, riz au beurre	Riso in bianco, riso al burro	Arroz blanco
Cannelloni (stuffed rolls of noodle dough)	Cannelloni (gefüllte Nudelteigrollen)	Cannelloni (sorte de gros macaroni farci)	Cannelloni	Canelones, canalones (rollos de pasta rellenos)
Florentine cannelloni	~ auf Florentiner Art	~ à la florentine	~ alla fiorentina	~ a la florentina
Cannelloni à la niçoise	~ auf Nizzaer Art	~ à la niçoise	~ alla nizzarda	~ a la nizarda
Crêpes with ham	Crêpes mit Schinken	Crêpes au jambon	Crêpes al prosciutto	Crêpes con jamón
~ with spinach	~ mit Spinat	~ à la florentine	~ con spinaci	~ con espinacas
Creole rice	Kreolenreis	Riz à la créole	Riso alla creola	Arroz a la criolla
Curried rice	Curryreis	Riz au curry	Riso al curry	Arroz al curry
Fish risotto	Fischrisotto	Risotto de poisson	Risotto di pesce	Risotto de pescado
Ginger rice	Ingwerreis	Riz au gingembre	Riso allo zenzero	Arroz con jengibre
Gnocchi (small dumplings)	Gnocchi	Gnocchi, gnocchis	Gnocchi	Ñoqui
Gnocchi à la parisienne (baked dumplings of choux pastry)	Pariser Gnocchi (gratinierte Klößchen aus Brandteig)	Gnocchi à la parisienne (gnocchi de pâte à choux fromagée)	Gnocchi alla parigina (gnocchi di farina gratinati)	Ñoqui a la parisiense (ñoquis de harina al gratén)
Gnocchi à la romaine (semolina dumplings)	Römische Gnocchi (gratinierte Grießklößchen)	Gnocchi à la romaine (à la semoule)	Gnocchi alla romana (gnocchi di semolino)	Ñoqui a la romana (ñoquis de sémola)
Green noodles	Grüne Bandnudeln	Nouilles vertes	Tagliatelle verdi	Tallarines
Hominy (crushed maize cooked with water or milk)	Maisgrießbrei (in Wasser oder Milch gekocht)	Hominy (bouillie de maïs à l'eau ou au lait)	Hominy (farina grossa di granturco cotta in acqua o latte)	Hominy (gachas de maíz cocidas en agua o leche)
Lasagne, noodles	Lasagne	Lasagnes, lasagne	Lasagne	Tallarines
Lenten ravioli	Fastenravioli	Ravioli farcis au maigre	Ravioli di magro	Ravioles de vigilia
Liver dumplings	Leberknödel	Boulettes de foie	Canederli di fegato	Albóndigas de hígado
Macaroni timbale	Makkaroni-Pastete	Timbale de macaroni	Timballo di maccheroni	Timbal de macarrones
Macaroni	Makkaroni	Macaroni	Maccheroni	Macarrones
~ with butter	~ mit Butter	~ au beurre	~ al burro	~ con mantequilla
~ cheese, ~ au gratin	~ gratiniert	~ au gratin	~ gratinati	~ al gratén
~ with tomato sauce	~ mit Tomatensauce	~ à la napolitaine	~ al pomodoro	~ con salsa de tomate

Farinaceous dishes	Teigwaren und Reis	Pâtes et riz	Pasta e riso	Pastas italianas, arroz
Noodles	Bandnudeln	Nouilles	Tagliatelle	Tallarines
~ with butter	~ mit Butter	Nouilles au beurre	Tagliatelle al burro	~ con mantequilla
~ in cream sauce	~ in Rahmsauce	Nouilles à la crème	Tagliatelle alla panna	~ a la crema
Pilaff, pilau	Pilaf (Pilaw, Pilau)	Riz pilaf, riz pilaw	Riso pilaf	Arroz pilav
Polenta (maize porridge)	Polenta (Maisbrei)	Polenta	Polenta	Polenta (gachas de maíz)
Potato dumplings	Kartoffelklößchen	Gnocchi à la piémontaise	Gnocchi di patate	Ñoqui de patatas
Ravioli	Ravioli	Ravioli, raviolis	Ravioli	Ravioles
Cheese-filled ravioli	~ mit Quarkfüllung	~ au fromage blanc	~ di ricotta	~ de requesón
Rice croquettes	Reiskroketten	Croquettes de riz	Crocchette di riso	Croquetas de arroz
Rice ring	Reisring	Bordure (ou turban) de riz	Corona di riso	Corona de arroz
~ ring with mushrooms	~ mit Pilzen	~ de riz aux champignons	~ di riso con funghi	~ de arroz con setas
Rice timbale, rice pie	Reis-Pastete	Timbale de riz	Timballo di riso	Timbal de arroz
Rice	Reis	Riz	Riso	Arroz
Greek rice	~ auf griechische Art	~ à la grecque	~ alla greca	~ a la griega
Rice with mushrooms	~ mit Steinpilzen	~ aux cèpes	~ con funghi porcini	~ con rodellones
Risotto	Risotto	Risotto	Risotto	Risotto
Chicken-liver risotto	~ mit Hühnerleber	~ aux foies de volaille	~ coi fegatini	~ con higadillos de ave
Saffron risotto	~ auf Mailänder Art (mit Safran gewürzt)	~ à la milanaise (risotto safrané)	~ alla milanese (con zafferano)	~ a la milanesa (con azafrán)
Mushroom risotto	~ mit Steinpilzen	~ aux cèpes	~ con funghi porcini	~ con rodellones
Truffle risotto	~ mit Trüffeln	~ aux truffes	~ coi tartufi	~ con trufas
Saffron rice	Safranreis	Riz au safran	Riso allo zafferano	Arroz con azafrán
Spaghetti	Spaghetti	Spaghetti, spaghettis	Spaghetti	Spaghetti, espaguetis
~ with bolognese sauce	~ auf Bologneser Art (mit Fleischsauce)	~ à la bolonaise (avec petit ragoût de bœuf)	~ alla bolognese, ~al ragù	~ a la boloñesa (con salsa de carne)
~ with meat sauce				
~ with anchovies	~ mit Sardellen	~ aux anchois	~ con le acciughe	~ con anchoas
~ with tomato sauce	~ mit Tomatensauce	~ sauce tomate	~ al pomodoro	~ con salsa de tomate
Spätzle (small flour dumplings)	Spätzle	Spätzle (petits gnocchi de farine)	Spätzle (gnocchetti à base di farina)	Spätzle (ñoquis pequeños de harina)
Tagliatelle, noodles	Tagliatelle	Tagliatelles	Tagliatelle	Tallarines

Farinaceous dishes	Teigwaren und Reis	Pâtes et riz	Pasta e riso	Pastas italianas, arroz

Tortilla
    (thin flat maize cake)
Tyrolean dumplings
Vermicelli
	Tortilla
	    (Maisfladen)
	Tiroler Knödel
	Fadennudeln
		Tortilla
		    (Galette de maïs)
		Boulettes à la tyrolienne
		Vermicelle, vermicelles
			Tortilla sottile
			    (focaccia di mais)
			Canederli tirolesi
			Vermicelli
				Tortilla
				    (torta de maíz)
				Albóndigas tirolesas
				Fideos

Salads	Salate	Salades	Insalate	Ensaladas
Asparagus salad	Spargelsalat	Salade d'asperges	Insalata d'asparagi	Ensalada de espárragos
Beetroot salad	Rote-Rüben-Salat	~ de betterave	~ di barbabietole	~ de remolacha
Belgian endive salad	Chicoréesalat	~ d'endives	~ d'indivia belga	~ de endibia de Bruselas
Black and white salad (potatoes & black truffles. Mayonnaise)	Schwarzweißer Salat (Kartoffeln und Trüffeln. Mayonnaise)	~ demi-deuil (pommes de terre et truffes noires. Mayonnaise)	~ bianca e nera (patate e tartufi neri. Maionese)	~ medio luto (ensalada de patatas y trufas negras con mayonesa)
Black salsify salad	Schwarzwurzelsalat	Salade de salsifis	Insalata di scorzonera	Ensalada de salsifí negro
Cabbage salad, coleslaw	Krautsalat	~ de choux	~ di cavoli	~ de coles
Caesar salad (cos lettuce, anchovies, egg)	Cäsarsalat (Römischer Salat, Sardellen, Ei)	Salade César (romaine, anchois, œuf)	~ alla Cesare (lattuga romana, acciughe, uovo)	~ César (lechuga romana, anchoas, huevo)
Carmen salad (red peppers, breast of chicken, peas & rice)	Carmen-Salat (rote Paprikaschoten, Hühnerfleisch, Erbsen, Reis)	~ Carmen (poivrons rouges, blanc de poule, petits pois, riz)	~ Carmen (peperoni rossi, petto di pollo, piselli e riso)	~ Carmen (carne de ave, pimientos, arroz, guisantes)
Cauliflower salad	Blumenkohlsalat	Salade de choux-fleurs	Insalata di cavolfiori	Ensalada de coliflor
Celery salad	Selleriesalat	~ de céleri	~ di sedano	~ de apio
Celeriac salad	~ (Knollensellerie-)	~ de céleri-rave	~ di sedano rapa	~ de apio-nabo
Corn salad, lamb's lettuce salad	Feldsalat	~ de mâche, ~ de doucette	~ di dolcetta, ~ di gallinelle	~ de hierba de los canónigos
Cos (lettuce) salad[74]	Römischer Salat	~ romaine	~ di lattuga romana	~ de lechuga romana
Cos lettuce salad, romaine salad	Sommerendiviensalat	~ romaine	~ di lattuga romana	~ de lechuga romana
Cucumber salad	Gurkensalat	~ de concombres	~ di cetrioli	~ de pepino
Dandelion salad	Löwenzahnsalat	~ de pissenlit	~ di dente di leone	~ de diente de león
Endive salad	Friséesalat	~ (de chicorée) frisée	~ d'indivia	~ de endibia
Escarole salad	Eskariolsalat	~ d'escarole	~ di scarola	~ de escarola
Escarole salad, endive salad	Winterendiviensalat	~ d'escarole	~ di scarola	~ de escarola
Fancy salad	Bunter Salat	Salade mêlée	Insalata capricciosa	Ensalada variada
Fennel salad	Fenchelsalat	~ de fenouil	~ di finocchi	~ de hinojo

Salads	Salate	Salades	Insalate	Ensaladas
Francillon salad (pota-toes, mussels, truffles)	Francillon-Salat (Kartoffeln, Miesmu-scheln, Trüffeln)	Salade Francillon (pommes de terre, moules et truffes)	Insalata Francillon (patate, cozze e fettine di tartufi)	Ensalada Francillon (patatas, mejillones y trufas)
French bean salad	Bohnensalat, grüner	~ de haricots verts	~ di fagiolini	~ de judías verdes
Garden cress salad	Gartenkressesalat	~ de cresson alénois	~ di crescione d'orto	~ de mastuerzo
Green pepper salad	Paprikasalat	~ de poivrons	~ di peperoni	~ de pimientos
Green salad	Grüner Salat	~ verte	~ verde	~ verde
Lettuce salad	Kopfsalat	~ de laitue	~ di lattuga	~ de lechuga
Lettuce salad in cream	~ in Sahne	~ de laitue à la crème	~ di lattuga alla panna	~ de lechuga a la crema
Lettuce-tomato salad	Tomaten-Kopfsalat	~ de tomate et laitue	~ di pomodori e lattuga	~ de lechuga y tomate
Lorette salad (lamb's let-tuce, celery, beetroot. French dressing)	Lorette-Salat (Rapunzel, Staudensellerie, rote Rüben)	~ Lorette (mâche, céleri, betterave. Vinai-grette)	~ Lorette (valerianella, sedano, barbabietole. Olio e aceto)	~ Lorette (hierba de los canónigos, apio y remolacha)
Mixed salad	Gemischter Salat	~ mêlée, ~ panachée	~ mista	~ variada
Niçoise salad (a: string beans, potatoes, toma-toes, olives; b: raw tomatoes, onions and green peppers with anchovies and black olives)	Nizzaer Salat (a: Kartoffeln, grüne Bohnen, Toma-ten, Oliven; b: rohe Tomaten, Papri-kaschoten und Zwiebeln mit Sardellen und schwarzen Oliven)	~ niçoise (a: haricots verts, pommes de terre, to-mates, olives; b: tomates, poivrons, oignons crus avec anchois et olives noires)	~ nizzarda (a: fagiolini, patate, pomodori, olive; b: pomodori, cipolle, peperoni crudi con acciughe e olive nere)	~ nizarda (a: patatas, judías verdes, tomates, aceitunas; b: tomates, cebollas, pimientos crudos con anchoas y aceitunas negras)
Ninon salad (lettuce & orange salad)	Ninon-Salat (Kopfsalat und Orangenspalten)	Salade Ninon (salade de laitue à l'orange)	Insalata Ninon (lattuga e spicchi d'arance)	Ensalada Ninon (lechuga y naranja)
Potato salad	Kartoffelsalat	~ de pommes (de terre)	~ di patate	~ de patatas
Rachel salad (celery, artichoke bottoms, potatoes, asparagus tips)	Rachel-Salat (Sellerie, Artischockenböden, Kartoffeln und Spargelspitzen)	~ Rachel (céleri, pommes de terre, fonds d'artichauts, pointes d'asperges)	~ Rachel (sedano, pata-te, fondi di carciofo, punte d'asparagi. Maionese)	~ Rachel (apio, patatas, fondos de alcachofas, puntas de espárragos. Mayonesa)
Radish salad	Radieschensalat	~ de radis (roses)	~ di ravanelli	~ de rabanitos
Red cabbage salad	Rotkohlsalat	~ de choux rouges	~ di cavoli rossi	~ de lombarda
Red chicory salad	Radicchio-Salat[75]	~ de trévise	~ di radicchio rosso	~ de achicoria de Treviso

Salads	Salate	Salades	Insalate	Ensaladas
Rice salad	Reissalat	Salade de riz	Insalata di riso	Ensalada de arroz
Russian salad (mixed vegetable salad dressed with mayonnaise)	Russischer Salat (Gemüse-salat mit Mayonnaise angemacht)	Salade russe (salade de légumes divers liée à la mayonnaise)	Insalata russa (insalata di verdure miste legata con maionese)	Ensalada rusa (ensalada de hortalizas variadas adere-zada con mayonesa)
Salad in season	Salat der Saison	~ de saison	~ di stagione	~ del tiempo
Spinach beet salad	Mangoldsalat	~ de bettes	~ di bietole	~ de acelgas
Springtime salad	Frühlingssalat	~ printanière	~ primaverile	~ primaveral
Tomato and cucumber salad	Gurken-Tomaten-Salat	~ de concombres et tomates	~ di pomodori e cetrioli	~ de tomate y pepino
Tomato salad	Tomatensalat	~ de tomates	~ di pomodori	~ de tomate
Tosca salad (celery, poul-try, truffles, Parmesan. Mayonnaise)	Tosca-Salat (Sellerie, Ge-flügel, Trüffeln, Par-mesan. Mayonnaise)	~ Tosca (céleri, volaille, truffes, parmesan. Mayonnaise)	~ Tosca (sedano, pollo, tartufi, parmigiano. Maionese con senape)	~ Tosca (apio, carne de ave, trufas blancas, parmesano)
Waldorf salad (apples, celeriac & walnuts. Mayonnaise)	Waldorf-Salat (Äpfel, Knollensellerie, Walnüsse. Mayonnaise)	~ Waldorf (pommes reinettes, céleri-rave, noix. Mayonnaise)	~ Waldorf (sedano rapa, mele e noci. Maionese)	~ Waldorf (apio-nabo, manzanas y nueces. Mayonesa)
Watercress salad	Brunnenkressesalat	~ de cresson (de fontaine)	~ di crescione	~ de berros

[74]) or romaine salad.
[75]) Zichoriensalat mit rotweißen Blättern.

Cheese	Käse	Fromages	Formaggi	Quesos
Blue cheese	Edelpilzkäse	Bleu	Formaggio erborinato	Queso con mohos
Cheese board	Käseplatte	Plateau de fromages	Formaggi assortiti	Surtido de quesos
Cheese-puffs	Käsewindbeutel	Choux au fromage	Choux al formaggio	Buñuelos de queso
Cheese soufflé	Käse-Auflauf	Soufflé au fromage	Soufflé di formaggio	Soufflé de queso
Cheese spread	Streichkäse	~ à tartiner, ~ fondu	Formaggio da spalmare	Queso blando
Cheese-straws	Käsestangen	Paillettes au fromage	Bastoncini al formaggio	Barritas de queso
Choice of cheese	Käseauswahl	Assortiment de fromages	Assortimento di formaggi	Selección de quesos
Cottage cheese, curd(s)	Quark	Fromage blanc	Ricotta	Requesón
Cream-cheese	Rahmkäse	Fromage à la crème	Formaggio alla crema	Queso de nata
Dutch cheese	Holländer Käse	Hollande	Formaggio olandese	Queso de Holanda
Edam cheese	Edamer	Édam	Edam	Queso de bola
Emmenthal	Emmentaler	Emmenthal, emmental	Emmenthal	Emmenthal
Ewe's milk cheese	Schafkäse	Fromage de brebis	Pecorino	Queso de oveja
Goat-cheese	Ziegenkäse	Fromage de chèvre	Formaggio di capra	Queso de cabra
Gorgonzola (blue cheese)	Gorgonzola (Blauschimmelkäse)	Gorgonzola (fromage persillé)	Gorgonzola (formaggio con venature verdi)	Gorgonzola (queso con mohos)
Green cheese	Kräuterkäse	Fromage aux herbes	Formaggio alle erbe	Queso de hierba
Liptauer (curds of ewe's milk with paprika & caraway seeds)	Liptauer (Quark aus Schafmilch, mit Paprika und Kümmel)	Liptauer (fromage blanc de brebis, additionné de paprika et cumin)	Liptauer (ricotta di latte di pecora mista con paprica e comino)	Liptauer (requesón de leche de oveja con pimentón y comino)
Parmesan (cheese)	Parmesankäse	Parmesan	Parmigiano	Parmesano
Petit-suise (soft full-cream cheese)	Petit-suisse (milder frischer Rahmkäse)	Petit-suisse (fromage frais très gras)	Petit-suisse (formaggio ricco di panna)	Petit-suisse (queso fresco de nata)
Ramekins, cheese tartlets	Käsetörtchen	Ramequins	Tartelette al formaggio	Tartaletas de queso
Roquefort (blue cheese of ewe's milk)	Roquefort (Blauschimmel-käse aus Schafmilch)	Roquefort (fromage persillé)	Roquefort (formaggio di latte di pecora)	Queso de Roquefort (queso con mohos)
Smoked cheese	Räucherkäse	Fromage fumé	Formaggio affumicato	Queso curado al humo
Swiss cheese, gruyère	Gruyère (Greyerzer)	Gruyère	Groviera, gruviera	Queso suizo
Swiss fondue	Fondue (Käsefondue)	Fondue savoyarde	Fondue	Fondue a la suiza

Sweets & ice-creams	Süßspeisen, Eisspeisen	Entremets et glaces	Dolci e gelati	Dulces y helados
Almond cake	Mandeltorte	Gâteau aux amandes	Torta di mandorle	Tarta de almendras
Almond soufflé	Mandel-Auflauf	Soufflé aux amandes	Soufflé alle mandorle	Soufflé de almendras
Angel (food)cake	Engelskuchen (leichtes Biskuit)	Biscuit mousseline	Pan degli angeli	Bizcocho
Apple charlotte (stewed apples enclosed in bread slices)	Apfel-Charlotte (Apfelmus in Brotscheibenhülle)	Charlotte aux pommes (marmelade de pommes dans enveloppe de tranches de pain)	Charlotte di mele (passato di mele in involucro di fette di pane)	Carlota de manzanas (puré de manzanas en envoltura de rebanadas de pan)
Apple crumble	Apfel mit Streuseln	Gratin de pommes[77])	Gratin di mele	Gratén de manzanas
Apple pie	Apfelpie	Pie aux pommes	Torta di mele	Tarta de manzanas
Apple fritters	Apfelringe, gebacken	Beignets de pommes	Frittelle di mele	Buñuelos de manzanas
Apple fritters	Apfelbeignets	Beignets de pommes	Frittelle di mele	Buñuelos de manzana
Apple strudel	Apfelstrudel	Strudel aux pommes	Strudel di mele	Strudel de manzana
Apple tart	Apfeltorte	Tarte aux pommes	Torta di mele	Tarta de manzana
Apple turnover	Apfeltasche	Chausson aux pommes	Fagottino di mele	Pastelillo de manzana
Apricot dumplings	Marillenknödel	Boulettes aux abricots	Gnocchi alle albicocche	Albóndigas de albaricoques
Apricot soufflé	Aprikosenauflauf	Soufflé aux abricots	Soufflé di albicocche	Soufflé de albaricoques
Apricot tart	Aprikosentorte	Tarte aux abricots	Torta di albicocche	Tarta de albaricoques
Assorted pastries	Auswahl an Backwerk	Pâtisserie assortie	Pasticceria assortita	Pastelería fina
Variety of pies and cakes	~ an Torten	Gâteaux variés	Assortimento di torte	Tartas diversas
Baked apple	Bratapfel	Pomme au four	Mela al forno	Manzana asada
Baked ice cream[76]) (ice cream covered with meringue and baked)	Überraschungs-Omelette (Eis mit Eierschnee bedeckt und gebacken)	Omelette surprise[78]) (glace meringuée, colorée au four)	Omelette a sorpresa (gelato meringato al forno)	Tortilla Alaska (helado merengado dorado en el horno)
Baked stuffed apple (filled with butter and sugar)	Apfel nach Hausfrauenart (Bratapfel mit Butter und Zucker gefüllt)	Pomme à la bonne femme (pomme au four remplie beurre et sucre)	Mela alla bonne femme (mela al forno ripiena di burro e zucchero)	Manzana asada (rellena de mantequilla y azucar)
Meringue apple	~ mit Meringue	~ meringuée	~ meringata	Manzana merengada
Apple dumpling (apple baked in pastry)	~ im Schlafrock	Pomme en surprise	~ in gabbia	Manzana vestida

Sweets & ice-creams	Süßspeisen, Eisspeisen	Entremets et glaces	Dolci e gelati	Dulces y helados
Banana fritters	Bananenbeignets	Beignets de bananes	Frittelle di banane	Buñuelos de plátanos
Banana split	Banana split	Bananesplit	Banane split	Banane split
(split bananas with ice cream and whipped cream)	(aufgeschnittene Banane mit Eis und Schlagsahne)	(banane fendue garnie de glace et de chantilly)	(banane tagliata longetudinalmente con gelato e panna)	(banane tagliata longitudinalmente con gelato e panna)
Bananas flambé	Bananen, flambiert	Bananes flambées	Banane alla fiamma	Plátanos flameados
Bavarian chocolate cream	Schokoladenbavarois	Bavarois au chocolat	Bavarese al cioccolato	Crema bávara de chocolate
Bavarian cream (custard with gelatine & whipped cream added)	Bayerische Creme[79]) (kalte Süßspeise aus Eiercreme und Schlagsahne)	Bavarois[80]) (entremets froid à base de crème anglaise et chantilly)	Bavarese (dolce freddo a base di crema inglese e panna montata)	Crema bávara (crema inglesa mezclada con gelatina y nata batida)
Ribboned Bavarian cream	~ Schichtcreme	Bavarois rubané	Bavarese variegata	~ bávara tricolor
Bavarian chocolate cream	~ Schokoladencreme	~ au chocolat	Bavarese al cioccolato	~ bávara de chocolate
Bavarian vanilla cream	~ Vanillecreme	~ à la vanille	Bavarese alla vaniglia	~ bávara de vainilla
Bavarian strawberry cream	Erdbeer-Bavarois	Bavarois aux fraises	Bavarese di fragole	Crema bávara de fresas
Bavarian vanilla cream	Vanille-Bavarois	Bavarois à la vanille	Bavarese alla vaniglia	Crema bávara de vainilla
Biscuits, Am. cookies	Kekse	Gâteaux secs, biscuits	Biscotti	Galletas, bizcochos
Biscuits, Am. cookies	Biskuits	Gâteaux secs, biscuits	Biscotti	Galletas, bizcochos
Black Forest cake (with cherries)	Schwarzwälder Kirschtorte	Gâteau de la Forêt-Noire (aux cerises)	Torta della Selva Nera (torta di ciliege)	Tarta de la Selva Negra (con cerezas)
Bombe (cone-shaped ice cream)	Eisbombe (zwei Eissorten in Halbkugelform)	Bombe glacée (glace composée)	Bomba (gelato a due sapori, in forma di cono)	Bomba (helado de dos sabores, hecho en molde)
Bombe Nesselrode (chestnut and vanilla ice cream)	~ Nesselrode (außen Kastanieneis, innen Vanilleeis)	Bombe Nesselrode (glace aux marrons, bombe vanille)	Bomba Nesselrode (gelato di marroni e vaniglia)	~ Nesselrode (helado de castaña y vainilla)
Brioche	Brioche	Brioche [beurre	Brioche	Brioche
Butter-cream cake	Buttercremetorte	Gâteau à la crème au	Torta di crema al burro	Tarta de crema
Cabinet pudding (made of custard, sponge biscuits and candied fruits)	Diplomatenpudding (aus Eiercreme, Löffelbiskuits, kandierten Früchten)	Pudding de cabinet (fait de crème anglaise, biscuits et fruits confits)	Budino diplomatico (fatto di crema inglese, savoiardi e canditi)	Budin diplómatico (hecho de natillas, bizcochos y fruta confitada)

Sweets & ice-creams	Süßspeisen, Eisspeisen	Entremets et glaces	Dolci e gelati	Dulces y helados
Cake, gateau, pie	Torte	Gâteau, tarte	Torta	Tarta, pastel
Cake tart	Kuchen	Gâteau, tarte	Torta, dolce	Tarta, pastel
Tart, flan, shortcake	~ (Mürbeteig-)	Tarte, flan	Crostata	Tarta
Caramel custard[81])	Karamelcreme	Crème renversée au caramel[82])	Crème caramel	Flan (al caramelo)
Cassata (ice-cream slice with candied fruits)	Cassata (Eisschnitte mit kandierten Früchten)	Cassate (glace composée aux fruits confits)	Cassata (gelato di panna con frutta candita)	Cassata (mantecado con fruta confitada)
Champagne sherbet	Champagner-Sorbet	Sorbet au champagne	Sorbetto allo champagne	Sorbete al champaña
Chantilly, whipped cream	Schlagsahne	Crème chantilly[83])	Panna montata	Chantillí, nata batida
Charlotte russe (custard with casing of sponge biscuits)	Charlotte russe (Vanille-creme in Biskuithülle)	Charlotte russe (bavarois à la vanille dans enve-loppe de biscuits)	Charlotte alla russa (crema alla vaniglia in involucro di savoiardi)	Carlota rusa (crema de vainilla en envoltura de bizcochos)
Cheesecake	Quarkkuchen	Gâteau au fromage blanc	Torta di ricotta	Tarta de queso alemana
Cheesecake	Topfenkuchen	Gâteau au fromage blanc	Torta di ricotta	Tarta de queso
Cheesecake	Käsekuchen	Gâteau au fromage blanc	Torta di ricotta	Tarta de queso
Cheese strudel (filled with sweet curds)	Topfenstrudel	Strudel au fromage blanc	Strudel di ricotta	Strudel de requesón
Cherries jubilee (flaming cherries)	Kirschen auf Jubiläumsart (flambierte Kirschen)	Cerises jubilé (flambées au kirsch)	Ciliege giubileo (bagnate di kirsch e infiammate)	Cerezas jubileo (cerezas flameadas)
Cherry strudel	Kirschstrudel	Strudel aux cerises	Strudel di ciliege	Strudel de cerezas
Cherry tart, cherry pie	Kirschtorte	Tarte aux cerises	Torta di ciliege	Tarta de cerezas
Cherry tartlet	Kirschtörtchen	Tartelette aux cerises	Tarteletta con ciliege	Tartaleta de cerezas
Chocolate cake	Schokoladentorte	Gâteau au chocolat	Torta di cioccolato	Tarta de chocolate
Chocolate cream	Schokoladencreme	Crème au chocolat	Crema al cioccolato	Crema de chocolate
Chocolate éclairs	Schokoladeneclairs	Èclairs au chocolat	Éclairs al cioccolato	Éclairs de chocolate
Chocolate ice cream	Schokoladeneis	Glace au chocolat	Gelato di cioccolato	Helado de chocolate
Chocolate mousse	Schokoladenmousse	Mousse au chocolat	Mousse al cioccolato	Mousse de chocolate
Chocolate pudding	Schokoladenpudding	Pudding au chocolat	Budino di cioccolato	Budín de chocolate
Chocolate sauce	Schokoladensauce	Sauce au chocolat	Salsa al cioccolato	Salsa de chocolate
Chocolate soufflé	Schokoladenauflauf	Soufflé au chocolat	Soufflé al cioccolato	Soufflé de chocolate
Chocolate truffles	Schokoladentrüffeln	Truffes au chocolat	Tartufi di cioccolato	Trufas de chocolate

Sweets & ice-creams	Süßspeisen, Eisspeisen	Entremets et glaces	Dolci e gelati	Dulces y helados
Christmas cake	Weihnachtsbaumstamm	Bûche de Noël	Tronco di Natale	Tronco de Navidad
Christmas pudding (steamed pudding with raisins currants, spices)	Weihnachtspudding (aus Rosinen, Zitronat, Gewürzen)	Christmas pudding (à base de roisins secs, de farine, de fruits confits, d'épices)	Budino natalizio (con uva passa, canditi e spezie)	Budín de Navidad (con pasas; fruta confitada, especias)
Coconut cake	Kokosnußtorte	Gâteau à la noix de coco	Torta alla noce di cocco	Tarta de coco
Coffee ice cream	Kaffee-Eis, Mokkaeis	Glace au café	Gelato al caffè	Helado de café
Coffee parfait	Mokkaparfait	Parfait au café	Parfait al caffè	Parfait de café
Coffee soufflé	Mokkasoufflé	Soufflé au café	Soufflé al caffè	Soufflé de café
Coupe Jacques (ice cream with fruit salad)	Eisbecher mit Früchten	Coupe Jacques (macédoine garnie de glace)	Coppa Jacques (macedonia al gelato)	Copa Jacques (helado con ensalada de fruta
Jamaica coupe	~ Jamaika	~ Jamaïque	~ Giamaica	~ Jamaica
Crème Beau rivage (custard with whipped cream)	Creme Beau-Rivage (Vanillecreme mit Schlagsahne)	Crème Beau rivage (crème renversée à la vanille, décorée de chantilly)	Crema Beau rivage (crema alla vaniglia con panna montata)	Crema Beau-rivage (flan adornado de nata batida)
Crêpes (French pancakes)	Crêpes	Crêpes	Crêpes, crespelle	Crêpes
Crêpes Georgette (with slices of pineapple)	~ Georgette (mit Ananasscheiben)	~ Georgette (fourrées tranches d'ananas)	~ Georgette (con fettine d'ananas)	~ Georgette (crêpes con piña)
Pancakes with jam	~ mit Konfitüre	~ aux confitures	~ alla marmellata	~ con mermelada
Norman pancakes (with apples)	~ auf normannische Art (mit Äpfeln)	~ à la normande (aux pommes)	~ alla normanna (con mele)	~ a la normanda (con manzanas)
Crêpes-Suzette (spread with orange buttercream)	~ Suzette (mit Orangen-Buttercreme be-strichen)	~ Suzette (tartinées avec un beurre d'orange au curaçao)	~ Suzette (spalmate di burro all'arancio e al curaçao)	~ Suzette (crêpes a la naranja)
Cream-cake, cream gateau	Sahnetorte	Gâteau à la crème	Torta alla panna	Tarta de crema
Cream cornet, cream roll	Schaumrolle	Cornet à la crème	Cannolo alla panna[86])	Rollo de crema
Cream-slice	Cremeschnitte	Millefeuille, mille-feuille	Millefoglie	Milhojas
Currant jelly	Johannisbeer-Gelee	Gelée de groseilles	Gelatina di ribes	Jalea de grosellas
Currant tart	Johannisbeer-Torte	Tarte aux groseilles	Torta di ribes	Tarta de grosellas
Custard (sauce)	Vanille-Sauce	Sauce anglaise[84])	Salsa alla vaniglia	Salsa de vainilla
Custard, vanilla cream	Vanille-Creme	Crème anglaise[85])	Crema alla vaniglia	Natillas (pl.)

Sweets & ice-creams	Süßspeisen, Eisspeisen	Entremets et glaces	Dolci e gelati	Dulces y helados
Custard	Creme, englische	Crème anglaise	Crema inglese	Natillas (pl.)
Custard	Eiercreme	Crème anglaise	Crema inglese	Natillas (pl.)
Custard	Englische Creme	Crème anglaise	Crema inglese	Natillas (pl.)
Doughnuts	Krapfen (Faschings-)	Beignets viennois	Krapfen, bombolone	Buñuelos de Berlin
Doughnuts	Berliner Pfannkuchen	Beignets viennois	Krapfen, bombolone	Buñuelos de Berlin
Doughnuts	Faschingskrapfen	Beignets viennois	Krapfen, bombolone	Buñuelos de Berlin
Éclairs[87])	Eclairs	Éclairs	Éclairs	Éclairs
Coffee éclairs	~ (Mokka-)	~ au café	~ al caffè	~ de café
Chocolate éclairs	~ (Schokoladen-)	~ au chocolat	~ al cioccolato	~ de chocolate
Filbert soufflé	Haselnuß-Auflauf	Soufflé aux avelines	Soufflé di nocciole	Soufflé de avellanas
Fool (fruit purée mixed with cream)	Fool (Art Mousse aus Obstpüree und Schlagsahne)	Fool (mousse fait d'une purée de fruits et de crème fouettée)	Fool (purè di frutta mescolata con panna montata)	Fool (puré de fruta mezclado con nata batida)
Floating island (meringue shells in custard sauce)	Schnee-Eier (eierförmige Meringen auf englischer Creme)	Œufs à la neige (meringues en forme d'œuf sur crème anglaise)	Uova alla neve (meringhe a forma d'uovo su crema inglese)	Huevos de nieve (merengues en forma de huevo sobre natillas)
Flummery of semolina and fruit sauce	Flammeri (Grieß-) mit Fruchtsaft	Flamri[88] sauce aux fruits rouges	Budino di semolino con salsa di frutta	Budín de sémola con salsa de fruta
French blancmange (almond milk & gelatine)	Blancmanger (Mandelmilch mit Gelatine)	Blanc-manger (gelée aux amandes)	Biancomangiare (latte di mandorle e gelatina)	Manjar blanco (leche de almendras y gelatina)
French toast	Arme Ritter	Pain doré, pain perdu	Pan dorato, pan perduto	Torrijas
Fritters, beignets	Beignets	Beignets	Frittelle	Buñuelos
Fritters	Krapfen (Küchel)	Beignets	Frittelle	Buñuelos
Fruit salad	Obstsalat	Fruits rafraîchis[89])	Macedonia di frutta	Ensalada de frutas[90])
Exotic fruit salad	~ exotisch	Salade de fruits exotiques	~ di frutta esotica	~ de frutas exóticas
Fruit salad with champagne	~ mit Schaumwein	~ de fruits au champagne	~ di frutta allo champagne	~ de frutas al champán
Fruit crumble	Obst mit Streuseln	Gratin de fruits, crumble aux fruits	Gratin di frutta	Gratén de fruta
Fruit ice-cream	Frucht-Eis	Glace aux fruits	Gelato di frutta, sorbetto	Helado de frutas, sorbete
Fruit jelly	Obstgelee	Gelée de fruits	Gelatina di frutta	Jalea de fruta

Sweets & ice-creams	Süßspeisen, Eisspeisen	Entremets et glaces	Dolci e gelati	Dulces y helados
Fruit tart, fruit pie	Obstkuchen	Tarte aux fruits	Torta di frutta	Tarta de fruta
Fruit meringue pie	~ mit Meringe	~ aux fruits meringuée	~ di frutta meringata	~ de fruta merengada
Fruit tartlet	Obsttörtchen	Tartelette aux fruits	Tarteletta di frutta	Tartaleta de fruta
Gingerbread	Lebkuchen	Pain d'épice	Panpepato	Alajú
Gingerbread	Pfefferkuchen	Pain d'épice	Panpepato	Alajú
Gooseberry fool	Stachelbeer-Mousse	Mousse aux groseilles à maquereau	Mousse di uva spina	Espuma di uva espina
Gooseberry tart, gooseberry pie	Stachelbeertorte	Tarte aux groseilles à maquereau	Torta di uva spina	Tarta de uva espina
Granita	Granita (Gramolata)	Granité	Granita, gramolata	Granizado
Gugelhupf (yeast cake with raisins)	Gugelhupf	Kouglof, kugelhopf	Kugelhupf (dolce di pasta lievitata)	Kugelhupf (pastel de molde alto)
Harlequin soufflé (half vanilla, half chocolate)	Harlekin-Auflauf (Vanille und Schokolade)	Soufflé Arlequin (moitié vanille, moitié chocolat)	Soufflé Arlecchino (vaniglia e cioccolato)	Soufflé arlequín (mitad vainilla, mitad chocolate)
Hazelnut cream	Haselnuß-Creme	Crème aux noisettes	Crema di nocciole	Crema de avellanas
Hazelnut ice cream	Haselnuß-Eis	Glace aux noisettes	Gelato di nocciola	Helado de avellanas
Ice-cream meringue	Eisbaiser	Meringue glacée	Meringa col gelato	Merengue con helado
Ice-cream tart	Eistorte	Gâteau glacé	Torta gelato	Tarta helada
Ice cream	Sahneeis	Glace à la crème	Gelato di crema	Mantecado
Ice cream [cream	Eis	Glace	Gelato [panna	Helado
Iced coffee with whipped	Eiskaffee	Café liégeois	Caffè freddo con gelato e	Café frío con helado y nata
Ice-soufflé	Eisauflauf	Soufflé glacé	Soufflé gelato	Soufflé helado
Iced chocolate cake	Sacher-Torte	Sachertorte (gâteau viennois au chocolat)	Torta di cioccolato	Tarta de chocolate
Iced melon	Melone (eisgekühlte)	Melon frappé	Melone ghiacciato	Melón helado
Kaiserschmarren (raisin omelette cut up into pieces)	Kaiserschmarren (Rosinen-Omelette in Stücke zerkleinert)	Kaiserschmarren (omelette aux raisins coupée en morceaux)	Kaiserschmarren (omelette spezzettata all'uvetta)	Kaiserschmarren (tortilla de pasas cortada en trozos)
Key lime pie	Limettentorte	Tarte au citron vert	Torta al limone verde	Tarta de lima
Kirsch cake	Zuger Kirschtorte	Gâteau au kirsch de Zoug	Torta al kirsch di Zug	Tarta al kirsch

Sweets & ice-creams	Süßspeisen, Eisspeisen	Entremets et glaces	Dolci e gelati	Dulces y helados
Kirsch soufflé	Kirschwasserauflauf	Soufflé au kirsch	Soufflé al kirsch	Soufflé al kirsch
Lemon cream	Zitronen-Creme	Crème au citron	Crema al limone	Crema de limón
Lemon ice-cream	Zitronen-Eis	Glace au citron	Gelato di limone	Helado de limón
Lemon sherbet	Zitronen-Sorbet	Sorbet au citron	Sorbetto al limone	Sorbete de limón
Lemon soufflé	Zitronen-Auflauf	Soufflé au citron	Soufflé al limone	Soufflé de limón
Linzer tart (latticed jam tart made of short pastry with nuts and cinnamon)	Linzer Torte (Mürbeteig mit Zimt und Nüssen, mit Marmelade bestrichen)	Linzertarte (tarte en pâte sablée à la cannelle, garnie de confiture)	Torta di Linz (torta di pasta frolla profumata con cannella e coperta di marmellata)	Tarta de Linz (tarta de mermelada hecha de pastaflora con nueces y canela)
Macaroons	Makronen	Macarons	Amaretti	Mostachones, macarrones
Madeira cake, pound cake	Sandkuchen	Quatre-quarts	Torta paradiso[91]	Bizcocho cuatro cuartos
Melon ice-cream	Meloneneis	Glace au melon	Gelato di melone	Helado de melón
Meringue Chantilly	Sahne-Baiser	Meringue Chantilly	Meringa con la panna	Merengue con nata
Meringue Chantilly	Baiser mit Schlagsahne	Meringue Chantilly	Meringa con la panna	Merengue con nata
Meringue	Meringe	Meringue	Meringa	Merengue
Mille-feuille (cake of puff pastry)	Tausendblätterkuchen	Millefeuille, mille-feuille	Millefoglie (torta di pasta sfoglia)	Milhojas (pastel de hojaldre y crema)
Mince pie (small pie filled with raisins, spices, candied peel)	Mince pie (Törtchen gefüllt mit Rosinen Orangeat, Gewürzen)	Mince pie (tartelette garnie de raisins secs, fruits confits, épices)	Mince pie (tarteletta ripiena d'un trito di uva passa, canditi e spezie)	Mince pie (tarteleta rellena de pasas, fruta confitada y especias)
Mixed ice-cream	Gemischtes Eis	Glace panachée	Gelato misto	Helado variado
Mocha cake	Mokkatorte	(Gâteau) moka	Torta al caffè	Tarta de moca
Mont-Blanc (mashed chestnuts with cream)	Montblanc (Kastanien-püree mit Schlagsahne)	Mont-blanc (purée de marrons garnie de chantilly)	Montebianco (passato di marroni con panna)	Negro en camisa (puré de castañas con nata batida)
Mousse (frozen whipped cream mixture)	Mousse (gefrorene aroma-tisierte Schlagsahne)	Mousse glacée	Mousse (gelato a base di panna montata)	Mousse (helado a base de nata batida)
Napfkuchen (yeast cake with raisins)	Napfkuchen	Napfkuchen (baba allemand)	Napfkuchen (dolce di pasta lievitata)	Napfkuchen (dulce de pasta levada)

Sweets & ice-creams	Süßspeisen, Eisspeisen	Entremets et glaces	Dolci e gelati	Dulces y helados
Neapolitan ice (ice-cream made in layers of different flavours)	Neapolitanisches Eis (Eisschnitte aus drei verschiedenfarbigen Lagen)	Tranche napolitaine (glace à trois parfums disposée en couches)	Gelato alla napoletana (gelato a strati di differente sapore)	Helado napolitano (tajada de helado hecho de tres diferentes sabores)
Nut cake	Nußtorte	Gâteau aux noix	Torta di noci	Tarta de nueces
Oatcakes	Hafergebäck	Galettes d'avoine	Biscotti all'avena	Galletas de avena
Omelet(te)	Omelette	Omelette	Omelette	Tortilla
Baked ice-cream, Am. baked Alaska	~ mit Eis[92])	~ norvégienne, ~ surprise	~ a sorpresa (gelato al forno)	~ Alaska (helado merengado)
Omelette flambé	~ flambiert	~ flambée	~ alla fiamma, ~ flambé	~ flameada
Omelette with cherries	~ mit Kirschen	~ Montmorency	~ con ciliege	~ con cerezas
Jam omelette	~ mit Konfitüre	~ aux confitures	~ con marmellata	~ con mermelada
Rum omelette	~ mit Rum	~ au rhum	~ al rum	~ al ron
Soufflé omelette	~ soufflée	~ soufflée	~ soufflée	~ soufflée
Stephanie omelette	~ Stephanie (mit Erdbeeren)	~ Stéphanie (aux fraises)	~ Stefania (con fragole)	~ Estefanía (con fresas)
Orange cake	Orangentorte	Gâteau à l'orange	Torta all'arancia	Tarta de naranja
Pancake	Pfannkuchen	Pannequet	Crêpe (frittatina)	Crepe
Pancake with jam	~ mit Konfitüre	Pannequet aux confitures	Crêpe alla marmellata	~ con mermelada
Pancakes with jam	Palatschinken	Pannequets aux confitures	Crêpes con marmellata	Crepes con mermelada
Parfait	Parfait	Parfait	Parfait	Parfait
Parfait; mousse	Halbgefrorenes	Parfait; mousse glacée	Semifreddo; mousse	Semifrío
Pastry	Backwerk	Pâtisserie, petit gâteau	Pasta	Pasta
Peach Alexandra (on vanilla ice-cream, with strawberry purée)	Pfirsich Alexandra (auf Vanilleeis, mit Erdbeerpüree)	Pêche Alexandra (sur glace vanille, avec purée de fraises)	Pesca Alessandra (con gelato di vaniglia e purè di fragole)	Melocotón Alejandra (con mantecado y puré de fresas)
Peach flambé	~ flambiert	~ flambée	~ alla fiamma, ~ flambé	~ flameado
Peach Cardinal (with raspberry sauce and slivered almonds)	~ nach Kardinalsart (mit Himbeerpüree und Mandelsplittern)	~ à la cardinal (avec purèe de framboises et amandes effilées)	~ alla cardinale (con sciroppo di lampone e mandorle a filetti)	~ a la cardenal (con puré de frambuesas y almendras)

Sweets & ice-creams	Süßspeisen, Eisspeisen	Entremets et glaces	Dolci e gelati	Dulces y helados
Peach Melba (with vanilla ice-cream and raspberry sauce)	~ Melba (auf Vanille-eis mit Himbeersaft)	~ Melba (sur glace vanille avec purée de framboises)	~ Melba (con gelato di vaniglia e sciroppo di lampone)	~ Melba (con helado de vainilla y puré de frambuesas)
Pear Alma (stewed in port wine, decorated with whipped cream)	Birne Alma (in Port-wein pochiert, mit Schlagsahne verziert)	Poire Alma (pochée au porto, décorée de crème Chantilly)	Pera Alma (cotta nel vino di Porto, decorata con panna montata)	Pera Alma (cocida en vino de Oporto, decorada con nata)
Pear Alma Condé (pear on rice border with fruit sauce)	Birne Alma Condé (Birne auf Reisrand mit Fruchtsauce)	Poire Alma Condé (dressée sur socle de riz et arrosée de sirop)	Pera Alma Condé (su zoccolo di riso con sciroppo di frutta)	Pera Alma Condé (sobre zócalo de arroz con jarabe de fruta)
~ Helena (pear on vanilla ice-cream with hot chocolate sauce)	~ Helene (auf Vanilleeis, mit heißer Schokoladen-sauce)	~ Bella-Hèlène (sur glace vanille avec sauce au chocolat chaude)	~ Elena (su gelato di vaniglia con salsa calda di cioccolato)	~ Helena (sobre helado de vainilla con salsa de chocolate)
Pecan pie	Pecannußtorte	Tarte à la noix de pacane	Torta alle noci di pecan	Tarta de pacana
Petits fours, fancy biscuits	Teegebäck	Petits fours	Pasticcini da tè	Pastas de té
Petits fours	Petits fours	Petits fours	Petits-fours	Pastas secas, pastas de té
Pineapple cake	Ananastorte	Gâteau à l'ananas	Torta all'ananas	Tarta de piña
Pineapple fritters	Ananasbeignets	Beignets d'ananas	Frittelle d'ananas	Buñuelos de piña
Pineapple tartlets	Ananastörtchen	Tartelettes à l'ananas	Tartelette all'ananas	Tartaleta de piña
Pineapple with kirsch	Ananas mit Kirsch	Ananas au kirsch	Ananas al kirsch	Piña al kirsch
~ with whipped cream	~ mit Schlagsahne	Ananas à la Chantilly	~ con panna	~ con nata
Pistachio ice-cream	Pistazien-Eis	Glace aux pistaches	Gelato al pistacchio	Helado de pistachos
Plum-cake, fruit-cake	Königskuchen	Cake	Plum-cake	Plum-cake
Plum dumplings	Zwetschgenknödel	Boulettes aux prunes	Gnocchi alle prugne	Albóndigas de ciruelas
Plum pudding	Plumpudding	Plum-pudding	Plum pudding	Plum pudding
Plum tart, plum flan	Pflaumenkuchen, Zwetsch-gentorte	Tarte aux prunes	Torta di prugne, torta di susine	Tarta de ciruelas
Poppy-seed cake	Mohntorte	Gâteau au pavot	Torta al papavero	Tarta de adormidera
Prince Pückler ice cream (vanilla, strawberry & chocolate ice-cream)	Fürst-Pückler-Eis (Vanille-, Erdbeer- und Schokoladeeis)	Glace prince Pückler (glace vanille, fraise et chocolat)	Gelato alla Pückler (gelato di vaniglia, fragola e cioccolato)	Helado Pückler (de vainilla, fresas y chocolate)

Sweets & ice-creams	Süßspeisen, Eisspeisen	Entremets et glaces	Dolci e gelati	Dulces y helados
Profiteroles au chocolat (small cream-puffs with chocolate sauce)	Profiteroles au chocolat (Windbeutel mit Schokoladensauce)	Profiteroles au chocolat (choux à la crème nappés de sauce chocolat)	Profiteroles al cioccolato (bignè alla crema con salsa di cioccolato)	Profiteroles au chocolat (lionesas de crema con salsa de chocolate)
Pudding Nesselrode pudding (iced chestnut pudding)	Pudding ~ Nesselrode (Maronen-Eispudding)	Pudding (pouding) ~ Nesselrode (pudding glacé aux marrons)	Budino ~ Nesseirode (budino gelato di marroni)	Budín ~ Nesselrode (budín frío de castañas)
Puff, choux Cream-puff	Windbeutel ~ mit Sahne	Chou (pl. choux) Chou à la crème	Bignè, bignola, chou Bignè alla panna	Lionesa, chou Lionesa con crema
Pumpkin pie	Kürbistorte	Tarte au potiron	Torta di zucca	Tarta de calabaza
Punch-cake	Punschtorte	Gâteau au punch	Torta al punch	Tarta al ponche
Raspberry ice-cream	Himbeer-Eis	Glace aux framboises	Gelato di lampone	Helado de frambuesas
Raspberry jelly	Himbeer-Gelee	Gelée de framboises	Gelatina di lamponi	Jalea de frambuesas
Rhubarb pie	Rhabarbertorte	Tarte à la rhubarbe	Torta al rabarbaro	Tarta de ruibarbo
Rhubarb tartlet	Rhabarber-Törtchen	Tartelette à la rhubarbe	Tarteletta al rabarbaro	Tartaleta de ruibarbo
Rice pudding	Reisauflauf	Gâteau de riz	Dolce di riso	Budín de arroz
Rice pudding	Milchreis	Riz au lait	Riso al latte	Arroz con leche
Rice Trauttmansdorff (rice pudding mixed with cream, gelatine, candied fruits)	Reis Trauttmansdorff (Milchreis mit Schlagsahne und Gelatine vermischt)	Riz à l'impératrice (riz au lait additionné de crème fouettée et gélatine)	Riso all'imperatrice (riso al latte con aggiunta di panna, gelatina e canditi)	Arroz a la emperatriz (arroz con leche adicionado de nata y fruta confitada)
Rum baba[93]	Baba mit Rum	Baba au rhum	Babà al rum	Babá al ron
Saint-honoré (rich cream cake bordered with small puffs)	St. Honoré-Torte (Cremetorte mit Windbeutelchen garniert)	Saint-honoré (gâteau à la crème avec bordure) de petits choux)	Saint-honoré (torta alla crema guarnita tutt'intorno di bignè)	Sanhonorato (tarta de crema guarnecida de pequeñas lionesas)
Salzburg sweet dumplings (kind of floating islands)	Salzburger Nockerln (eine Art Schnee-Eier)	Noques à la viennoise (sorte d'œufs à la neige)	Gnocchi di Salisburgo (specie di uova di neve)	Ñoqui de Salzburgo (especie de huevos de nieve)
Savarin (ring-shaped yeast cake soaked in liqueur)	Savarin (Hefekranz, mit Likör getränkt)	Savarin	Savarin (varieta di babà)	Savarin (dulce de pasta levada mojado de licor)
~ with fruits	~ mit Früchten	~ aux fruits	~ alla frutta	~ con fruta
~ with whipped cream	~ mit Schlagsahne	~ Chantilly	~ alla panna	~ con nata, ~ con Chantillí

Sweets & ice-creams	Süßspeisen, Eisspeisen	Entremets et glaces	Dolci e gelati	Dulces y helados
Semolina pudding	Grießpudding	Pudding de semoule	Budino di semolino	Budín de sémola
Sherbet, sorbet	Sorbet(t)	Sorbet	Sorbetto	Sorbete
Shortbread	Mürbegebäck	Sablés, biscuits sablés	Frollini	Galletas de pastaflora
Silvester bombe	Silvester-Eisbombe	Bombe Saint-Sylvestre	Bomba San Silvestro	Bomba San Silvestre
Soufflé Rothschild (vanilla soufflé with candied fruits)	Rothschild-Auflauf (Vanilleauflauf mit kandierten Früchten)	Soufflé Rothschild (soufflé vanille aux fruits confits)	Soufflé Rothschild (soufflé alla vaniglia con canditi)	Soufflé Rothschild (soufflé de vainilla con fruta confitada)
Sponge biscuits, ladyfingers	Löffelbiskuits	Biscuits à la cuiller	Savoiardi	Bizcochos
Sponge cake	Biskuittorte	Biscuit de Savoie	Pan di Spagna	Bizcocho de Saboya
Strawberries and cream	Erdbeeren mit Sahne	Fraises à la Chantilly	Fragole con la panna	Fresas con nata
Strawberry-cream	Erdbeer-Creme	Crème aux fraises	Crema di fragole	Crema de fresas
Strawberry ice cream	Erdbeer-Eis	Glace aux fraises	Gelato di fragola	Helado de fresas
Strawberry mousse	Erdbeer-Mousse	Mousse aux fraises	Mousse di fragole	Espuma de fresas
Strawberry parfait	Erdbeerhalbgefrorenes	Parfait aux fraises	Semifreddo alle fragole	Parfait de fresas
Strawberry shortcake	Erdbeer-Biskuittorte	Biscuit mousseline aux fraises	Pan di Spagna alle fragole	Bizcocho con fresas
Strawberry tart	Erdbeer-Torte	Tarte aux fraises	Torta di fragole	Tarta de fresas
Sundae, coupe	Eisbecher	Coupe glacée	Coppa di gelato	Copa de helado
Surprise melon (filled with fruit salad)	Überraschungs-Melone (mit Obstsalat gefüllt)	Melon en surprise (farci de macédoine)	Melone a sorpresa (ripieno di macedonia)	Melon en sorpresa (relleno de ensalada de fruta)
Surprise oranges (filled with orange ice cream)	Überraschungs-Orangen (mit Orangeneis gefüllt)	Oranges en surprise (remplies de glace à l'orange)	Arance a sorpresa (ripiene di gelato d'arancia)	Naranjas en sorpresa (rellenas de sorbete de naranja)
Swiss roll (baked jam roll)	Biskuitrolle	Biscuit roulé	Rotolo con marmellata[94]	Brazo de gitano
Syllabub (dessert of cream or milk whipped with wine and sugar)	Syllabub (schaumige Creme aus Milch oder Sahne, Wein, Zucker)	Syllabub (sorte de sabayon fait de crème ou lait, vin et sucre)	Syllabub (sorta di Zabaione a base di panna o latte, vino, zucchero)	Syllabub (espuma hecha de nata o leche, vino y azucar)
Tangerine ice cream	Mandarinen-Eis	Glace aux mandarines	Gelato di mandarino	Helado de mandarinas

Sweets & ice-creams	Süßspeisen, Eisspeisen	Entremets et glaces	Dolci e gelati	Dulces y helados
Tartlet	Törtchen (Tortelett)	Tartelette	Tarteletta	Tartaleta
Tipsy cake, see trifle				
Treacle tart	Melassekuchen	Tarte à la mélasse	Torta alla melassa	Tarta de melaza
Trifle (sponge cake soaked in wine and topped with custard)	Trifle (kalte Süßspeise aus likörgetränkten Biskuit und Creme)	Trifle (entremets froid fait de génoise imbibée de liqueur et de crème pâtissière)	Zuppa inglese (dolce fatto di strati di crema e di savoiardi intrisi di liquore)	Trifle (dulce frío hecho de bizcochos mojados en licor y de natillas)
Upside-down cake	Gestürzter Obstkuchen	Tarte renversée aux fruits	Torta di frutta	Tarta de fruta
Vacherin (rounds of meringue alternated with whipped cream	Vacherin (Schichttorte aus Meringeböden und Schlagsahne)	Vacherin Chantilly (cercles de meringue superposés, garnis de chantilly)	Vacherin (dischi di meringa alternati con panna montata)	Vacherin (tarta hecha de capas alternadas de merengue y nata)
~ with ice	~ mit Eis	~ glacé	~ al gelato	~ con helado
Vanilla ice cream	Vanille-Eis	Glace à la vanille	Gelato di vaniglia	Helado de vainilla, mantecado
Vanilla soufflé	Vanille-Auflauf	Soufflé à la vanille	Soufflé alla vaniglia	Soufflé de vainilla
Variety of pies and cakes	Verschiedene Torten	Gâteaux variés	Torte assortite	Tartas diversas
Waffles	Waffeln	Gaufres	Cialde	Barquillos
Wedding cake	Hochzeitstorte	Gâteau de mariage	Torta nuziale	Pastel de boda
Zabaglione, sabayon (foamy wine sauce of egg-yolk, sugar & wine)	Zabaglione[95]) (schaumige Creme aus Eigelb, Zucker und Wein)	Sabayon (crème mousseuse de jaunes d'œufs, sucre et vin)	Zabaione (crema di tuorli d'uovo, zucchero e vino)	Crema sabayon (hecha de yemas, azucar y vino)
Iced zabaglione	~ gefroren	Sabayon glacé	Zabaione gelato	Crema sabayon helada

[76]) Am. baked Alaska.
[77]) on crumble aux pommes.
[78]) dite omelette norvégienne.
[79]) auch Bavarois.
[80]) appelé aussi „Moscovite".
[81]) or baked custard.
[82]) dite aussi flan au caramel.

[83]) ou crème fouettée.
[84]) ou sauce vanille.
[85]) ou crème à la vanille.
[86]) o cannoncino alla panna.
[87]) small cakes of choux pastry filled with cream & iced.
[88]) flan de semoule.
[89]) ou salade de fruits et macédoine de fruits.

[90]) o macedonia de frutas.
[91]) o quattro quarti.
[92]) siehe Überraschungsomelette
[93]) small yeast-raised cake soaked in rum syrup.
[94]) o salame inglese.
[95]) auch Zabaione und Sabayon.

Fruit	Obst	Fruits	Frutta	Frutas
Almond	Mandel	Amande	Mandorla	Almendra
Apple	Apfel	Pomme	Mela	Manzana
Baked apple	~ gebraten	Pomme au four	Mela al forno	~ asada
Apricot	Aprikose	Abricot	Albicocca	Albaricoque
Assorted fruits	Gemischtes Obst	Fruits assortis	Frutta mista	Frutas variadas
Assorted nuts	Gemischte Nüsse	Fruits secs	Frutta secca	Fruta seca
Avocado (pl. avocados)	Avocado	Avocat	Avocado	Aguacate
Banana	Banane	Banane	Banana	Plátano
Bilberry, blueberry	Heidelbeere	Myrtille, airelle	Mirtillo	Arándano
Blackberry	Brombeere	Mûre sauvage	Mora di rovo	Zarzamora
Brazil nut	Paranuß	Noix du Brésil	Noce del Brasile	Nuez del Brasil
Candied fruit	Kandierte Früchte	Fruits confits	Frutta candita	Fruta confitada
Cherry (pl.cherries)	Kirsche	Cerise	Ciliegia	Cereza
Chestnut	Marone	Marron	Marrone	Castaña
Chestnut	Kastanie	Châtaigne	Castagna	Castaña
Citron	Zitronatzitrone	Cédrat	Cedro	Cidra
Clementine	Klementine	Clémentine	Mandarancio, clementina	Clementina
Coconut	Kokosnuß	Noix de coco	Noce di cocco	Coco
Cranberry	Preiselbeere	Airelle (rouge)	Mirtillo rosso	Arándano rojo
Currant	Johannisbeere	Groseille	Ribes	Grosella
Redcurrant	~ (rote)	Groseille rouge	Ribes rosso	Grosella roja
Blackcurrant	~ (schwarze)	Cassis, groseille noire	Ribes nero	Grosella negra
Currants	Korinthen	Raisins de Corinthe	Uva di Corinto	Pasas de Corinto
Date	Dattel	Datte	Dattero	Datil
Damson	Damaszenerpflaume	Prune de Damas	Susina damaschina	Ciruela damascena
Early fruits	Frühobst	Primeurs	Primizie	Primicias, fruta temprana
Fig	Feige	Figue	Fico	Higo
Fresh fruits	Frisches Obst	Fruits frais	Frutta fresca	Frutas frescas
Fruit in season	Obst der Saison	Fruits de saison	Frutta di stagione	Fruta del tiempo
Fruit in syrup	Obst in Sirup	Fruits au sirop	Frutta sciroppata	Fruta en almíbar

Fruit	Obst	Fruits	Frutta	Frutas
Fruit salad, macedoine	Obstsalat	Salade de fruits, macédoine de fruits	Macedonia di frutta	Ensalada de frutas, macedonia de frutas
Gooseberry	Stachelbeere	Groseille à maquereau	Uva spina	Uva espina
Grapefruit	Grapefruit	Grape-fruit, pamplemousse	Pompelmo	Granada
Grapes (pl.)	Trauben	Raisin	Uva	Uva
Black grapes	~ (blaue)	Raisin noir	Uva nera	~ negra
White grapes	~ (weiße)	Raisin blanc	Uva bianca	~ blanca
Greengage	Reineclaude (Reneklode)	Reine-claude (pl. reines-claudes)	Prugna regina Claudia	Ciruela claudia
Guava	Guave, Guajave	Goyave	Guaiava	Guayaba
Hazelnut, filbert	Haselnuß	Noisette, aveline	Nocciola	Avellana
Hothouse fruit, forced fruit	Treibhausobst	Fruits de serre	Frutta di serra	Fruta de invernadero
Kiwi	Kiwi	Kiwi	Kiwi, kivi	Kiwi
Lemon	Zitrone	Citron	Limone	Limón
Lychee	Litchi	Litchi	Litchi (prugna cinese)	Lichi
Mango	Mango	Mangue	Mango	Mango
Medlar	Mispel	Nèfle	Nespola	Níspola, níspero
Loquat, Japanese	~ (japanische)	Nèfle du Japon	Nespola del Giappone	Níspola del Japón
Melon	Melone	Melon	Melone, popone	Melón
Mirabelle	Mirabelle	Mirabelle	Mirabella (sorta di susina)	Ciruela amarilla
Mulberry	Maulbeere	Mûre	Mora di gelso	Mora
Muscat grapes, muscatel	Muskatellertrauben	Muscat	Uva moscata	Uva moscatel
Nectarine	Nektarine	Nectarine, brugnon	Pesca nettarina, pesca noce	Briñón, griñón
Orange salad	Orangensalat	Salade d'oranges	Insalata d' arance	Ensalada de naranjas
Orange	Apfelsine	Orange	Arancia, arancio	Naranja
Orange	Orange	Orange	Arancia, arancio	Naranja
Blood orange	~ (Blutorange)	Orange sanguine	Arancia sanguigna	Naranja sanguina
Papaya	Papaya	Papaye	Papaia	Papaya
Passion-fruit, granadilla	Passionsfrucht	Fruit de la passion	Frutto della passione	Granadilla
Peach	Pfirsich	Pêche	Pesca [arachide	Melocotón

Fruit	Obst	Fruits	Frutta	Frutas
Peanut	Erdnuß	Cacahuète, arachide	Nocciolina americana,	Cacahuete, Am. maní
Pear	Williams Christbirne	Poire williams	Pera William	Pera
Pear	Birne	Poire	Pera	Pera
Persimmon	Kakipflaume	Kaki	Cachi	Caqui
Pineapple	Ananas	Ananas	Ananas	Piña, ananás
Plum	Pflaume, Zwetsch(g)e	Prune	Prugna, susina	Ciruela
Prune	~ (gedörrte)	Pruneau	Prugna secca	Ciruela pasa
Pomegranate	Granatapfel	Grenade	Melagrana	Toronja, pomelo
Prune	Backpflaume	Pruneau	Prugna secca	Ciruela pasa
Quince	Quitte	Coing	Cotogna, mela cotogna	Membrillo
Raisins	Rosinen	Raisins secs	Uva passa	Pasas
Raspberry	Himbeere	Framboise	Lampone	Frambuesa
Rhubarb	Rhabarber	Rhubarbe	Rabarbaro	Ruibarbo
Sour cherry, morello (pl. morellos)	Sauerkirsche	Griotte	Amarena, visciola, marasca	Guinda
Stewed fruits, compote	Kompott	Compote	Composta, frutta cotta	Compota, fruta cocida
Stewed apples	~ (Apfel-)	~ de pommes	Composta di mele	Compota de manzanas
Stewed prunes	~ (Backpflaumen-)	~ de pruneaux	Composta di prugne	~ de ciruelas
Stewed pears	~ (Birnen-)	~ de poires	Composta di pere	~ de peras
Mixed stewed fruits	~ (gemischtes)	~ assortie	Composta mista	~ variada
Stewed cherries	~ (Kirschen-)	~ de cerises	Composta di ciliegie	~ de cerezas
Stewed cranberries	~ (Preiselbeer-)	~ d'cirelles	Composta di mirtillo rosso	~ de arándanos rojos
Stewed quinces	~ (Quitten-)	~ de coings	Composta di cotogne	~ de membrillo
Strawberries with cream	Erdbeeren mit Sahne	Fraises à la Chantilly	Fragole con la panna	Fresas con nata
Strawberry	Erdbeere	Fraise	Fragola	Fresa, fresón
Wild strawberry	~ (Walderdbeere)	Fraise des bois	Fragola di bosco	Fresa silvestre
Sultanas	Sultaninen	Raisins de Smyrne	Uva sultanina	Pasas de Esmirna
Tangerine, mandarin(e)	Mandarine	Mandarine	Mandarino	Mandarina, tangerina
Walnut, nut	Nuß (Walnuß)	Noix	Noce	Nuez (pl. nueces)
Watermelon	Wassermelone	Pastèque, melon d'eau	Cocomero, anguria	Sandía, melón de agua

Bread	Brot	Pain	Pane	Pan
Breadcrumbs	Paniermehl, Semmelbrösel	Chapelure	Pan grattato, pangrattato	Pan rallado
Breadcrumbs	Brösel	Chapelure	Pan grattato, pangrattato	Pan rallado
Brown bread, black bread	Schwarzbrot	Pain noir	Pane nero	Pan moreno, pan bazo
Bun	Rosinenbrötchen	Petit pain aux raisins secs	Panino all'uvetta	Panecillo con pasas
Cheese sandwich	Käsebrot	Sandwich au fromage	Panino al formaggio	Emparedado de queso
Corn bread	Maisbrot	Pain de maïs	Pane di granturco	Pan de maíz
Crescent roll, croissant	Hörnchen	Croissant	Cornetto, croissant	Medialuna, cuerno
Croissant	Croissant	Croissant	Croissant, cornetto	Medialuna, croissant
Croque-monsieur (toasted ham and cheese sandwich)	Croque-monsieur (getoasteter Schinken-Käse-Sandwich)	Croque-monsieur[99] (sandwich grillé au jambon et fromage)	Toast (coppia di fette di pane tostate con formaggio e prosciutto)	Croque-monsieur (emparedado tostado de jamón y queso)
Croûtons	Croûtons[97]	Croûtons	Crostini	Trocitos de pan frito
Double-decker	Doppeldecker	Double-decker	Sandwich doppio	Emparedado doble
Fresh bread, new bread	Frisches Brot	Pain-frais	Pane fresco	Pan fresco
Grissini (crisp bread in long thin sticks)	Grissini (knuspriges Stangenbrot)	Gressins (pain en forme de bâtonnet sec)	Grissini	Grissini (pan en forma de barritas)
Ham sandwich	Schinkenbrot	Sandwich au jambon	Panino al prosciutto	~ de jamón
Home-made bread	Hausbackenes Brot	Pain de ménage	Pane casereccio	Pan casero
Knäckebrot (Swedish wholemeal crackers)	Knäckebrot (schwedisches Schrotbrot)	Knäckebrot (galettes de farine non blutée)	Knäckebrot (gallette di farina integrale)	Knäckebrot (especie de pan integral sueco)
Milk-roll	Milchbrötchen	Petit pain au lait	Panino al latte	Bollo de leche, mollete
Muffin (bun toasted and buttered)	Muffins[98] (Brötchen geröstet und mit Butter bestrichen)	Muffin (petit pain grillé et beurré)	Muffin (panino tostato e imburrato)	Muffin (panecillo tostado y con mantequilla)
Poppy-seed roll	Mohnbrötchen	Petit pain au pavot	Panino al papavero	Panecillo con adormidera
Pretzel, bretzel[96]	Brezel	Bretzel	Brezel	Rosca
Pumpernickel (wholemeal rye-bread)	Pumpernickel	Pumpernickel (pain noir de seigle broyé)	Pane di segale (molto scuro)	Pan moreno de Westfalia
Roll, French roll	Semmel	Petit pain	Panino	Panecillo, mollete
Roll	Brötchen	Petit pain	Panino	Panecillo, mollete
Rye-bread	Roggenbrot	Pain de seigle	Pane di segale (o di segala)	Pan de centeno

Bread	Brot	Pain	Pane	Pan
Sandwich (pl. sandwiches)	Sandwich	Sandwich	Sandwich, panino	Bocadillo, emparedado, sandwich
Sandwich (pl. sandwiches)	Belegtes Brötchen (Semmel)	Sandwich	Panino (imbottito), sandwich	Emparedado, sandwich
Sandwich loaf	Kastenbrot	Pain de mie, pain anglais	Pane a cassetta[100])	Pan de molde, pan inglés
Sandwich loaf	Toastbrot	Pain de mie, pain anglais	Pane a cassetta, pan carré	Pan inglés
Seed-roll	Kümmelbrötchen	Petit pain au cumin	Panino al comino	Panecillo al comino
Slice of bread	Brotschnitte	Tranche de pain	Fetta di pane	Rebanada de pan
Toast	Röstbrot	Toast, rôtie	Pane tostato	Toast, tostada
Toast	Toast	Toast, rôtie	Fetta di pane tostato	Toast, tostada
Buttered toast	~ mit Butter	Toast beurré	~ di pane tostato con burro	~ con mantequilla
White bread, wheat bread	Weißbrot	Pain blanc	Pane bianco	Pan blanco
Wholemeal bread	Vollkornbrot	Pain complet	Pane integrale	Pan completo, pan integral
Wholemeal bread	Schrotbrot	Pain complet	Pane integrale	Pan completo
Wholemeal bread	Grahambrot	Pain complet	Pane integrale	Pan completo, pan integral

[96]) crisp knot-shaped biscuit.
[97]) geröstete Brotwürfel.
[98]) (pl.)
[99]) ou croque-madame.
[100]) o pan carré.

Spices & condiments	Gewürze	Epices et condiments	Spezie e condimenti	Especias y condimentos
Angelica	Angelika (Engelwurz)	Angélique	Angelica	Angélica
Anise, aniseed	Anis	Anis	Anice	Anís
Basil	Basilikum	Basilic	Basilico	Albahaca
Bay-leaf	Lorbeerblatt	Feuille de laurier	Foglia d'alloro	Hoja de laurel
Bay	Lorbeer	Laurier	Alloro	Laurel
Borage	Borretsch	Bourrache	Borragine	Borraja
Burnet	Pimpinelle	Pimprenelle	Salvastrella	Pimpinela
Burnet	Bibernelle	Pimprenelle	Salvastrella	Pimpinela
Candied citron peel	Zitronat	Cédrat confit	Cedro candito	Cidra confitada
Capers	Kapern	Câpres	Capperi	Alcaparras
Cardamom	Kardamom	Cardamome	Cardamomo	Cardamomo
Chervil	Kerbel	Cerfeuil	Cerfoglio	Perifollo
Chive	Schnittlauch	Ciboulette	Erba cipollina	Cebollino (ajo moruno)
Cinnamon	Zimt	Cannelle	Cannella	Canela
Clove	Nelke	Clou de girofle	Chiodo di garofano	Clavo (de especia)
Clove	Gewürznelke	Clou de girofle	Chiodo di garofano	Clavo de especia
Coriander	Koriander	Coriandre	Coriandolo	Coriandro
Cumin, caraway	Kümmel	Cumin	Comino, cumino	Comino
Curry(-powder)	Curry	Curry, cari, cary	Curry	Curry
Dill	Dill	Aneth	Aneto	Eneldo
Fennel	Fenchel	Fenouil	Finocchio	Hinojo
Garlic; clove of garlic	Knoblauch; Knoblauchzehe	Ail; gousse d'ail	Aglio; spicchio d'aglio	Ajo; diente de ajo
Gherkins	Cornichons	Cornichons	Cetriolini sott'aceto	Pepinillos en vinagre
Ginger	Ingwer	Gingembre	Zenzero	Jengibre
Horseradish	Meerrettich (Kren)	Raifort	Rafano, cren	Rábano picante
Hot pepper, red pepper	Pfefferschote	Piment rouge	Peperoncino	Guindilla, ñora
Hot pepper, red pepper	Chili(schote)	Piment fort, piment rouge	Peperoncino	Guindilla, ñora
Juniper berries	Wacholderbeeren	Baies de genièvre	Bacche di ginepro	Bayas de enebro
Juniper	Wacholder	Genièvre	Ginepro	Enebro
Lemon balm	Zitronenmelisse	Mélisse, citronnelle	Melissa, cedronella	Toronjil, melisa
Lovage	Liebstöckl	Livèche, ache de montagne	Levistico, sedano di monte	Levístico, apio de montaña

Spices & condiments	Gewürze	Epices et condiments	Spezie e condimenti	Especias y condimentos
Mace	Muskatblüte	Macis	Macis	Macis, macia
Marjoram	Majoran	Marjolaine	Maggiorana	Mejorana
Mint	Minze	Menthe	Menta	Menta, hierbabuena
Mixed pickles	Mixed-Pickles	Pickles	Sottaceti	Encurtidos (en vinagre)
Mugwort	Beifuß	Armoise	Artemisia	Artemisa
Mustard	Senf	Moutarde	Senape, senapa, mostarda	Mostaza
Nutmeg	Muskatnuß	(Noix de) muscade	Noce moscata	Nuez moscada
Oregano, wild marjoram	Oregano (Origano)	Origan	Origano	Orégano
Paprika	Paprika(pulver)	Paprika	Paprica, paprika	Pimentón, paprika
Parsley	Petersilie	Persil	Prezzemolo	Perejil
Pepper	Pfeffer	Poivre	Pepe	Pimienta
Cayenne pepper	~ (Cayenne-)	~ de Cayenne	~ di Caienna	~ de Cayena
Whole pepper	~ (ganzer)	~ en grains	~ in grani	~ en grano
Pimento, allspice	Nelkenpfeffer	Piment	Pimento	Pimienta de Jamaica
Pimento, allspice	Piment	Piment	Pimento	Pimienta de Jamaica
Pimento, Jamaica pepper	Jamaikapfeffer	Piment	Pepe della Giamaica	Pimienta de Jamaica
Pine-nuts	Pignolen (Pinienkerne)	Pignons	Pinoli, pignoli	Piñones
Pistachio (pl. pistachios)	Pistazie	Pistache	Pistacchio	Pistacho
Poppy(-seed)	Mohn	Pavot	Papavero	Adormidera
Rosemary	Rosmarin	Romarin	Rosmarino	Romero
Rue	Weinraute	Rue	Ruta	Ruda
Saffron	Safran	Safran	Zafferano	Azafrán
Sage	Salbei	Sauge	Salvia	Salvia
Shallot	Schalotte	Échalote	Scalogno	Escaloña, chalote
Summer savory	Bohnenkraut	Sarriette	Santoreggia	Ajedrea
Sweet herbs, fine herbs	Kräuter (Gewürz-)	Fines herbes	Erbe aromatiche	Hierbas aromáticas
Tarragon	Estragon	Estragon	Dragoncello, estragone	Estragón, dragoncillo
Thyme	Thymian	Thym, serpolet	Timo	Tomillo
Turmeric	Kurkuma	Curcuma	Curcuma	Cúrcuma
Vanilla	Vanille	Vanille	Vaniglia	Vainilla
Woodruff	Waldmeister	Aspérule	Asperula, stellina odorosa	Asperilla, rubilla

Alcoholic drinks	Alkoholische Getränke	Boissons alcooliques	Bevande alcoliche	Bebidas alcohólicas
Anisette	Anisette (Anislikör)	Anisette	Anisetta	Anisete
Aperitif	Aperitif	Apéritif	Aperitivo	Aperitivo
Beer	Bier	Bière	Birra	Cerveza
Light beer, pale ale	~ (helles)	~ blonde	~ chiara	~ dorada
Dark beer, stout	~ (dunkles)	~ brune	~ scura	~ negra
Draught beer	~ (vom Faß)	~ à la pression	~ alla spina	~ de barril
Munich beer	~ (Münchner)	~ de Munich	~ di Monaco	~ de Munich
Bordeaux, claret	Bordeaux	Bordeaux	Bordeaux	Burdeos
Bottled beer	Flaschenbier	Bière en bouteilles	Birra in bottiglia	Cerveza en botellas
Bottled wine	Flaschenwein	Vin en bouteilles	Vino in bottiglia	Vino embotellado
Brandy	Schnaps	Eau-de-vie	Acquavite	Aguardiente
Brandy	Weinbrand	Eau-de-vie	Acquavite	Aguardiente
Brandy	Branntwein	Eau-de-vie	Acquavite	Aguardiente
Burgundy	Burgunder	Bourgogne	Borgogna	Borgoña
Champagne	Champagner	Champagne	Champagne	Champaña, champán
Cider	Apfelwein	Cidre	Sidro	Sidra
Cognac, French brandy	Cognac	Cognac	Cognac	Coñac
Cup (chilled drink of wine with various flavourings)	Bowle (kaltes Getränk aus Wein und Früchten)	Cup (boisson froide à base de vin et fruits)	Bowle (bevanda fredda di vino bianco e frutta)	Bowle (bebida fría de vino blanco y fruta)
Peach cup	~ (Pfirsich-)	Cup aux pêches	Bowle di pesca	Bowle de melocotón
Woodruff cup	~ (Waldmeister-)	Cup à l'aspérule	Bowle di asperula	Bowle de asperilla
Dessert wine	Dessertwein	Vin de dessert	Vino da dessert	Vino de postre
Dessert wine	Strohwein	Vin de paille	Passito, vinsanto	Vino blanco generoso
Fortified wine	Likörwein	Vin de liqueur	Vino liquoroso	Vino generoso
Gin	Gin	Gin, genièvre	Gin	Ginebra
Irish coffee, gaelic coffee (hot coffee with Irish whiskey and cream on top)	Irish coffee (heißer Kaffee mit einem Schuß Whiskey und Schlagsahne)	Irish coffee (café bouillant avec whiskey et crème fraîche)	Irish coffee (caffè bollente con whiskey e panna)	Café irlandés (café hirviendo con whiskey y nata batida)
Kirsch(wasser)	Kirsch(wasser)	Kirsch	Kirsch	Kirsch
Kümmel	Kümmel	Kummel	Kümmel	Kummel, cúmel
Liqueur	Likör	Liqueur	Liquore	Licor

Alcoholic drinks	Alkoholische Getränke	Boissons alcooliques	Bevande alcoliche	Bebidas alcohólicas
Local wine	Landwein	Vin de pays	Vino nostrano, vino locale	Vino del país
Madeira	Madeira	Madère	Madera	Vino de Madera
Malmsey, malvoisie	Malvasier	Malvoisie	Malvasia	Malvasía
Maraschino (liqueur from sour cherries)	Maraschino (Likör aus der Sauerkirsche)	Marasquin (liqueur de griottes)	Maraschino (liquore di marasche)	Marrasquino (licor de guindas)
Marc brandy, grappa	Tresterbranntwein	Marc	Grappa	Aguardiente de orujo
Moselle	Moselwein	Vin de Moselle	Vino della Mosella	Mosela
Mulled wine	Glühwein	Vin chaud	Vino brûlé, vino caldo	Vino caliente
Muscatel, muscat	Muskateller	Muscat	Moscato	Vino moscatel
Must (new wine)	Most	Moût	Mosto	Mosto
Port	Portwein	Porto	Porto	Oporto
Punch	Punsch	Punch	Punch, ponce	Ponche
Red wine	Rotwein	Vin rouge	Vino rosso, vino nero	Vino tinto
Rhine wine, hock	Rheinwein	Vin du Rhin	Vino del Reno	Vino del Rin
Rosé	Rosé(wein)	Vin rosé	Rosé, rosatello, rosato	Vino rosado
Rum	Rum	Rhum	Rum, rhum	Ron
Sherry	Sherry	Xérès	Sherry	Jerez
Sparkling wine	Schaumwein	Vin mousseux	Spumante	Vino espumoso
Sweet wine	Süßwein	Vin doux	Vino dolce	Vino dulce
Table wine	Tischwein	Vin de table	Vino da pasto	Vino de pasto, vino de mesa
Vermouth, vermuth	Wermut	Vermouth	Vermut	Vermut
Vodka	Wodka	Vodka	Vodka	Vodka
Whisky, whiskey	Whisky	Whisky	Whisky	Whisky
Whisky and soda	~ mit Soda	~ and soda	Whisky e soda	~ con soda
White wine	Weißwein	Vin blanc	Vino bianco	Vino blanco
Wine in carafe	Schoppenwein	Vin ouvert, vin en carafe	Vino in caraffa, vino sciolto	Vino de la cuba
Wine	Wein	Vin	Vino	Vino
Green wine, young wine	~ (neuer)	~ jeune	~ nuovo, ~ giovane	~ nuevo
Wine in carafe	~ (offener)	~ ouvert, ~ en carafe	~ sciolto, ~ in caraffa	~ de la cuba

Non-alcoholic drinks[101])	Alkoholfreie Getränke	Boissons sans alcool	Bevande analcoliche	Bebidas sin alcohol
Blackcurrant syrup	~ schwarz	Sirop de cassis	Sciroppo di ribes nero	~ de grosellas negras
Bottled sodas	Brauselimonaden	Sodas, boissons gazeuses	Bibite gassale	Limonadas efervescentes
Buttermilk	Buttermilch	Babeurre	Latticello	Suero de manteca
Camomile tea	Kamillentee	Tisane de camomille	Infuso di camomilla	Infusión de manzanilla
Condensed milk	Kondensmilch	Lait concentré	Latte condensato	Leche condensada
Cappuccino	Cappuccino	Cappuccino	Cappuccino	Cappuccino
Cocoa	Kakao	Cacao	Cacao	Cacao
Coffee	Kaffee	Café	Caffè	Café
Black coffee	~ (schwarzer)	~ noir, ~ nature	~ nero	~ solo, ~ negro
Coffee with brandy	~ mit Schuß	~ arrosé	~ corretto	~ con gota
Coffee with cream[102])	~ mit Sahne	~ crème	Caffè con panna	~ con crema
Coffee without caffeine[103]	~ (koffeinfreier)	décaleiné	~ decalleinato	~ descafeinado
Coffee with milk	Milchkaffee	Café au lait, ~ crème	Caffelatte	Café con leche
Continental breakfast[104])	~ komplett	~ complet	Caffelatte completo	~ completo
Currant syrup	Johannisbeersaft, rot	Sirop de groseilles	Sciroppo di ribes	Jarabe de groseltas
Drip coffee	Filterkaffee	Café filtre	Caffè filtro	Café filtro
Espresso	Espresso	Café express	Espresso	Café exprés
Fizzy lemonade	Brauselimonade	Limonade gazeuse	Gassosa, gazzosa	Gaseosa
Fruit juice	Fruchtsaft	Jus de fruits	Succo di frutta	Zumo de fruta
Apple juice, sweet cider	~ (Apfel-)	~ de pommes	~ di mete	~ de manzanas
Grape juice	~ (Trauben-)	~ de raisin	~ d'unva	~ de uva
Grapefruit juice	~ (Grapefruit-)	~ de grape-fruit	~ di pompelmo	~ de toronja
Orange juice	~ (Orangen-)	~ d'oranges	~ d'arancia	~ de naranja
Grenadine (pomegranate syrup)	Grenadine (Granatapfelsirup)	Grenadine (sirop de grenade)	Granatina (sciroppo di melagrana)	Granadina (jarabe de granada)
Hot chocolate	Schokolade	Chocolat	Ciocoolata	Chocolate
Ice	Eis	Glace	Ghiaccio	Hielo
Iced tea	Eistee	Thé glacé	Té ghiacciato	Té helado
Lemon squash	Zitronensaft, frisch gepreßt	Citron pressé	Spremuta di limone	Zumo fresco de limón
Lemonade	Limonade	Citronnade, limonade	Limonata	Limonada
Lime tea, linden-tea	Lindenblütentee	Tisane de tilbeul	Infuso di tiglio	Infusión de tila

Non-alcoholic drinks[101]	Alkoholfreie Getränke	Boissons sans alcool	Bevande analcoliche	Bebidas sin alcohol
Milk-shake	Milch-Shake	Milk-shake	Frullato, frappé	Batido
Milk	Milch	Lait	Latte	Leche
Pasteurized milk	~ (pasteurisierte)	~ pasteurisé	~ pastorizzato	~ pasterizada
Mineral water	Mineralwasser	Eau minérale	Acqua minerale	Agua mineral
Mint tea	Pfefferminztee	Thé de menthe	Tè di menta	Té de menta
Orange squash	Orangensaft, frisch ge-preßt	Orange pressée	Spremuta d'arancia	Zumo fresco de naranja
Orangeade	Orangeade	Orangeade	Aranciata	Naranjada
Raspberry syrup	Himbeersaft	Sirop de framboises	Sciroppo di lampone	Jarabe de frambuesas
Rose-hip tea	Hagebuttentee	Thé de cynorrhodons	Infuso di rosa canina	Infusión de escaramujo
Seltzer (water)	Selterswasser	Eau de Seltz, eau gazeuse	Selz, seltz	Agua de Seltz
Skimmed milk	Magermilch	Lait écrémé	Latte scremato	Leche desnatada
Soda(-water)	Sodawasser	Soda	Soda	Soda
Sour cherry syrup	Weichselsirup	Sirop de griottes	Sciroppo di amarene	Jarabe de guindas
Sweet cider	Apfelsaft (Süßmost)	Cidre doux	Succo di mele	Jugo de manzanas
Syrup, Am. sirup	Sirup	Sirop	Sciroppo	Jarabe
Tea	Tee	Thé	Tè	Té
Tea, rolls, jam and butter	~ komplett	~ complet	~ completo	~ completo
Tea with lemon	~ mit Zitrone	~ au citron	~ con limone	~ con limón
Tea with milk	~ mit Milch	~ au lait	~ con latte	~ con leche
Tomato juice	Tomatensaft	Jus de tomates	Succo di pomodoro	Jugo de tomate
Vegetable juice	Gemüsesaft	~ de légumes	~ di verdura	Jugo de legumbres
Water	Wasser	Eau	Acqua	Agua
Whole milk	Vollmilch	Lait entier	Latte intero	Leche sin desnatar
Yoghurt	Joghurt	Yaourt, yogourt	Yogurt, iogurt	Yogur

[101] or soft drinks.
[102] or white coffee.
[103] or decaffeinated coffee.
[104] coffee, hot milk, rolls and butter.

Breakfast	Frühstück	Petit déjeuner	Prima colazione	Desayuno
Bacon	Speck (geräucherter)	Bacon (lard fumé)	Bacon	Bacon, tocino ahumado
Bacon	Bacon	Bacon	Bacon	Bacon (tocino ahumado)
Biscuits, Am. cookies	Kekse	Gâteaux secs	Biscotti	Galletas, bizcochos
Boiled ham	Schinken (gekochter)	Jambon cuit	Prosciutto cotto	Jamón en dulce, ~ cocido
Smoked ham	~ geräucherter)	~ fumé	~ affumicato	~ ahumado, ~ serrano
Raw ham	~ (roher)	~ cru	~ crudo	~ natural, ~ crudo
Bread	Brot	Pain	Pane	Pan
Brown bread	Schwarzbrot	Pain noir	Pane nero	Pan moreno, pan bazo
Bun, brioche	Brioche	Brioche	Brioche	Brioche
Butter	Butter	Beurre	Burro	Mantequilla, manteca
Cappuccino	Cappuccino	Cappuccino	Cappuccino	Cappuccino
Cereals	Getreideflocken	Céréales	Fiocchi di cereali	Cereales
~ with cream	~ mit Sahne	~ à la crème	~ di cereali con panna	~ con nata
Cocoa	Kakao	Cacao	Cacao	Cacao
Coffee with milk	Milchkaffee	Café au lait, café crème	Caffelatte	Café con leche
Coffee	Kaffee	Café	Caffè	Café
Coffee without caf-feine[103]	~ (koffeinfreier)	~ décaféiné	~ decaffeinato	~ descafeinado
Continental breakfast[104]	~ komplett	~ complet	Caffelatte completo	~ completo
Coffee with milk[102]	~ mit Milch	~ au lait, ~ crème	Caffelatte	~ con leche
Coffee with cream[102]	~ mit Sahne	~ crème	Caffè con panna	~ con crema
Black coffee	~ (schwarzer)	~ noir, ~ nature	~ nero	~ solo, ~ negro
Cream	Sahne	Crème fraîche	Panna, crema	Nata, crema
Whipped cream, chan-tilly	~ (Schlagsahne)	~ fouettée, ~ chantilly	Panna montata	Nata batida
Crescent roll, croissant	Hörnchen	Croissant	Cornetto, croissant	Medialuna, croissant, cuerno
Crescent roll, croissant	Kipfel	Croissant	Cornetto, croissant	Cuerno, medialuna
Drip coffee	Filterkaffee	Café filtre	Caffè filtro	Café filtro
Eggs	Eier	Œufs	Uova (sing. uovo)	Huevos
~ cooked to order	~ nach Wunsch	~ au choix	Uova a piacere	Huevos a elección

105

Breakfast	Frühstück	Petit déjeuner	Prima colazione	Desayuno
Espresso	Espresso	Café express	Espresso	Café exprés
Fried eggs	Setzeier	Œufs sur le plat, œufs poêlés	Uova al tegame	Huevos al plato, huevos estrellados
Ham and eggs	~ mit Schinken	Œufs poêlés au jambon	Uova al prosciutto	Huevos con jamón
Bacon and eggs	~ mit Speck	Œufs poêlés au bacon	Uova al bacon	Huevos al plato con bacon
Fruit juice	Fruchtsaft	Jus de fruits	Succo di frutta	Zumo de fruta
Grapefruit juice	~ (Grapefruit-)	~ de grape-fruit	~ di pompelmo	~ de toronja
Orange juice	~ (Orangen-)	~ d'oranges	~ d'arancia	~ de naranja
Grape juice	~ (Trauben-)	~ de raisin	~ d'uva	~ de uva
Fruit juices	Fruchtsäfte	Jus de fruits	Succhi di frutta	Zumos de fruta
Ham	Schinken	Jambon	Prosciutto	Jamón
Grilled ham	~ (gegrillter)	~ grillé	~ alla griglia	~ a la parrilla
Hard-boiled eggs	Harte Eier	Œufs durs	Uova sode	Huevos duros
Honey	Honig	Miel	Miele	Miel
Hot chocolate	Schokolade	Chocolat	Cioccolata	Chocolate
Iced grapefruit	Grapefruit, eisgekühlt	Grape-fruit frappé	Pompelmo ghiacciato	Toronja helada
Jam, preserve	Konfitüre (Marmelade)	Confiture	Confettura, marmellata	Mermelada, confitura
Apricot jam	~ (Aprikosen-)	~ d'abricots	~ d'albicocche	~ de albaricoques
Strawberry jam	~ (Erdbeer-)	~ de fraises	~ di fragole	~ de fresas
Raspberry jam	~ (Himbeer-)	~ de framboises	~ di lamponi	~ de frambuesas
Redcurrant jam	~ (Johannisbeer-)	~ de groseilles	~ di ribes	~ de grosellas
Cherry jam	~ (Kirsch-)	~ de cerises	~ di ciliege	~ de cerezas
(Orange) marmalade	~ (Orangen-)	~ d'oranges	~ di arance	~ de naranjas
Peach jam	~ (Pfirsich-)	~ de pêches	~ di pesche	~ de melocotón
Plum jam	~ (Pflaumen-)	~ de prunes	~ di prugne	~ de ciruelas
Knäckebrot (Swedish wholemeal crackers)	Knäckebrot (schwedisches Schrotbrot)	Knäckebrot (galettes de farine non blutée)	Knäckebrot (gallette di farina integrale)	Knäckebrot (especie de pan integral sueco)
Lemon squash	Zitronensaft, frisch gepreßt	Citron pressé	Spremuta di limone	Zumo fresco de limón
Medium-boiled eggs	Weiche Eier (5–6 Min.)	Œufs mollets	Uova bazzotte	~ encerados, ~ blandos
Milk-roll	Milchbrötchen	Petit pain au lait	Panino al latte	Bollo de leche

Breakfast	Frühstück	Petit déjeuner	Prima colazione	Desayuno
Milk	Milch	Lait	Latte	Leche
Pasteurized milk	~ (pasteurisierte)	~ pasteurisé	~ pastorizzato	~ pasterizada
Omelet(te)	Omelett	Omelette	Omelette	Tortilla
Plain omelette	~ natur	~ nature	~ semplice	~ sencilla, ~ al natural
Ham omelette	~ mit Schinken	~ au jambon	~ con prosciutto	~ con jamón
Orange squash	Orangensaft, frisch gepreßt	Orange pressée	Spremuta d'arancia	Zumo fresco de naranja
Pastry	Backwerk	Pâtisserie, petit gâteau	Pasta	Pasta, Am. masita
Poached eggs	Verlorene Eier	Œufs pochés	Uova affogate	Huevos escalfados
Porridge (boiled oatmeal)	Porridge (Haferbrei)	Porridge	Porridge (farinata d'avena)	Porridge (copos de avena)
Roll, French roll	Semmel	Petit pain	Panino	Panecillo
Roll, French roll	Brötchen	Petit pain	Panino	Panecillo, mollete
Rye-bread	Roggenbrot	Pain de seigle	Pane di segale	Pan de centeno
Scrambled eggs	Rühreier	Œufs brouillés	Uova strapazzate	Huevos revueltos
Soft-boiled eggs	Weiche Eier (2–3 Min.)	Œufs à la coque	Uova alla coque	Huevos pasados por agua
Sugar	Zucker	Sucre	Zucchero	Azúcar
Tea	Tee	Thé	Tè	Té
Tea, rolls, jam and butter	~ komplett	~ complet	~ completo	~ completo
Tea with milk	~ mit Milch	~ au lait	~ con latte	~ con leche
Tea with rum	~ mit Rum	~ au rhum	~ con rum	~ con ron
Tea with lemon	~ mit Zitrone	~ au citron	~ con limone	~ con limón
Toast	Toast	Toast, rôtie	Fetta di pane tostato	Toast, tostada
Buttered toast	~ mit Butter	Toast beurré	~ di pane tostato con burro	~ con mantequilla
Tomato juice	Tomatensaft	Jus de tomates	Succo di pomodoro	Jugo de tomate
Vegetable juice	Gemüsesaft	~ de légumes	Succo di verdura	Jugo de legumbres
White bread, wheat bread	Weißbrot	Pain blanc	Pane bianco	Pan blanco
Wholemeal bread	Vollkornbrot	Pain complet	Pane integrale	Pan completo
Yoghurt	Joghurt	Yaourt, yogourt	Yogurt, iogurt	Yogur
Zwieback, biscuit rusks	Zwieback	Biscottes	Fette biscottate	Bizcochos tostados

[102]) or white coffee.　　　[103]) or decaffeinated coffee.　　　[104]) coffee, hot milk, rolls and butter.

according to amount	Menge, je nach	selon quantité	secondo quantità	según cantidad
according to size	Größe, je nach	selon grosseur (S.G.)	secondo grandezza (S.G.)	según tamaño
appetite	Appetit m	appétit m	appetito m	apetito m
aroma, flavouring	Aroma n	arôme m	aroma m	aroma m
aromatic	aromatisch	aromatique	aromatico	aromático
ashtray	Aschenbecher m	cendier m	portacenere, posacenere	cenicero m
aspic, jelly	Aspik m	aspic m, gelée f	gelatina f, aspic m	gelatina f, aspic m
assorted, mixed	gemischt	assorti, varié, mêlé	assortito, misto	mixto, variado, surtido
at choice, at pleasure	Wahl, nach	au choix	a scelta	a elección
at choice, at pleasure	Wunsch, nach	au choix	a piacere, a volontà	a elección
at once, immediately	sofort	tout de suite	subito	en seguida
at pleasure	Belieben, nach	à discrétion	a volontá	a voluntad [biente
at room temperature	temperiert	chambré	a temperatura ambiente	a la temperatura del am-
au gratin, gratinated	gratiniert	au gratin, gratiné	gratinato, al gratin	al gratén, gratinado
au gratin, gratinated	überbacken	au gratin, gratiné	gratinato, al gratin	al gratén, gratinado
bacon	Speck m	lard m	lardo m	lardo, tocino m
bad	schlecht	mauvais	cattivo	malo
bain-marie	Bainmarie n (Wasserbad)	bain-marie m	bagnomaria m	baño (de) maría
banquet	Bankett n	banquet m	banchetto m	banquete m
batter	Backteig m	pâte à frire	pastella f	pasta de buñuelos
bicarbonate of soda	Natron n	bicarbonate de soude m	bicarbonato di sodio m	bicarbonato de sosa
big, large	dick	gros (f. grosse)	grosso	grueso
bill, Am. check	Rechnung f	addition f; (Hotel-) note f	conto m	cuenta f
will you sign the bill, sir?	wollen Sie bitte die Rechnung signieren?	s'il vous plaît, voulez-vous signer l'addition?	per favore, vuole siglare il conto?	¿por favor, quiere Vd. firmar la cuenta?
we will charge this to your hotel account	wir werden es auf die Hotelrechnung setzen	on va le mettre sur la note de la chambre	lo mettiamo sul conto della camera	lo incluimos en la cuenta del hotel
bill of fare	Speisekarte f	carte (des mets) f	lista (delle vivande) f	lista de platos
bitter	bitter	amer (f. amère)	amaro	amargo
boiled	gesotten	bouilli	lessato, bollito	hervido, cocido
bone	Knochen m	os m	osso m	hueso m

bottle	Flasche f	bouteille f	bottiglia f	botella f
half-bottle (0,6 pints)	halbe Flasche	demi-bouteille	mezza bottiglia	media botella
bouquet (fragrance of wine)	Bouquet n (Bukett)	bouquet m	bouquet m	aroma m
braised	braisiert	braisé	brasato	braseado
braised	geschmort	braisé	brasato, stufato	estofado, braseado
bread-basket	Brotkorb m	corbeille à pain f	cestino del pane m	cestilla del pan f
breaded, crumbed	paniert	pané	impanato, panato	empanado
breadcrumbs	Semmelbrösel, Paniermehl	chapelure	pangrattato	pangrattato
(continental) breakfast	Frühstück n	petit déjeuner m	prima colazione f	desayuno m
brine, souse, pickle	Pökel m	saumure f	salamoia f	salmuera f, adobo m
brochette, skewer	Spießchen n	brochette f, attereau m	speidino m	broqueta, brocheta
bunch of herbs	Kräuterbündel	bouquet garni	mazzetto di odori	manojito de hierbas
burnt	verbrannt	brûlé	bruciato	quemado
butter	Butter f	beurre m	burro m	mantequilla, manteca f
cafeteria, self-service	Selfservice m	libre-service, self-service	self-service	selfservice, autoservicio
caramel (burnt sugar)	Karamel(zucker) m	caramel (sucre fondu)	caramello m	caramelo (azúcar tostado)
casserole, stewpan	Kasserolle f	casserole f, cocotte f	casseruola f	cacerola, cazuela f
casserole, stewpan	Schmortopf	casserole f, cocotte f	casseruola f	cazuela, cacerola f
cellar	Keller m	cave f	cantina f	bodega f
chafing-dish, hotplate	Tischrechaud (m und n)	réchaud, chauffe-plat	scaldapiatti m	calentador m
chair	Stuhl m	chaise f	sedia f	silla f
champagne-bucket	Sektkühler m	seau à champagne m	secchiello da champagne	cubo del champaña
(small) change, coppers	Kleingeld n	(petite) monnaie f	spiccioli m (pl)	dinero suelto, calderilla
chicken-frill, cutlet-frill	Kotelettmanschette f	papillote f, manchette f	papillote	papillote
choice	auserlesen	choisi	scelto	selecto
chopped, minced	gehackt	haché	tritato	picado
choux pastry	Brandteig	pâte à choux	pasta da bignè (o da chou)	pasta de lionesas
Christmas menu	Weihnachtsmenü	menu de Noël	menu di Natale	menú de Navidad
cigar	Zigarre f	cigare m	sigaro m	cigarro, puro m
cigarette	Zigarette f	cigarette f	sigaretta f	cigarrillo m
clean	rein (sauber)	propre	pulito	limpio

cloak-room	Garderobe f	vestiaire m	guardaroba m	guardarropa m
coated	überzogen	nappé, arrosé	cosparso	bañado, rociado
coffee pot	Kaffeekanne f	cafetière f	caffettiera f	cafetería f
coffee spoon	Kaffeelöffel m	cuiller à café f	cucchiaino m	cucharilla f
cold buffet	kaltes Buffet (od. Büfett)	buffet froid	buffet freddo	buffet, bufet(e) m
cold	kalt	froid	freddo	frío
cook	Koch m	cuisinier m	cuoco m	cocinero m
(female) cook	Köchin f	cuisinière f	cuoca f	cocinera f
cooked (boiled)	gekocht	cuit (gesotten: bouilli)	cotto (gesotten: bollito)	cocido, hervido
cooking	Kochen n	cuisson f	cottura f	cocción f
corkscrew	Korkenzieher m	tire-bouchon m	cavatappi m	sacacorchos, tirabuzón m
cork	Kork(en) m	bouchon m	turacciolo m, tappo m	corcho, tapón m
course	Gang m	service m, plat m	portata f	plato m
first course	~ (erster)	premier service	primo piatto	primero plato
second course	~ (zweiter)	deuxième service	secondo piatto	segundo plato
court-bouillon (fish-stock)	Fischsud m	court-bouillon m	court-bouillon	caldo corto
cover	Gedeck n	couvert m	coperto m	cubierto m
cream	Rahm m	crème f	panna f, crema f	nata, crema f
cream	Sahne f	crème fraîche	panna f, crema f	nata, crema f
creamed, in cream	in Sahne	à la crème	alla panna, alla crema	a la crema, con crema
crisp	knusperig	croquant, croustillant	croccante	crujiente
croquette (fried ball of minced food)	Krokette f	croquette f	crocchetta f	croqueta f
cruet-stand	Essig- und Öl-Ständer m	huilier m, ménagère f	oliera f	vinagreras f (pl.)
cruet-stand	Menage f	ménagère f, huilier m	oliera f	vinagreras f (pl)
cup	Tasse f	tasse f	tazza f	taza f
curried, in curry	Curry, mit	au curry	al curry	con curry, al curry
cutlery, table silver	Besteck n	couvert m	posate f (pl)	cubierto m
day's bill of fare	Tageskarte f	carte du jour f	lista del giorno f	carta del día
decanter	Karaffe f	carafe f	caraffa f	garrafa f
decanter	Wasserflasche f	carafe f	caraffa f	jarra f, garrafa f

deep-frozen, quick frozen	tiefgekühlt	surgelé	surgelato	congelado
dessert	Dessert n	dessert m	dessert m	postres m (pl.)
dessert	Nachtisch m	dessert m	dessert m	postres m (pl)
diet	Diät f	régime m	dieta f	dieta f, régimen m
digestion	Verdauung f	digestion f	digestione f	digestión f
dining-room	Speisesaal m	salle à manger f	sala da pranzo f	comedor m
dinner	Abendessen n	dîner m	pranzo m	cena f, comida f
dinner	Diner n	dîner m	pranzo (di gala)	comida f
candlelight dinner	~ bei Kerzenlicht	~ aux chandelles	~ a lume di candela	cena con velas
dip (sauce)	Dip m	dip, assaisonnement	salsa	salsa
dish, Am. platter	Platte f	plat m	piatto m	plato
dish	Speise f (Gericht)	mets m, plat m	piatto m, pietanza f	plato, guiso
cold dish	~ (kalte)	plat froid	piatto freddo	plato frío
hot dish	~ (warme)	plat chaud	piatto caldo	plato caliente
dish (prepared) to order	~ auf Bestellung	plat sur commande	piatto da farsi	plato a pedido
dish	Gericht n (Speise)	mets m, plat m	piatto m, pietanza f	plato, manjar m
suggested dishes	empfohlene Gerichte	plats recommandés	piatti consigliati	platos recomendados
ready dishes	fertige Gerichte	plats tout prêts	piatti pronti	platos listos
don't mention it	bitte (nach „danke")	pas de quoi; de rien	prego, di nulla	no hay de qué, de nada
double	doppelt	double	doppio	doble
dozen; half-dozen	Dutzend; halbes Dutzend	douzaine f; demi-douzaine	dozzina f; mezza dozzina	docena f; media docena
dry	trocken	sec (f. sèche)	secco	seco
Easter menu	Ostermenü	menu de Pâques	menu di Pasqua	menú de Pascua
edible	eßbar	comestible	commestibile	comestible
egg-cup	Eierbecher m	coquetier m	portauovo m	huevera f
egg-yolk, yolk of egg	Eigelb n	jaune d'œuf m	rosso d'uovo, tuorlo m	yema de huevo f
en papillote (in paper casing)	Papillote, en (in Papier-hülse)	en papillote	al cartoccio	en papillote (asado en un papel)
excellent, very good	ausgezeichnet	excellent	eccellente, ottimo	excelente
excuse me (sir)	entschuldigen Sie	excusez-moi	scusi	¡ perdone (señor) !
extra charge	Zuschlag m	supplément m	supplemento m	suplemento m

fat, shortening, grease	Fett n	graisse f	grasso m	grasa f
fat	fett	gras (f. grasse)	grasso	graso
finger-bowl, finger-glass	Fingerschale f	rince-doigts m	sciacquadita m	lavadedos m
fish-bone	Gräte f	arête f	lisca, spina f	espina f
fish dish	Fischgericht n	plat de poisson	piatto di pesce	plato de pescado
fish-kettle	Fischkessel	poissonnière f	pesciera, pesciaiola f	besuguera f
fish knife and fork	Fischbesteck n	couvert à poisson	posate da pesce	cubierto de pescado
fish specialities	Fischspezialitäten	spécialités de poisson	specialità di pesce	especialidades de pescado
fish steak [tea	Fischschnitte f	darne f	trancia di pesce f	rodaja de pescado
five o'clock tea, afternoon	Fünfuhrtee	five o'clock, goûter	tè delle cinque	té de las cinco
flambé, flambéed	flambiert	flambé	alla fiamma, flambé	flameado
fleurons (small puff pastry crescents)	Fleurons (Blätterteig-Halbmonde)	fleurons m liquide	sfogliatine (a forma di mezzaluna)	fleurons (hojaldre en forma de media luna)
flour	Mehl n	farine f	farina f	harina f
fork	Gabel f	fourchette f	forchetta f	tenedor m
french dressing	Vinaigrette	vinaigrette	vinaigrette	vinagreta
fresh	frisch	frais (f. fraîche)	fresco	fresco
fricassee	Frikassee m	fricassée, blanquette f	fricassea f	fricasé m
fried …	Fritüre f	friture f	frittura f	fritura f, frito m
… from the trolley	… vom Wagen serviert	… de la voiture	… dal carrello	… del carrito
fruit basket	Früchtekorb m	corbeille à fruits f	cestino da frutta m	cestilla de frutas
fruit-dish	Obstschale f	fruitier m	fruttiera f	frutero m
frying pan, Am. skillet	Pfanne f (Brat-)	poêle f (spr. poal)	padella f	sartén f
full	voll	plein	pieno	lleno (de)
garnish	Beilage f	garniture f	contorno m, guarnizione f	guarnición f
garnished	mit Beilage	garni	guarnito, con contorno	guarnecido
gelatin(e)	Gelatine f	gélatine f	gelatina	gelatina f
giant, jumbo	Riesen …	géant	gigante	gigante
glazed: iced, frosted	glaciert (glasiert)	glacé	glassato	glaseado

glass	Glas n	verre m	bicchiere m	vaso, (mit Fuß) copa
per glass	pro Glas	le verre	al bicchiere	por vaso
liqueur-glass	~ (Likör-)	~ à liqueur	bicchierino	copita (para licor)
tumbler, water-glass	~ (Wasser-)	~ à eau	bicchiere da acqua	vaso para agua
wine-glass	~ (Wein-)	~ à vin	bicchiere da vino	copa para vino
good	gut	bon (f. bonne)	buono	bueno
good morning, madam	guten Tag, Fräulein!	bonjour, mademoiselle!	buon giorno, signorina!	buenos días, señorita
good evening, madam	guten Abend, gnädige Frau!	bonsoir, madame!	buona sera, signora!	buenas tardes, señora
good night, sir	gute Nacht, mein Herr!	bonne nuit, monsieur!	buona notte, signore!	buenas noches, señor
gourmet, gastronome	Feinschmecker m	gourmet	buongustaio	gastrónomo m
grated	gerieben	râpé	grattugiato, grattato	rallado
gravy, brown gravy	Bratensauce f	jus m	sugo di carne m	jugo de carne m
grilled, broiled	Grill, vom	grillé	alla griglia, ai ferri	a la parrilla, emparrillado
grilled, broiled	gegrillt	grillé	alla griglia, ai ferri	a la parrilla
grilled, broiled	Rost, vom	grillé, au gril	alla griglia, ai ferri, in gratella	a la parrilla
guest, customer	Gast m (Kunde)	hôte, client m	ospite m, cliente m	huésped m, cliente m
half	halb	demi	mezzo	medio
hard	hart	dur	duro	duro
head-cook, chef	Küchenchef m	chef (de cuisine) m	capocuoco, chef	jefe de cocina, chef
chef's ...	... des Chefs [empfiehlt	... du chef	... dello chef	... del chef
our chef suggests	unser Küchenchef	le chef recommande	lo chef consiglia	el chef propone
head-waiter	Oberkellner m	maître (d'hôtel)	capocameriere m	jefe de comedor, primer
help yourself	bedienen Sie sich	servez-vous	si serva	sírvase Vd. [camarero
here is (here are)	hier ist (hier sind)	voici	ecco, ecco qui	he aquí
home-made	hausgemacht	maison	fatto in casa	hecho en casa
honey	Honig m	miel m	miele m	miel f
hot	heiß	chaud	molto caldo, caldissimo	caliente
hotplate, chafing-dish	Wärmeplatte f	réchaud, chauffe-plat m	scaldapiatti m	calentador m
hour	Stunde f	heure f	ora f	hora f

ice bucket, ice-pail	Eiskübel m	seau à glace m	secchiello da ghiaccio	cubo de hielo
ice	Eis n	glace f	ghiaccio m	hielo m
iced, frozen, chilled	eisgekühlt	glacé, frappé	ghiacciato, gelato	helado
icing, frosting	Glace (Zuckerglasur)	glace f	glassa, ghiaccia f	glasa f
indigestible	unverdaulich	indigeste	indigesto	indigesto, difícil de digerir
ingredients	Zutaten f	ingrédients m	ingredienti m	ingredientes m
jelly	Gelee n	gelée f, aspic m	gelatina f	gelatina
jellied, in jelly	in Gelee	à la gelée, en gelée	in gelatina	en gelatina
juice	Saft m	jus m	sugo m, succo m	jugo m, Fruchtsaft: zumo
juicy	saftig	juteux (f. juteuse)	sugoso, succoso	jugoso, suculento
kitchen	Küche f (Raum)	cuisine f	cucina f	cocina f
good plain cooking	~ (bürgerliche)	~ bourgeoise	~ casalinga	cocina casera
real French cuisine	~ (echte französische)	véritable cuisine française	~ francese genuina	~ francesa auténtica
international cuisine	~ (internationale)	cuisine internationale	~ internazionale	~ internacional
knife	Messer n	couteau m	coltello m	cuchillo
lard	Schmalz (Schweine-)	saindoux	strutto m	manteca de cerdo
larded	gespickt	piqué, lardé	lardellato	mechado, lardeado
layer	Schicht f	couche f	strato m	capa f
lean	mager	maigre	magro	magro
Lenten dish, meatless dish	Fastenkost f	plat maigre m	platto di magro m	piato de vigilia (o de viernes)
light	leicht	léger	leggero	ligero
litre (bottle of 1¾ pints)	Liter n	litre m	litro m	litro m
liquid	flüssig	liquide	liquido	liquido
lukewarm, tepid	lauwarm	tiède	tiepido	templado, tibio
lunch, luncheon	Mittagessen n	déjeuner m	colazione f, pranzo m	almuerzo m
excuse me, are you here for lunch?	werden Sie zum Mittagessen hier sein?	pardon, est-ce que vous serez ici pour le déjeuner?	scusi, sarà qui per la colazione?	¿estará Vd. aquí para el almuerzo?
maître	Maître	maître	maître m	jefe de comedor
main course, main dish	Hauptgericht n	plat principal m	piatto forte m	plato fuerte
margarine	Margarine f	margarine f	margarina f	margarina f

marinade, pickle	Beize f	marinade f	marinata	marinada f
marinade, pickle	Marinade f	marinade f	marinata f	marinada f
pickled, marinated	mariniert	mariné	marinato	marinado, en escabeche
match; light	Zündholz n	allumette f	fiammifero m	cerilla f, fósforo m
may I come in?	gestattet? (ist es…)	pardon, puis-je entrer?	è permesso?, si può?	¿se puede?, ¿permiso?
meal	Mahlzeit f	repas m	pasto m	comida f
à la carte meal	~ nach der Karte	repas à la carte	pasto alla carta	comida a la carta
fixed price meal	~ zu festem Preis	repas à prix fixe	pasto a prezzo fisso	comida a precio fijo
meat dish	Fleischgericht n	plat de viande	piatto di carne	plato de carne
menu	Menü n	menu m	menu, menù m	menú m, minuta f
milk-jug	Milchkännchen	pot à lait m	bricco del latte m	jarrita de leche
moment, instant	Augenblick m	instant m	momento m, istante m	momento m, instante m
wait a minute, please	warten Sie bitte einen Augenblick	voulez-vous attendre un instant?	vuole attendere un momento?	haga el favor de esperar un momento
mould	Form f (Backform)	moule m, forme f	stampo m, forma f	molde m
mustard-pot	Senftopf	moutardier	mostardiera	mostacera f
mustard	Senf m	moutarde f	senape, senapa, mostarda	mostaza f
napkin	Serviette	serviette f	tovagliolo m, salvietta f	servilleta f
napkin, serviette	Deckserviette f	napperon m	coprimacchie m	cubre mantel m
number	Nummer f	numéro m	numero m	número m
your room number, please, sir?	welches ist Ihre Zimmernummer, bitte?	pardon, quel est le numéro de votre chambre?	scusi, qual è il numero della sua camera?	por favor, cuál es el número de su habitación?
nutcrackers (pl)	Nußknacker m	casse-noix, casse-noisette	schiaccianoci m	cascanueces m
oatmeal	Hafermehl	farine d'avoine	farina d'avena	harina de avena
occupied, engaged	besetzt	occupé, pris	occupato	ocupado
of easy digestion	verdaulich (leicht)	de facile digestion	di facile digestione	de fácil digestión
oil; olive oil	Öl n; Olivenöl	huile f; huile d'olive	olio m; olio d'oliva	aceite m; aceite de oliva
on request	Wunsch, auf	sur demande	a richiesta	a petición
on the spit	Spieß, vom	à la broche	allo spiedo	al asador
order	Bestellung f	commande f	ordinazione f, commanda f	pedido m
on request	auf Bestellung	sur commande	su ordinazione	a pedido

our special …	Art des Hauses, nach	… maison	… della casa	… de la casa
out of season	Saison, außer	hors de saison	fuori stagione	fuera de la temporada
oven	Backofen	four m	forno m	horno m
oven	Rohr (Bratröhre)	four m	forno m	horno m
paper napkin	Papier-Serviette f	serviette en papier f	tovagliolo di carta m	servilleta de papel
paste, pastry, dough	Teig m	pâte f	pasta f	masa, pasta f
pat (or roll) of butter	Butterröllchen n	coquille de beurre	ricciolo di burro m	bolilla de mantequilla
patron, regular customer	Stammgast m	habitué, client régulier	cliente abituale m	habitual m
peel, rind	Schale (vom Obst)	pelure f, écorce f	buccia f, scorza f	cáscara, corteza f
pepper shaker	Pfefferstreuer m	poivrière f	pepaiola f	pimentero m
pepper-mill	Pfeffermühle f	moulin à poivre m	macinapepe, macinino	molinillo de pimienta
per person, per head	Person, pro	par personne, par tête	a persona, a testa	por persona
piece; each	Stück n; pro Stück	morceau m, pièce f; la pièce	pezzo m; al pezzo	pieza; la pieza
pinch, dash	Prise f	pincée f, prise f	presa f, pizzico m	pellizca
pitcher	Krug m	cruche f	brocca f	jarra f
plate	Teller m	assiette f	piatto m	plato m
please; if you please	bitte	s'il vous plaît	prego; per favore	por favor
portion, helping	Portion f	portion f	porzione f	porción f
half-portion	halbe Portion	demi-portion	mezza porzione	media porción
pot	Topf (Koch-) m	marmite f	pentola f	marmita, olla f, puchero m
price, charge	Preis m	prix m	prezzo m	precio m
at fixed price	zu festem Preis	à prix fixe	a prezzo fisso	a precio fijo
puff pastry, flaky pastry	Blätterteig m	pâte feuilletée	pasta sfoglia f	pasta de hojaldre
purée	Püree n	purée f	purè m, purea f, passato m	puré m
quarter bottle	Viertelliterflasche f	bouteille d'un quart	bottiglia da un quarto	botella de un cuarto
quarter of a chicken	Viertel Huhn	quart de poulet	quarto di pollo	cuarto de pollo
rare, underdone	englisch (halb durch)	saignant	al sangue	poco hecho
rare, underdone	halb durch (englisch)	saignant	al sangue	poco hecho
raw	roh	cru	crudo	crudo
recipe	Rezept n	recette f	ricetta f	receta f
refrigerator	Kühlschrank m	réfrigérateur, frigidaire	frigorifero m	refrigerador m, nevera f

regional dish, local dish	Lokalgericht	mets local, plat local	piatto tipico	plato típico, plato local
remainder, change	Rest m (von Geld)	reste m, restant m	resto m	vuelta f, resto m
reserved	reserviert	réservé	riservato, prenotato	reservado
restaurant	Gasthaus n	restaurant m	trattoria f	fonda f
baked	gebacken	au four	al forno	al horno
fried, deep-fried, french-fried	~ im Fett	frit	fritto	frito
pickled, marinated,	gebeizt	mariné	marinato	marinado, adobado
roast, roasted	gebraten	rôti	arrostito, arrosto	asado
sauté, sautéed, pan-fried	~ (in Butter)	sauté	fritto nel burro, saltato	salteado
baked	~ (im Bratofen)	(rôti) au four	al forno	al horno
grilled, broiled	~ (auf dem Rost)	grillé	alla griglia, ai ferri	a la parrilla, emparrillado
restaurant	Restaurant n	restaurant m	ristorante m	restaurante m
open-air restaurant	~ im Freien	~ en plein air	ristorante all'aperto	~ al aire libre
vegetarian restaurant	~ (vegetarisches)	restaurant végétarien	ristorante vegetariano	~ vegetariano
ripe; over-ripe	reif; überreif	mûr; trop mûr	maturo; troppo maturo	maduro; muy maduro
room service	Zimmerservice m	service à l'étage	servizio in camera m	servicio en habitación
roux (flour fried in fat)	Einbrenne f	roux	roux (farina rosolata nel burro)	salsa rubia (harina rehogada en manteca)
salad bowl	Salatschüssel f	saladier m	insalatiera f	ensaladera f
salmi (ragout of game-birds)	Salmi n (Wildragout)	salmis m	salmì m	salmorejo (guisado de caza)
salt-cellar, salt-sifter	Salzstreuer m	salière f	saliera f	salero m
salt, cured	gepökelt	salé, saumuré	salato	salado, salpreso
salt	Salz n	sel m	sale m	sal f
sauce-boat	Soßenschüssel f	saucière f	salsiera f	salsera f
sauce-boat	Sauciere f	saucière f	salsiera f	salsera f
saucer	Untertasse f	soucoupe f	piattino m	platillo m
sauté, sautéed, pan-fried	geröstet (in der Pfanne)	sauté	saltato	salteado, rehogado
sauté, sautéed, pan-fried	sautiert	sauté	saltato, rosolato	salteado

seasoning	Würze f	assaisonnement m	condimento m	condimento m
service, attendance	Bedienung f	service m	servizio m	servicio m
service charge included	~ inbegriffen	service compris	servizio compreso	~ incluído
service charge not included	~ nicht inbegriffen	service non compris	servizio non compreso	~ no incluído
service table, side table	Serviertisch m	guéridon, table de service	tavolino di servizio m	mesita de servicio
sharp, hot, piquant	pikant	piquant	piccante	picante
short pastry	Mürbeteig m	pâte brisée, pâte sablée	pasta frolla f	masa quebrada, pastaflora
side table, service table	Beistelltisch m	guéridon m, table de service	tavolino di servizio m	mesita de servicio f
sieve	Sieb (Mehl-)	tamis m	setaccio m	tamiz m
siphon(-bottle)	Siphon m	siphon m	sifone m	sifón m
slice	Scheibe f	tranche f	fetta, trancia f, trancio m	lonja, tajada, Brot: rebanada
slice	Schnitte f	tranche f	fetta, trancia f, trancio m	loncha, lonja, Brot: rebanada
small, little	klein	petit	piccolo	pequeño
smell, odour	Geruch m	odeur f	odore m	olor m
smoked	geräuchert	fumé	affumicato	ahumado
snack, afternoon tea	Jause f	goûter m, five o'clock	merenda f	merienda, café (de las cinco)
snack	Imbiß m	collation f (casse-croûte)	spuntino m	colación f, refrigerio m
soft	weich	mou (f. molle)	molle, tenero	blando
soigné, carefully prepared	soigniert (gepflegt)	soigné	soigné, curato	esmerado
some more …?	noch etwas …?	encore du …?	ancora un po' di …?	¿algo más de …?
soufflé	Auflauf m	soufflé m	soufflé m	soufflé m
soup-plate	Suppenteller m	assiette creuse	piatto fondo m	plato sopero m
sour, acid	sauer	aigre, acide, sur	acido	agrio
speciality, specialty	Spezialität f	spécialité f	specialità f	especialidad f
spoon	Löffel m	cuiller f, cuillère f	cucchiaio m	cuchara f
stew, ragout	Ragout n	ragoût m, sauté m	stufato m, spezzatino m	ragout, ragú, guisado
stewed, smothered	gedünstet	étuvé, en ragoût	stufato, in umido	estofado, guisado
strainer	Seiher m	passoire f	colino m, passino m	colador m
(drinking-) straw	Stroh-, Trinkhalm m	chalumeau m, paille f	cannuccia f	pajita f
stuffed	gefüllt	farci	ripieno, farcito	relleno
stuffing, dressing, farce	Füllung	farce f	ripieno m, farcia f	relleno m

stuffing, farce, dressing	Farce f	farce f	farcia f, ripieno m	relleno m
suet	Nierenfett, Talg	graisse de rognon	grasso di rognone	grasa de riñones
sugar-bowl, sugar-basin	Zuckerdose f	sucrier m	zuccheriera f	azucarero m [dillo
sugar-icing, frosting	Glasur f (Zuckerguß)	glace f	glassa, ghiaccia f	baño
sugar-tongs	Zuckerzange f	pinces à sucré	mollette per lo zucchero	tenacillas del azúcar f
sugar	Zucker m	sucre m	zucchero m	azúcar m
caster (or castor) sugar	~ (Grieß-)	~ semoule	~ Semolato	~ granulado
sugar-candy	~ (Kandis-)	~ candi	~ candito	~ cande, ~ candi
icing-sugar	~ (Puder-, Staub-)	~ glace	~ a velo	~ de flour
cane-sugar	~ (Rohr-)	~ de canne	~ di canna	~ de caña
vanilla-sugar	~ (Vanille-)	~ vanillé	~ vanigliato	~ de vainilla,
lump sugar, cube sugar	~ (Würfel-)	~ en morceaux	~ in quadretti	~ en terrones,
sugar-bowl, sugar-basin				~ de cortadillo
sugared	gezuckert	sucré	zuccherato	azucarado
sweet, sweet dish, dessert	Süßspeise f	entremets m	dolce m	dulce m
sweet	süß	doux (f. douce)	dolce	dulce
table-cloth	Tischtuch n	nappe f	tovaglia f	mantel m
table	Tisch m	table f	tavolo m, tavola f	mesa f
engaged table	~ (besetzter)	~ occupée	tavolo occupato	~ ocupada
corner table	~ in der Ecke	~ dans le coin	~ d'angolo	~ de rinconera
table by the window	~ am Fenster	~ près de la fenêtre	~ vicino alla finestra	~ cerca de la ventana
free table	~ (freier)	~ libre	~ libero	~ libre
table for . . . people	~ für ... Personen	~ pour ... couverts	~ per ... persone	~ para ... personas
reserved table	~ (reservierter)	~ réservée	~ riservato	~ reservada
will this table be to your satisfaction, sir?	ist Ihnen dieser Tisch recht?	cette table-là va bien?	va bene questo tavolo?	¿le agrada esta mesa?
sit down at this table, please	bitte, wollen Sie hier Platz nehmen	veuillez-vous asseoir à cette table	prego, s'accomodi a questo tavolo	haga el favor de sentarse a esta mesa
taste, flavour	Geschmack m	goût m, saveur f	gusto m, sapore m	sabor m, gusto m
tasteless, flat, insipid	geschmacklos	fade, sans goût	insipido	insípido

tasty, savoury	schmackhaft	savoureux (f. savoureuse)	saporito, gustoso	sabroso
tea-pot	Teekanne f	théière f	teiera f	tetera f
tea-spoon	Teelöffel m	cuiller à thé f	cucchiaino m	cucharilla f
telephone	Telefon n	téléphone m	telefono m	
tender, soft	zart	tendre	tenero	tierno
thank you (very much)!	danke (bestens)!	merci (beaucoup)!	grazie (tante)!	(muchas) gracias
thick	dickflüssig	épais (f. épaisse)	denso	denso, espeso
thin	dünn	mince	sottile	delgado
tin-opener, can-opener	Dosenöffner m	ouvre-boîtes m	apriscatole m	abrelatas m
tinned, Am. canned	Dosen-…	en boîte	in scatola	en lata, en conserva
tip, gratuity	Trinkgeld n	pourboire m [la bière?	mancia f	propina f
tip included	~ inbegriffen	pourboire compris	mancia inclusa	servicio incluido
to add	hinzufügen	ajouter	aggiungere	añadir
to bake	backen (im Ofen)	cuire au four	cuocere in forno	cocer al horno
to be enough	genügen	suffire	bastare	bastar
is it enough?	genügt es so?	c'est bien tout?	basta cosí?	¿es bastante?
to be mistaken	irren, sich	se tromper	sbagliare	equivocarse
excuse me, I made a mistake	Entschuldigung bitte, ich habe mich geirrt	excusez-moi je me suis trompé	scusi, ho sbagliato	discúlpeme Vd. que me haya equivocado
to beat, to whip; beaten	schlagen; geschlagen	fouetter; fouetté	sbattere; sbattuto	batir; batido
to blanch [whipped	blanchieren	blanchir	scottare	blanquear
to bone	ausbeinen	désosser	disossare	deshuesar, desosar
to book, to reserve	reservieren	réserver, retenir	risérvare, prenotare	reservar
do you want to book a table?	wollen Sie einen Tisch reservieren?	voulez-vous réserver une table?	vuole riservare un tavolo?	¿quiere Vd. reservar una mesa?
I am sorry but they are already all reserved	es tut mir leid, es sind schon alle reserviert	je suis désolé mais elles sont déjà toutes réservées	mi dispiace, ma sono già tutti riservati	siento decirle que están todas reservadas
to breakfast	frühstücken	déjeuner	far colazione	desayunar (se)
to bring	bringen	apporter	portare	traer

to brown slightly	anbraten	faire revenir	soffriggere	sofreír, rehogar
to call	rufen	appeler	chiamare	llamar
excuse me, did you call?	haben Sie gerufen?	pardon, avez-vous appelé?	scusi, ha chiamato?	¿disculpe Vd., ha llamado?
to carve	tranchieren	découper	trinciare	trinchar
to carve	zerlegen	découper	trinciare	trinchar
to chill, to cool	abkühlen	refroidir	raffreddare	enfriar
to choose, to select	wählen	choisir	scegliere	escoger, elegir
to clear (away)	abräumen	desservir	sparecchiare	quitar la mesa
to cook	kochen	cuire	cuocere	cocer, guisar, hervir
to cover	zudecken	couvrir	coprire	cubrir
to cut	schneiden	couper	tagliare	cortar
to displease	bedauern	regretter	dispiacere	sentir, desagradar
I am afraid there is no more left	ich bedaure, das haben wir nicht mehr	je regrette, monsieur, il n'y en a plus	mi dispiace, ma non ne abbiamo più	siento decirle que este plato se ha acabado
sorry, it is not on the menu today	ich bedaure, das haben wir heute nicht	je regrette, mais ce n'est pas sur la carte	mi dispiace, ma questo non si serve oggi	lo siento pero hoy no servimos eso
to dress (the salad)	anmachen (den Salat)	assaisonner (la salade)	condire (l'insalata)	aderezar la ensalada
to drink	trinken	boire	bere	beber
anything to drink, sir?	etwas zu trinken?	quelque chose à boire?	qualcosa da bere?	¿algo de beber?
will you drink wine or beer, sir?	was wünschen Sie zu trinken, Wein oder Bier?	que désirez-vous boire, monsieur, du vin ou de la bière	cosa desidera bere, vino o birra?	¿toma Vd. vino o cerveza?
to eat	essen	manger	mangiare	comer
to abstain from meat	kein Fleisch essen	faire maigre	mangiare di magro	comer de vigilia
to fill (up)	füllen	remplir	riempire	rellenar
to flour	Mehl, bestreuen mit	enfariner	infarinare	enharinar
to fry (in deep fat)	fritieren	frire	friggere	freír
to fry (in deep fat)	backen (im Fett)	frire	friggere	freír
to garnish; garnished	garnieren; garniert	garnir; garni	guarnire; guarnito	guarnecer; guarnecido
to grill, to broil	grillen (grillieren)	griller	grigliare	emparrillar
to grind; ground	mahlen; gemahlen	moudre; moulu	macinare; macinato	moler; molido

121

Culinary and service terms

to have dinner, to dine	speisen [speist	dîner	pranzare	comer, cenar
dinner is served at ...	es wird um ... Uhr ge-	on dîne à ... heures	si pranza alle ...	se come a las ...
to lay the table, to lay up	decken (den Tisch)	mettre le couvert, dresser la table	apparecchiare la tavola	poner la mesa
to melt; melted	zerlassen; zerlassen	fondre; fondu	fondere; fuso	derretir, fundir; derretido, fundido
to melt	schmelzen	fondre	fondere	derretir, fundir
to mix, to blend	mischen	mélanger, mêler	mescolare	mezclar
to open	öffnen	ouvrir	aprire	abrir
to order	bestellen	commander	ordinare	pedir, ordenar
are you being attended, sir?	haben Sie schon bestellt?	monsieur a-t-il commandé?	il signore ha già ordinato?	¿ya ha ordenado Vd.?
to peel	schälen	éplucher	sbucciare	pelar, mondar
to pepper	pfeffern	poivrer	pepare [per il pepe	sazonar con pimienta
to poach	pochieren	pocher	sobbollire, bollire	hervir, cocer
to pour out	einschenken	verser	versar da bere	echar de beber
to prefer	vorziehen	préférer	preferire	preferir
to prepare	zubereiten	préparer	preparare, preparato al tavolo (del cliente)	preparar
prepared at guest table	am Tisch zubereiten	préparé à la table		preparado en la mesa del cliente
to put, to lay	legen	mettre	mettere	poner, meter
to recommend, to suggest	empfehlen	recommander	consigliare	recomendar
may I suggest the ...	ich möchte Ihnen ... empfehlen	je vais vous recommander le...	le consiglierei il ...	quisiera recomendar a Vd. el ...
to reduce	einkochen (eindicken)	réduire	ridurre, condensare	reducir
to roast; roast, joint	braten; Braten m	rôtir; rôti m	arrostire; arrosto m	asar; asado
to salt; salted	salzen; gesalzen	saler; salé	salare; salato	salar; salado
to season, to spice	würzen	assaisonner	condire, aromatizzare	sazonar, condimentar
to serve	auftragen	servir	servire	servir
to serve	bedienen	servir	servire	servir

to serve	servieren	servir	servire	servir
all grill orders are served with potatoes	alle Grilladen werden mit Kartoffeln serviert	toutes nos grillades sont garnies aux pommes	le carni alla griglia sono guarnite con patate	las carnes a la parrilla se sirven con patatas
to shape, to turn	tournieren	tourner	dar forma	tornear
to show	zeigen	montrer	mostrare	mostrar
to sift, to sieve	sieben	tamiser	passare al setaccio	tamizar
to spread	bestreichen	tartiner	spalmare	untar
to sprinkle, to dredge	bestreuen	saupoudrer	cospargere	espolvorear
to squeeze	pressen (auspressen)	presser	spremere	exprimir
to stew, to braise	dünsten	étuver	stufare	estofar
to stuff, to farce	farcieren	farcir	farcire	rellenar
to substitute, to replace	ersetzen	remplacer	sostituire	sustituir
to sugar; sugared	zuckern; gezuckert	sucrer; sucre	zuccherare; zuccherato	azucarar; azucarado
to taste	kosten, versuchen	goûter, (Wein) déguster	assaggiare	probar, gustar
to taste	schmecken (kosten)	goûter	assaggiare	gustar
is this soup to your liking, sir?	wie schmeckt Ihnen diese Suppe?	comment trouvez-vous cette soupe?	Le piace questa minestra?	¿le gusta esta sopa?
to the right	rechts	à droite	a destra	a la derecha
to thicken, to bind	legieren (binden)	lier	legare	ligar
to thin out	verdünnen	allonger	allungare	diluir
to turn sour	sauer werden	tourner à l'aigre	diventar acido, inacidire	agriarse, Milch: cuajarse
to uncork	entkorken	déboucher	stappare, sturare	destapar, descorchar
to unmould, to turn out	stürzen (aus der Form)	démouler	sformare	desmoldar
to warm up, to reheat	aufwärmen	réchauffer	riscaldare	recalentar
to write	schreiben	écrire	scrivere	escribir
write it down, please	schreiben Sie es mir bitte auf	écrivez-le moi, s'il vous plaît	me lo scriva, per favore	haga el favor de escribir-melo
today's special (ity)	Tagesgericht n	plat du jour m	piatto del giorno m	plato del día
toilet, lavatory, restroom	Toilette f	lavabo m, toilette f	toilette f, gabinetto m	retrete m, lavabo
tomato paste	Tomatenmark n	concentré de tomates	conserva di pomodoro	conserva de tomate f

tray	Tablett n	plateau m	vassoio m	bandeja f
where shall I put the tray?	wo darf ich das Tablett hinstellen?	où dois-je mettre le plateau?	dove devo mettere il vassoio?	¿donde puedo poner la bandeja?
may I take the tray away?	darf ich das Tablett abservieren?	puis-je enlever le plateau?	posso togliere il vassoio?	¿puedo quitar la bandeja?
too, too much	zu viel (zu sehr)	trop	troppo	demasiado
toothpick	Zahnstocher m	cure-dent (pl. cure-dents)	stuzzicadenti m	palillo, mondadientes m
tough	zäh (hart)	coriace	duro, tiglioso	duro
to wish, to desire	wünschen	désirer [sieur?	desiderare	desear
what would you like, sir?	was wünschen Sie?	que désirez-vous, mondésirez-vous autre chose?	che cosa desidera?	¿qué desea Vd.?
do you want anything else?	wünschen Sie noch etwas?		desidera altro?	¿qué más desea Vd.?
do you wish some more?	wünschen Sie noch ein wenig?	en désirez-vous encore un peu?	ne desidera ancora un poco?	¿toma Vd. algo más de ...?
what would you like for dessert, sir?	was wünschen Sie zum Nachtisch?	que désirez-vous comme dessert?	che cosa desidera per dessert?	¿qué quiere Vd. de postre?
what do you wish instead of ...?	was wünschen Sie anstatt...?	que désirez-vous à la place de ...?	che cosa desidera avere al posto di ...?	¿qué quiere Vd. en lugar de ...?
(just) as you like	wie Sie wünschen	comme vous voulez	come Lei desidera	como Vd. quiera, Vd. manda
trolley, rolling cart, wagon	Wagen m	voiture f	carrello m	carrito de servicio m
truffled	getrüffelt	truffé	tartufato, con tartufi	trufado
(soup-)tureen	Suppenschüssel f	soupière f	zuppiera f	sopera f
vegetable fat	Pflanzenfett n	graisse végétale f	grasso vegetale m	grasa vegetal f
vegetarian	vegetarisch	végétarien	vegetariano	vegetariano
vinegar	Essig m	vinaigre m	aceto m	vinagre m
vintage date	Weinjahr n	millésime m, année f	annata f	año
waiter	Kellner m	garçon m	cameriere m	camarero, Am. auch mozo
waiting time ... minutes	Zubereitungszeit: ... Minuten	... minutes d'attente	... minuti d'attesa	... minutos de esperea
waitress	Kellnerin f	serveuse f	cameriera f	camarera (¡señorita!)

124

warm	warm	chaud	caldo	caliente
to put in warm	~ stellen	mettre au chaud	mettere in caldo	calentar
well done	gut durchgebraten	bien cuit	ben cotto	bien hecho
white of egg	Eiweiß n	blanc d'œuf m	chiara d'uovo f, albume m	clara de huevo f
whole, entire	ganz (ungeteilt)	entier, tout	intero, tutto	entero
wine-bucket	Weinkühler m	seau à champagne m	secchiello da champagne	cubo del champaña m

Alsacienne (à l'):	dish garnished with sauerkraut.
Amphitryon:	a munificent host.
Anglaise (à l'):	vegetables cooked in salt water; fish coated in egg-and-breadcrumb and then sautéd or deep-fried.
Argenteuil:	dish garnished with asparagus. (Town, northwest of Paris, renowned for its asparagus fields.)
Bacchus:	Roman god of wine.
béarnaise (à la):	dish served with sauce béarnaise. (From Béarn, a former French province.)
Béchamel (Louis de):	Marquis de Béchamel, steward of Louis XIV. He is supposed to have invented the béchamel sauce.
Beignet:	from the Celtic bigne (tumour, swelling).
Bellevue, en:	dish of fish or poultry in jelly, richly garnished.
Bercy:	suburb of Paris.
Bernhardt (Sarah):	celebrated French actress (1844−1923).
Bigarade:	bitter kind of orange.
Bismarck (Otto):	Fürst von Bismarck, first chancellor of The German Empire (1815−1898).
Bourguignonne (à la):	dish cooked in red wine, usually garnished with small onions and button mushrooms.
Bretonne (à la):	dish garnished with white beans, whole or mashed.
Brillat-Savarin (Anthelme):	French lawyer, politician, and writer, author of the celebrated work *Physiologie du goût* (1755−1826).
Brunoise:	vegetables cut into small cubes.
Canapés:	small (toasted) slices of bread topped with a savoury
Cantaloup:	a variety of melon. The name derives from Cantalupo, near Rome.
Cardinal:	dish of marine fish garnished with lobster.

Carême (Marie-Antoine):	famous French chef, author of many works on gastronomy (Le Maître d'hôtel français, Le cruisinieur parisien, etc.); 1784–1833.
Chantilly (à la):	dish with sweetened or flavoured whipped cream. (From Chantilly, near Paris, celebrated for its château and racecourse.)
Chateaubriand (François-René):	French diplomat and author, born in Saint-Malo (1768–1848).
Chaud-froid:	dish of cold cooked meat, poultry, fish or game served in jelly.
Civet:	hare or game stew cooked with red wine and the animal's blood.
Clamart:	dish garnished with peas. (A southwest suburb of Paris.)
Colbert (Jean-Baptiste):	French statesman, minister of finance to King Louis XIV (1619–1683).
Conti:	dish with mashed lentils. (Princes de Conti, a junior branch of the House of Condé.)
Cordon bleu:	the 'blue ribbon' worn by the Knights-grand-cross of the Holy Ghost. Applied by extension to a first-class cook.
Court-bouillon:	stock flavoured with wine (or vinegar) and spices, used in fish dishes.
Crapaudine, en:	pigeon or chicken shaped like a toad and grilled. From the French crapaud (toad).
Crécy:	dish garnished with carrots (Crécy-en-Ponthieu, town in the French Somme department).
Curry:	hot Indian mixture of ground spices containing turmeric, cardamom, coriander, ginger, cumin, etc. Also a dish flavoured with this.
Diana:	Roman goddess of hunting, the Greek Artemis.
Du Barry:	dish garnished with cauliflower. (Comtesse du Barry, mistress of the French king Louis XV, condemned by the Revolutionary Tribunal of Paris and guillotined; 1743–1793.)
Dubois (Urbain François):	French cook, author of several books on the culinary art (1818–1901).
Dugléré (Adolphe):	celebrated French chef of the Café Anglais in Paris (1805–1884).

Duxelles:	sautéd chopped mushrooms used as a stuffing or a garnish.
Entrée:	dish served before the joint.
Entremets:	sweet dish.
Esau:	in the Old Testament, son of Isaac and Rebekah. He sold his birthright to his brother Jacob for a lentil dish.
Escoffier (Auguste):	French chef, known as 'the king of chefs and the chef of kings, author of the famous *Le guide culinaire*, translated into all languages (1847–1935).
Flamande (à la):	dish garnished with cabbage. (From Flanders, an ancient countship.)
Fleurons:	puffs of pastry-work for use as a garnish.
Florentine (à la):	dish garnished with spinach.
Forestière (à la):	dish with wild mushrooms, chiefly chanterelles and morels.
Gastronomy:	the art and science of good eating and drinking, including the preparation and service of food.
Gourmet:	a connoisseur of fine wine and food.
Grimod de la Reynière:	French gourmet, author of the *Almanach des gourmands* (1758–1837).
Helder:	Dutch port, naval battle between an Anglo-French and a Dutch fleet in 1673.
Holstein:	1) Freidrich Holstein, German diplomat; 1837–1909. 2) German region, now part of Schleswig-Holstein.
Hongroise (à la):	dish flavoured with paprika.
Indienne (à l'):	dish flavoured with curry and usually served with rice.
Jardinière (à la):	dish garnished with various vegetables.
Joinville:	François d'Orléans, Prince de Joinville, third son of Louis-Philippe, king of the French (1818–1900).

Judic (à la):	dish garnished with braised lettuce. (Anna Judic, French comedienne; 1850–1911.)
Julienne, en:	vegetables (or truffles and other foodstuffs) cut into thin strips.
Lady Curzon:	wife of Lord Curzon, Great Britain's viceroy of India (1859–1925).
Londonderry:	Charles William Vane, Marquis of Londonderry, English statesman (1778–1854).
Lucullus:	Roman general, famous for the luxury of his banquets (106–57 BC).
Lyonnaise (à la):	dish with sautéd onions. (From Lyon, capital of the French Rhône department.)
Macaire (Robert):	character in the play L'Auberge des Adrets, made popular by the French actor Frédérick Lemaître (1800–1876).
Macédoine:	mixture of fruit or vegetables cut up small. (From Macedonia, multiracial area of the Balkan Peninsula.)
Maintenon:	Françoise d'Aubigné, Marquise de Maintenon, secretly married to Louis XIV of France (1635–1719).
Malossol:	delicate, slightly salted caviar. From the Russian malosolny (slightly salted).
Maltaise (à la):	dish containing blood oranges.
Marengo:	village in northern Italy, where Napoleon Bonaparte defeated the Austrians (June 14, 1800).
Maryland:	Middle Atlantic state of the US.
Masséna (André):	duc de Rivoli, prince d'Essling, a leading French general (1758–1817).
Melba:	Dame Nellie Melba, stage name of Helen Armstrong Mitchell, Australian operatic soprano, born near Melbourne (1861–1931).
Meyerbeer (Giacomo):	German opera composer, born in Berlin (1791–1864).
Mirabeau (Honoré-Gabriel):	French politician, one of the greatest orators of the National Assembly (1749–1791).
Mireille:	opera by Charles Gounod, based on the Provençal poem by Mistral.

Mirepoix:	mixture of sautéd chopped carrots, onions, celery, and bacon, used in sauces etc. (Duc de Mirepoix, Marshal of France; 1699–1757.)
Montmorency:	dish containing cherries. (1 – Town in the French Seine-et-Oise department, renowned for its cherries. 2 – Distinguished French family.)
Mornay:	dish covered with Mornay sauce (a cheese-flavoured white sauce) and gratinated.
Mulligatawny:	East Indian soup highly seasoned with curry. From Tamil milagu-tannir (pepper-water)
Nantua (à la):	dish garnished with crayfish. (Town in the French Ain department.)
Natives:	top-quality oysters reared in British waters.
Navarin:	French stew of mutton and vegetables. From Navarino, a Greek port, where the Anglo-French defeated the Turco-Egyptian fleet in 1827.
Nesselrode:	dish with mashed chestnuts. (Comte von Nesselrode, Russian diplomat; 1780–1862.)
Newburgh:	city, southeastern New York, US on the Hudson River.
Niçoise (à la):	dish with tomatoes, garlic, olives, and anchovies. (From Nice, a French town on the Mediterranean coast.)
Normande (à la):	dish with cream, cider, calvados, apples, etc. (From Normandy, a former province of northern France.)
Orlov:	noble Russian family.
Paillard:	well-known restaurant in Paris.
Parmentier:	dish with potatoes. (Antoine Augustin Parmentier, French agronomist, developed the growing of potatoes in France; 1737–1831.)
Périgourdine (à la):	dish served with a truffle sauce. (From Périgord, a district in the southwest of France, well-known for its truffloo.)
Piémontaise (à la):	dish garnished with risotto. (From Piemonte, name of a region in northern Italy.)

Polonaise (à la):	boiled vegetables coated with fried breadcrumbs.
Pont Neuf:	second-oldest bridge across the Seine River in Paris.
Portugaise (à la):	dish containing tomatoes.
Printanière (à la):	dish garnished with mixed vegetables.
Provençale (à la):	dish with olive oil, tomato and garlic. (From Provence, a former province in the southeast of France.)
Rachel (Elisa):	French tragedienne (1820–1858).
Ravigote:	from the verb ravigoter (to strengthen).
Richelieu:	Louis-François-Armand, duc de Richelieu, Marshal of France and grand-nephew of cardinal de Richelieu; 1696–1788.
Rossini:	dish garnished with truffles, foie gras and Madeira sauce. (Italian operatic composer and gourmet, celebrated for his comic operas; 1792–1868.)
Rothschild:	name of a famous European banking dynasty, founded by Mayer Anselm Rothschild, born in Frankfurt am Main in 1743.
Saint-Germain:	dish with mashed peas.
Saint-Honoré:	Parisian gateau, named after the baker's patron saint.
Saint-Hubert:	dish consisting of game. (Name of the hunter's patron saint.)
Sandwich:	named after John Montagu, Earl of Sandwich, said to have eaten sandwiches when he once spent 24 hours at the gaming-table. (1718–1792).
Savoury:	savoury dish served at the beginning or end of dinner.
Sévigné:	Marie de Rabutin-Chantal, Marquise de Sévigné, famous for her letters to her daughter Mme de Grignan (1626–1696).
Soubise (à la):	dish with mashed onions. (Charles de Rohan, prince de Soubise, Marshal of France; 1715–1787.)

Strasbourgeoise (à la):	dish garnished with sauerkraut and goose liver.
Stroganov:	a wealthy Russian merchant family.
Tabasco:	very pungent sauce made from hot red peppers. (Tabasco, name of a river and state of Mexico.)
Thermidor:	the eleventh month of the French revolutionary calendar (from July 19 to August 17). From Greek thermos (heat) and doron (gift).
Turbigo:	town of Lombardy in Italy where the French defeated the Austrians in 1800 and 1859.
Vichy (à la):	dish garnished with carrots. (Spa is the department of Allier in France.)
Villeroi (à la):	dish coated with sauce Villeroi, then breaded and deep-fried. (François de Neufville, duc de Villeroi, Marshal of France 1644–1730.)
Waldorf(-Astoria):	name of a prestigious hotel in New York, built in 1931.

Flambé cookery

Nowadays a good chef is supposed to be able to prepare dishes on the chafing-dish. Therefore, there is an increased demand for such recipes.

Classic cookery books do not usually contain any recipes of this kind. Only maîtres and their assistants are expert in the field, and so we have asked them to contribute some recipes to the book. The following dishes have been chosen because they can be prepared easily and quickly. In this culinary art there of course no limits to one's creativity and imagination.

Useful hints

Spirits to be used for flambé dishes must have a high alcoholic content. Should the spirit contain too little alcohol, pure alcohol or a stronger spirit must be added. Some maîtres concoct their own special mixtures.

If you hold the pan in a slanting position and accompany the flame with the spoon filled with spirit, it will flare up more easily.

Sweets should be surrounded by lumps of sugar, which absorb the alcohol and function as wicks to feed the flames.

It is a good idea to sprinkle castor sugar – from as high as possible – over crêpes or omelettes while they flambé. The sugar will burn with a slight crackle.

If you do not have much time at your disposal, prepare only desserts. They are served at the end of the meal thus allowing you to work without time pressure.

For the 'mise en place':

salt, pepper, paprika
icing, castor and lump sugar
spirits
tomato ketchup, Worcester sauce and other sauces
peeled tomatoes
cream
lemons and oranges
a small lemon-squeezer

Other ingredients, such as mustard, curry, etc. according to the dishes to be prepared.

Fish

BASS VESUVIUS

Clean the fish, remove the bones and grill (prepared in the kitchen).
To make the sauce put some knobs of butter in the chafing-dish pan,
add some Worcester sauce, fennel seeds and lemon juice.

Put the grilled fish in the sauce, pour cognac over it and ignite. Serve
as soon as the flame dies down.

TROUT IN CHABLIS*

Place some butter in the pan and the lightly floured fish fillets.

When the fillets are browned, remove them, and add cubes of
tomatoes, basil leaves, salt and pepper to the sauce.

Let the sauce boil, lay the fillets in it again and pour Chablis over
them.

TROUT FOUR SEASONS

Finely chop half a bayleaf, a little parsley, some garlic and onion, one
celery leaf and the green of a fennel bulb. Add nutmeg and pepper.
Bring a brown or lake-trout to the boil in the appropriate amount of
water. Remove the fish before it is completely cooked, put it on a
covered plate.

Melt some butter in an (oval) pan, add a little cream and the chopped
herbs, stirring all the time. Salt to taste.

Now lay the trout in the sauce, cover the pan and simmer gently.

When it is done, put the fish on a hot dish, pour the sauce over it and
serve with green peas and boiled potatoes.

SPINY LOBSTERS BELLE EPOQUE

Chop finely one shallot and some parsley, put them into the pan and
add butter and oil. As soon as they are browned, add tomato sauce and
a glass of dry white wine. Stir well.

Remove the tails from small lobsters (150–200 g) and put them into
the pan. Add salt and pepper, turn the heat up and simmer, stirring all
the time.

When they are cooked, add brandy and ignite. Serve at once
sprinkled with chopped parsley or chervil.

DEVILLED SCAMPI

Melt some butter in the pan and add a finely chopped onion.

As soon as it begins to brown, add previously boiled and halved
scampi. Sprinkle with salt, pepper and curry. Let them brown slightly.

Pour brandy into the pan, and set light to it.

Serve with quarters of lemon and fresh parsley.

* Fillets of sole may be similarly prepared. Add lemon juice instead of tomato.

MEAT

CALF'S KIDNEYS NAPOLEON

Melt butter in the pan, turn the heat up high and fry the thickly sliced kidneys. Add cognac and ignite. When the flame dies down, put the kidneys on a dish and keep them warm.

Add a spoonful of finely chopped, browned onion, broth and a dash of Worcester sauce to the sauce in the pan, bring it to the boil, then add a little cream.

Leave the sauce on the heat until it is thick then pour it over the kidneys.

CALF'S LIVER AMBASSADOR

Melt butter in the pan and add the thinly sliced liver. Brown it, turning the heat up.

When it is nearly done, pour cognac over it and ignite. Remove the liver and keep it warm on a dish.

Add broth and finely chopped onion to the gravy, boil it up, then stir in a spoonful of sour cream.

Pour the sauce over the liver.

FILLET OF VEAL BELLE POMPADOUR

Melt butter in the pan, put the fillet slices in and brown over a high flame. When they are browned on both sides, pour in a generous amount of cognac and ignite. Remove the meat and keep it warm.

Add broth, let it boil, then add a spoonful of cream, stirring lightly, so that it thickens.

Just before serving, add a pinch of curry and then pour the sauce onto the slices of fillet.

FILLET STEAK VORONOV

Brown a knob of butter in the pan and lay the fairly thickly cut fillet steaks in it. Remove when they are browned and keep warm on a dish.

Add a few teaspoonfuls of mustard (of different kinds if available) and cook for 2 or 3 minutes.

Put the steaks back into the pan, letting them absorb the sauce. Pour a liberal amount of brandy into the pan and serve.

FILLET STEAK SPLENDID

Heat some butter and a tablespoon of olive oil in a covered stewpan. Place the salted and lightly floured fillet steak in it. When it is browned, put it to one side.

Now prepare the sauce with the following ingredients: ½ glass of dry white wine; bayleaf, sage and rosemary; Worcester sauce; nutmeg and pepper.

Pour the wine into the saucepan, then add all the other ingredients, stirring well. When the sauce begins to thicken, add cream and some black olives.

Put the fillet steak back into the pan, cover and let it simmer. Finally check the seasoning and add salt if necessary.

Serve the steak on a slice of fried bread, coat with the sauce and garnish with the olives.

BEEF FILLET EN BOÎTE

Heat the stewpan and melt a knob of butter and a little oil. Do not put the fillet into the pan before it is really hot to prevent the juice of the meat from seeping.

Meanwhile in another pan prepare a mustard sauce using French mustard, a little Worcester sauce, nutmeg, salt, pepper, and a few drops of oil.

When the fillet is almost done add the sauce, turn the meat, prick it with a fork to allow the sauce to penetrate into the centre. Finally add cognac.

Serve directly from the stewpan, holding it close to the guest to enable him to enjoy the appetizing aroma.

Béarnaise sauce (or mustard) can be served with this dish, separately.

MEDALLION OF VEAL DOMINIC

Put butter, rosemary, and a medallion of veal covered with a slice of ham in the pan. As soon as it begins to fry, remove the rosemary and add salt and pepper.

When it is done, pour on cognac. Finally add mushrooms and a sour cream sauce.

TOURNEDOS CATHERINE THE GREAT

Pour vodka on a cooked tenderloin steak, light it, cover and set aside.

Fry onions and parsley in butter. Add salt, pepper, curry, English mustard, Worcester sauce, and a little broth. When the sauce has thickened, pour it over the tournedos.

MARCO POLO SKEWERS

Thread on the skewers pieces of calf's liver and kidney alternated with pieces of bacon-fat and sage leaves. Put butter, salt, pepper, nutmeg and the skewers into the pan.

When they are done, pour whisky over them, ignite and serve flambé.

QUEEN SKEWERS

Prepare as for Marco Polo skewers, but use pre-cooked chicken and veal instead of liver and kidney.

CHICKEN MEPHISTOPHELES

Carve a roast chicken and keep it warm on a hotplate.

Melt some butter in the pan. Add a spoonful of French mustard and half a small tin of pâté de foie gras. Add 1 or 2 glasses of white wine and season with pepper, oregano, cayenne, curry and other spices to your liking.

Put the pieces of chicken into this sauce, pour on whisky and set light to it.

Lastly, add some cream and serve immediately.

FONDUE BOURGUIGNONNE

Fill a copper fondue-pot with olive oil and put it on the fondue stand. Cut a beef fillet into small cubes (approx. 150 g per person) and prepare the fondue forks or skewers.

Each guest skewers a meat cube, dips it into the boiling oil and fries it to his liking.

Mixed pickles, chips, and various sauces, such as ketchup, Worcester sauce, mayonnaise, tartare and béarnaise sauce may be served with the fondue.

CHINESE FONDUE

Proceed as with fondue bourguignonne, but use chicken broth instead of olive oil.

BACCHUS FONDUE

Cut veal fillets into small pieces (150 g per person). Heat a litre of white wine (do not let it boil) and add a whole onion, a bayleaf and a clove.

The same sauces as for Fondue bourguignonne can be served as side dishes.

SWEETS

BANANAS FLAMBÉ

Prepare the bananas beforehand as follows: cut them lengthwise into two halves, flour them, dip in a beaten egg and then once more in flour. Brown them in butter and place them side by side in the pan.

In the dining-room put the pan onto the stand. Sprinkle the bananas generously with icing sugar, pour some kirsch over them and ignite.

Keep spooning the kirsch over the bananas until the flame goes out.

BANANAS FLAMBÉ ELIZABETH

Heat castor sugar in the pan and when it just begins to caramelize add some knobs of butter, the juice of an orange and a glass of Grand Marnier (or another liqueur).

Put the halved bananas into the sauce and cook for 3 or 4 minutes.

Now add a glass of cognac and ignite.

PEACHES FLAMBÉ VENUS

Melt some butter in the pan. Before it browns, put in halved or quartered tinned peaches.

Let them brown slightly, pour a glass of liqueur over them and ignite. Before the alcohol has completely evaporated, put out the flame with the lid of the pan. Remove the peaches and keep them warm.

Add the syrup to the remaining sauce, then some cream until the mixture becomes thick. Pour it over the peaches and serve.

GOURMET'S PEAR

Put halved pears and some butter mixed with sugar into the pan. Heat it well, then pour cognac over them, ignite and let the flame burn. Remove the pears and put them on a dish.

Pour a hot chocolate sauce into the rest of the sauce, mix well and add a little cognac, if you like.

Coat the pears with this sauce and decorate with whipped cream.

PINEAPPLE HAWAIIAN PARADISE

Melt butter in the pan, then add a few lumps of sugar which have been previously rubbed with an orange peel. When the sugar has almost melted, add the tinned pineapple slices and brown slightly on both sides.

Pour on rum and ignite. Add the pineapple syrup and cook for another 3 or 4 minutes. Put 1 or 2 slices of pineapple onto each plate, garnish with a plum in the middle of each slice, pour the sauce over them and serve.

RUM OMELETTE CORDON BLEU

Heat the pan well, then put in a pre-cooked omelette, fold it in half, sprinkle generously with castor sugar and with a hot iron put a dèsign on it for decorative effect.

When the pan is sufficiently hot, pour some rum in and ignite. Spoon the rum over the omelette several times. Serve it on a warm plate.

CRÊPES SUZETTE (I)

Prepare the following cream in advance: mix butter, icing sugar, Curaçao and the grated peel of an orange or tangerine.

In the dining-room put part of this mixture into the pan. As soon as it begins to boil, add the previously cooked pancakes, one at a time, and let them absorb the flavour. With a spoon and a fork fold each pancake in four and line them up on the edge of the pan.

Spoon the sauce over the pancakes and move them all to the middle of the pan.

Pour an orange liqueur (such as Grand Marnier or Curaçao) plus some other kind of the guest's choice over the pancakes, slant the pan and ignite. Sprinkle the burning pancakes with castor sugar, letting it shower over the pancakes for effect. It will crackle slightly as it burns. Allow 3 pancakes per person.

CRÊPES SUZETTE (II)

Let castor sugar caramelize slowly. Add some butter and a little orange juice, stirring continuously.

Then rub lumps of sugar with orange peel and put them into the pan.

Sprinkle them with orange liqueur and kirsch and crush the lumps with a fork. Cook the sauce till it thickens.

Finally put in the pancakes, one at a time, and proceed as in the above recipe.

Americano: aperitif consisting of equal quantities of bitters and Italian vermouth, diluted with soda.

Angostura: the bark of a Venezuelan tree from which a bitter tonic is extracted, often used in cocktails.

Applejack: American for apple brandy.

Armagnac: top-quality brandy, similar to cognac, from Armagnac, a region in the Gers department.

Arrack: a spirit which is very similar to rum, distilled from rice. Imported from Java (Batavia arrack) and India.

Bacardi: white rum produced in Cuba.

Bénédictine: fine herbal liqueur made in the Benedictine monastery in Fécamp in Normandy. The abbreviation D.O.M. stands for 'Deo Optimo Maximo'.

Bourbon: American whiskey chiefly distilled from corn. (From Bourbon County in Kentucky.)

Calvados: apple brandy produced in Calvados in France.

Cobbler: drink of wine or liqueur, sugar, lemon, pounded ice, and whatever fruit is in season.

Cocktail: alcoholic drink made of various spirits mixed in a shaker with pounded ice.

Cognac: high-quality French brandy produced in the Cognac area (Charente department). The choice variety is known as 'fine champagne'.

Cointreau: orange-flavoured French liqueur, similar to Curaçao; in cocktails it can be replaced by Triple sec.

Crème: liqueur with a high sugar content and a low alcohol content.

Curaçao: liqueur flavoured with the peel of bitter oranges, produced in the island of Curaçao in the Antilles.

Dubonnet: French aperitif.

Fizz: a refreshing drink, a mixture of a strong liqueur, sugar, lemon juice, and soda water. Gin fizz is the most famous of its kind.

Flip: drink made of a dessert wine (or a strong liqueur), sugar and a fresh egg-yolk mixed in the shaker.

Gin (London gin): English colourless spirit flavoured with juniper berries.

Grand Marnier: excellent French liqueur made from cognac and oranges.

Grenadine: pomegranate syrup, bright red in colour.

Highball: iced drink of spirits diluted with soda water.

Kirsch: cherry brandy. Swiss and Black Forest kirsch are the most famous varieties.

Long drink: cold alcoholic drink diluted with soda and served in a tall glass.

Ouzo: a Greek spirit flavoured with aniseed.

Orange bitters: liquor used as a flavouring in cocktails.

Pastis: French aperitif flavoured with aniseed.

Pernod: French aperitif with aniseed and vermouth which is drunk diluted with water.

Port: strong, sweet, fortified wine made in Oporto, city in Portugal.

Rum: strong liquor distilled from sugar-cane. Best-known varieties: Jamaica rum (dark-brown) and Cuban rum (light yellow).

Sake: national Japanese alcoholic drink distilled from rice, warmed before serving.

Sambuca: Italian liqueur flavoured with aniseed, a typical local drink from Civitavecchia and Viterbo.

Sherry: a Spanish fortified wine. (Anglicism of the word 'Jerez'.)

Syrup: thick sweet liquid made by dissolving sugar in boiling water.

Soft drink: a non-alcoholic drink.

Sour: drink of spirits with lemon- or lime-juice and sugar.

Straight whiskey: American for neat whiskey.

Tequila: national Mexican liquor with a very high alcohol content made from an agave plant.

Triple sec: a sweet liqueur with an orange aroma, similar to Curaçao and Cointreau.

Tumbler: drinking-glass without a handle.

Vermouth: strong sweet wine flavoured with wormwood. From the German Wermut (wormwood, absinth).

Vodka: a Russian or Polish spirit distilled from rye, wheat, barley, etc. The name is a diminutive of the Russian voda (water).

Whiskey: a spirit distilled from various grains and including the Scotch made from malted barley with a characteristic smoky flavour, the Irish distilled from fermented malt and subject to three distillations, the Canadian distilled from rye and barley and the American whiskey made either from rye (rye whiskey) or corn (bourbon).

Zest: orange or lemon peel used as a flavouring.

GIN-Cocktails

MARTINI DRY

Gin	4/5
French vermouth	1/5

Serve with an olive or lemon peel.
(Take whisky instead of gin and you get a Manhattan)

Alexandra

Gin	1/3
Crème de cacao	1/3
Fresh cream	1/3

(Take brandy instead of gin and you get an Alexander).

Bronx

Gin	3/6
French vermouth	1/6
Italian vermouth	1/6
Orange juice	1/6

(Can be served with orange or lemon peel)

Dubonnet

Gin	1/2
Dubonnet	1/2

Serve with lemon peel.

Negroni

Gin	1/3
Italian vermouth	1/3
Bitters	1/3

Orange blossom

Gin	2/3
Orange juice	1/3

(You can add a dash of grenadine).

Paradise

Gin	3/6
Apricot brandy	1/6
Orange juice	2/6

White lady

Gin	2/4
Triple sec (or Cointreau)	1/4
Lemon juice	1/4

(Take brandy instead of gin and you get a Sidecar)

BRANDY-Cocktails

Sidecar

Brandy	2/4
Triple sec (or Cointreau)	1/4
Lemon juice	1/4

(Take gin instead of brandy and you get a White Lady)

Alexander

Brandy	1/3
Crème de cacao	1/3
Fresh cream	1/3

(Take gin instead of brandy and you get an Alexandra)

Stinger

Brandy	2/3
Crème de menthe	1/3

Brandy cocktail

Brandy	1 glass
Angostura	2 dashes
Sugar syrup	1 teaspoonful

(Grenadine, curaçao or triple sec are usable instead of sugar syrup)

* For dry cocktails use a larger quantity of the main spirit and add French instead of Italian vermouth.

RUM-Cocktails

Daiquiri

Cuban rum	5/6
Lemon juice	1/6
Sugar syrup (or grenadine)	1 teaspoonful

Bacardi

Bacardi rum	3/6
Lemon juice	1/6
Grenadine	1 teaspoonful
Gin	2/6

Presidente

Bacardi rum	3/4
French vermouth	1/4
Grenadine	½ teaspoonful

(American add 1 or 2 dashes of curaçao)

Rum cocktail

Bacardi rum	1 glass
Angostura	1 dash
Sugar syrup	½ teaspoonful

WHISKY-Cocktails

Manhattan

Canadian whiskey	2/3
Italian vermouth	1/3
Angostura	1 dash

Serve with an olive.

Old-fashioned

Bourbon (or rye whiskey)	1 glass
Angostura	2 dashes
Sugar	1 teaspoonful

Squeeze lemon peel on it and garnish with a slice of orange.
(Take gin instead of whiskey and you get an old-fashioned gin-cocktail)

Rob Roy

Scotch whisky	2/3
Italian vermouth	1/3
Angostura	1 dash

Serve with a cherry.

Whisky cocktail

American whiskey	1 glass
Angostura	2 dashes
Sugar syrup	1 teaspoonful

(Grenadine or curaçao are usable instead of sugar syrup)

VODKA-Cocktails

Bloody Mary

Vodka	½ glass
Tomato juice	1½ glasses
Lemon juice	1 teaspoonful

Serve in a tumbler with salt and paprika.

Vodka sour

Vodka	1 glass
Juice of half a lemon	
Sugar syrup	1 teaspoonful

(If you want a gin sour, a brandy sour or a whisky sour take these other spirits instead of vodka)

* For dry cocktails use a larger quantity of the main spirit and add French instead of Italian vermouth.